Edge of Empire

Edge of Empire

ATLANTIC NETWORKS AND REVOLUTION
IN BOURBON RÍO DE LA PLATA

Fabrício Prado

UNIVERSITY OF CALIFORNIA PRESS

University of California Press, one of the most distinguished university presses in the United States, enriches lives around the world by advancing scholarship in the humanities, social sciences, and natural sciences. Its activities are supported by the UC Press Foundation and by philanthropic contributions from individuals and institutions. For more information, visit www.ucpress.edu.

University of California Press
Oakland, California

Earlier versions of chapter 6 appeared in *Topoí, Revista de História* 13, no. 25 (July–Dec. 2012): 168–84 (available at www.revistatopoi.org/numeros_anteriores/topoi25/artigo_09.php); and *Colonial Latin American Historical Review* 16, no. 3 (2007): 287–312.

Library of Congress Cataloging-in-Publication Data

Prado, Fabrício Pereira, author.
    Edge of empire : Atlantic networks and revolution in Bourbon Rio de la Plata / Fabricio Prado.
        p.   cm.
    Includes bibliographical references and index.
    ISBN 978-0-520-28515-6 (cloth, alk. paper) — ISBN 978-0-520-28516-3 (pbk., alk. paper) — ISBN 978-0-520-96073-2 (electronic)
    1. Rio de la Plata Region (Argentina and Uruguay—Economic conditions—18th century.   2. Rio de la Plata Region (Argentina and Uruguay)—History—18th century.   I. Title.
HC167.R5P73   2015
382.09895′1—dc23   2015012977

Manufactured in the United States of America

24   23   22   21   20   19   18   17   16   15
10   9   8   7   6   5   4   3   2   1

In keeping with a commitment to support environmentally responsible and sustainable printing practices, UC Press has printed this book on Natures Natural, a fiber that contains 30% post-consumer waste and meets the minimum requirements of ANSI/NISO Z39.48-1992 (R 1997) (*Permanence of Paper*).

Contents

Illustrations and Tables

TABLES

Acknowledgments

This project started as the continuation of my research on the Portuguese colony in Río de la Plata, Colônia do Sacramento. My initial idea was to investigate what happened in the aftermath of the expulsion of the Portuguese from the region after a century-long presence. I realized, however, that the presence of foreign subjects was crucial for regional processes of trade, identity, and community building. As a result, this project grew in unexpected ways, incorporating new methodologies, new ideas, and a new framework that complicated and offered more nuanced explanations for the questions it poses, situating Río de la Plata in the Atlantic World.

The outcome of this work was in part affected by my experience as a Brazilian studying the history of Río de la Plata in the United States. The networks of scholarship and friendship in which I became a participant made clear that state-centered approaches do not provide satisfactory answers; people were never imprisoned by imaginary limits that nation-states try to naturalize in our minds. In this work there are two implicit assumptions: the current mythology of nation-states is more recent and less powerful than historians believed in the twentieth century, and it is useless to think of social groups as being isolated, for societies and social groups, after all, only develop in relationship to each other. I tried to explore processes that unfolded before the nation-state claimed monopoly over the loyalty of people confined within its sphere. Some of the answers provided here might prove that some practices and strategies undertaken before the nation was established are still relevant to understanding social dynamics in Latin America and in the Atlantic World in the contemporary phase of globalization. Social networks preceded and probably will survive the height of the nation-states.

The making of this book was possible because of a great number of scholars, archivists, and friends who helped me in many ways. All the responsibility for the text is mine, but I am deeply indebted to all those who gave me suggestions, criticism, and support.

I would like to thank the Department of History at Emory University for its generous support. The Graduate School of Arts and Sciences, the Institute for Critical International Studies, and the Latin American and Caribbean Studies Program at Emory University provided crucial funds for field research.

The fellowships awarded by the Lilly Library and the Luso-American Foundation for Development allowed me to access great collections in the United States and in Lisbon. Two fellowships at the John Carter Brown Library (JCBL) not only allowed me to explore the library's important collection but also provided an excellent environment for scholarly work. To the JCBL staff and my fellow fellows of 2008 and 2013, a special thanks. At the Center for Historical Research, Ohio State University, I found a safe haven to finish writing the dissertation from which the present book developed and a supportive group of people who helped me through the journey known as the job market. I wish to thank Professors Ken Andrien and Alan Gallay. Joe Miller, Kittiya Lee, and Richard Gordon provided stimulus and great ideas.

This project started back in Porto Alegre, and I would like to thank Susana Bleil da Souza and the memory of Sandra Pesavento for their initial support of my endeavor to break the aquarium walls and try swimming in the big ocean. Susana deserves special thanks for being such a great mentor; it was through her kind and effective advice that I was introduced to the world of historical research. My friends Fabio Kuhn and Eduardo Neumann: your camaraderie and love for history made this journey easier and certainly much more fun. Your generosity and rigorous scholarship were surpassed only by your friendship.

To the South Atlantic crew, Fabio Pesavento, Tiago Gil and Martha Hameister, my words of gratitude are not enough. Fabio, Tiago, and Martha are good friends and generous colleagues with whom I shared documents and ideas.

In Rio de Janeiro, I would like to thank the staff of the Arquivo Nacional and the Arquivo Histórico do Itamaraty. I am indebted to Professors Manolo Florentino and João Fragoso for their support, advice, and generosity in different stages of this research. To Carolina Veiga and Flavio Santos, my special thanks; the Gaucho embassy of Humaitá will always be remembered with affection.

My days in São Paulo would not be same if it was not for the baron Filipinho Diefenbach. *Aquele abraço!*

In Montevideo, I am indebted to the staff of the Archivo General de la Nación and the Archivo Histórico de la Catedral. I thank Nelsys Buby Fusco for his support and generosity. Ana Frega gave me crucial advice in our *charlas en la facultad* and helped me sharpen my arguments. Arturo Bentancur was always generous and supportive of my research since my first trip, when I was a master's student asking questions about Sacramento. Arturo, talking to you about "our friends" from the eighteenth century always renewed my confidence in the feasibility of the project. *¡Muchíssimas gracias!*

In Buenos Aires, I would like to thank the staff of the Archivo General de la Nación. Professor Jorge Gelman provided friendly support for my work, and I continue to be indebted to his challenging questions, which have allowed me to see beyond the obvious horizon. To Gabriel Di Meglio, the lines of Atmosphere are still echoing in the routes of the Atlantic. *Gracias mi amigo.* Gustavo Paz, thanks for friendship and advice. The old *guerrero*, my dear friend Rodrigo Vergara, made Buenos Aires feel like home once again.

In Lisbon, my days would not be the same without the hospitality and friendship of Paulo Souza and Antonio. Without the generosity and advice of Erika Dias, my research at Arquivo Historico Ultramarino would not have produced even half of the results I was able to achieve. Many thanks to Professor Pedro Cardim for helpful comments and academic support. The staff at Torre do Tombo also deserve my infinite gratitude. Nandini Chaturvedula made my stay in Lisbon and archival research much more fun.

In Spain, Rodrigo Ceballos was a good archive partner and a good friend with whom to investigate the variety of tapas available in Sevilla. Professor Manoel Herrero Sanchez deserves special thanks for his generosity and advice about the European contraband trade. The staff of the Archivo General de Indias was also crucial for this work.

My friends and colleagues from Atlanta provided support and shared thoughts, documents, and life stories. Uri and the Rosenheck family proved to be great friends. My good friend, Alex Borucki, deserves a special thanks for his generosity in sharing documents and the exchanges of ideas about *la tierra purpurea*. The Van Welie family gifted me with friendship on a transatlantic scale. Peter Knaup deserves special thanks for his endless kindness and support since my arrival in Atlanta. Daniel Domingues was my partner since the first day of graduate school. Thanks to Lena Suk for editorial help and for being such a great friend. Alicia Monroe, Agnes Czeblakow, and Mollie Lewis were excellent friends.

My thanks to my Atlanta friends would not be complete without mentioning the crew of the 132. My roommate and great friend, Bruno Camargo, thanks for friendship and support. And thanks to Ilan Vassermann and Rachel Hershenberg who completed the 132 family.

In Providence, Julia Timpe, Luca Prazeres, Julia Garner, Ana Leticia Fauri, Hal Langfur, Guadalupe Pinzón, and David Mittleman made the summers of 2008 and 2013 memorable and academically enriching.

Heidi Scott provided friendship and generous comments. To Viviana Grieco, my friend and helpful colleague, my special thanks for all the chats, opinions, and documents that have enriched this work. I also would like to thank Matthew Brown for his comments on parts of this work.

The book has benefited greatly from editorial work at University of California Press; I would like to thank especially Kate Marshall and Cindy Fulton. At William and Mary, I would like to thank my colleagues for their generosity as intellectuals and colleagues, especially Leisa Meyer, Cindy Hahamovich, Fred Corney, Brett Rushforth, and Paul Mapp. Nadine Zimmerli deserves special mention for her sharp and expert advice while I was preparing the manuscript. To Ed Pompeian, a special thanks for help sharpening the text and for the generous exchange of ideas and information about contraband trade in the Atlantic. Marco Millones and Carleigh Snead at the Center of Geospatial Analysis at William and Mary produced the maps in this book, and I am grateful for their attention and dedication to this project. Annie Blazer and Eric Han deserve a special mention for being such great friends and generous colleagues.

Professors David Eltis and Jeffrey Lesser helped me expand my historiographic horizons, framing Latin America within the larger Atlantic, and provided generous advice.

Professor Lyman Johnson offered support, advice, and camaraderie during the different phases of my research. I am especially thankful for his mentorship in helping me bring this project to book form. *Un fuerte abrazo*, Lyman!

I want to give special thanks to my adviser, Susan Migden Socolow. Her generosity and deep knowledge about history are unsurpassed. *¡Muchíssimas gracias!*

To my old friends Augusto Canani, Marcelo Fruet, Camila Giugliani, and João Geraldo Segala-Moreira, *não teria tido graça nenhuma sem vocês aí para atucanar!* Alexandre Zagoury, Frederico Antunes, Jorge Bucksdricker, and Daniel Sperb, thank you for your friendship.

My brothers, José Emílio Prado Júnior and Christiano Prado, have been lifelong friends. Chris deserves special thanks for support and *parceria* in the United States.

I dedicate this book to my parents, José Prado and Clóris Pereira.

Introduction

During the weeks of July 15 and July 30, 1821, representatives of all the towns in the Banda Oriental (roughly the territory of present-day Uruguay) convened to decide on the political future of the former Spanish province. According to one representative, Geronimo Bianqui, the Banda Oriental needed to decide whether to become an independent nation or join an already existing one: "These are the alternatives that the circumstances permit; we should ponder if Montevideo and its countryside can become a Nation and maintain its Independence, or if it cannot, to what Nation would [it] be most profitable to join, and which one would offer less dangers."[1] The assembly, unsurprisingly, decided in favor of formal annexation to the Luso-Brazilian empire under the name Cisplatine Province. The representative's rhetoric is revealing of the existing political options available to the pueblos of the province.[2] The Banda Oriental, in opposition to its former viceregal capital, Buenos Aires, opted to keep old commercial networks to Portuguese America and monarchical institutions instead of pursuing revolution and republicanism. During the revolutionary decades, the emergence of new political identities and changing institutions transformed the political and economic landscape of the Atlantic World. Transimperial networks of trade were at the core of these

1

dynamics and shaped the emergence of the new political geography during the age of revolution.

It was in Buenos Aires, capital of the most recently created Spanish viceroyalty (1776), that the local population overthrew the viceroy in 1810, becoming the first Spanish colony to effectively end Spanish rule. The revolutionary government of Buenos Aires, however, was not able to control the main port city in the former viceroyalty of Río de la Plata, Montevideo. After the creation of the revolutionary Buenos Aires Junta in 1810, across the Río de la Plata, Montevideo adopted several political projects in opposition to the authority of the former viceregal capital. Montevideo became the bastion of Spanish loyalism in the South Atlantic (1810–14) and later maintained monarchism by joining the Portuguese empire (1816–25). Eventually, Montevideo emerged as the capital of the independent republic of Uruguay (1828). During this process, while old colonial rivalries between the Montevideo and Buenos Aires communities contributed to these cities' divergent political paths, strong networks of trade with Brazil, England, and other foreign countries played a critical role in allowing Montevideo merchants to resist the old viceregal capital. (See map 1.)

Most historians of Iberian America have studied the processes of independence in colonial empires individually and have emphasized regional factors and imperial policies in shaping autonomist movements.[3] While these explanations illuminate important regional and Atlantic interconnections within the Spanish empire, they fall short in their failure to acknowledge the strength of transimperial and transnational interactions in the transition from colony to nation in Iberian America. *Edge of Empire* analyzes the role and significance of transimperial dynamics during the last decades of colonial rule and the revolutionary decades in the disputed Río de la Plata region (present-day Argentina, Uruguay, Paraguay, and southern Brazil). My analysis of Portuguese and Spanish commercial and political networks in Río de la Plata between 1760 and 1825 reveals the importance of transimperial interactions in shaping the very definition of empire, ideas of sovereignty, and political projects during these revolutionary years.

Because of the central role of trade for Atlantic empires in the eighteenth century, local merchants and authorities were able to use their con-

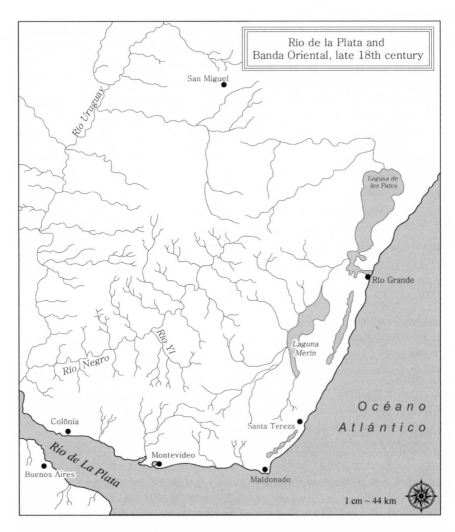

Map 1. Río de la Plata and the Banda Oriental, late Eighteenth Century.

SOURCE: Alonso Pacheco. Plano en que se demuestra la demarcación ejecutada por las primeras partidas de España y Portugal. 1757. Agustín Ybañez. Mapa del Territorio ocupado por los portugueses. 1804.

trol over networks of transimperial commerce, both legal and illegal, as leverage to obtain increased political and fiscal autonomy from centers of colonial power. As a result, the political fragmentation that occurred as the Spanish empire disintegrated has to be considered in light of the significance of exogenous processes in tandem with internal imperial dynamics already in motion during the last decades of the colonial period.

This book examines the dynamics of transimperial and transnational interactions by highlighting the ways in which regional communities used their political, familial, religious, and commercial networks with foreign subjects to enhance their political and economic position in the regional context. Transimperial connections allowed communities in colonial borderlands to resist colonial centers of power, the viceregal capitals. I argue that transimperial interaction shaped colonial identities and political culture in the last decades of Spanish rule and the emergence of new polities in the era of revolution in the Atlantic.

In politically peripheral areas, colonial subjects developed social and commercial transimperial networks that allowed them to devise other political and economic options than the ones prescribed by imperial centers. The case of Montevideo and its adjacent hinterland, the Banda Oriental, illustrates the ways local elites progressively gained autonomy from the viceregal capital of Buenos Aires by making use of their access to networks with foreigners. Colonial elites of Montevideo used their commercial, familial, religious, and political networks with Portuguese Brazil in combination with new political institutions in the wake of the Bourbon reforms to expand their city's jurisdiction over territory on the borderlands with Brazil and over commercial regulations. My analysis of Montevideo's political development in the late colonial period reveals that transatlantic trade networks were crucial in shaping the process of political emancipation of republican and monarchist polities in the Americas.

Montevideo and its hinterlands make for an especially salient case study to investigate the impact of transimperial trade networks on independence movements. Although some scholars have perceived it as merely peripheral in the Spanish mercantile system, Río de la Plata was actually one of the most disputed areas in the Atlantic World throughout the early modern period. In fact, the region was a stage for colonial disputes between Spain and Portugal and an area of concentrated interest for the

British and the French. By the end of the eighteenth century, Río de la Plata had become a hub of transimperial interactions and the fastest growing region in the Spanish empire.[4]

By the end of the eighteenth century, Montevideo and the Banda Oriental had been the subject of disputes between the Spanish and the Portuguese for more than one hundred years. Between 1680 and 1777 Colônia do Sacramento, a Portuguese town located across from Buenos Aires and 130 miles north of Montevideo, assured the region's importance in the diplomatic scene. It was the subject of five international treaties involving Spain, Portugal, Britain, and France in the eighteenth century alone.[5] The Banda Oriental was the locus of interaction between Portuguese and Spanish subjects, as well as other Europeans, Africans, and indigenous groups. The importance of local alliances in war, legal and illegal commerce, and imperial politics marked the emergence of regional interests and communities. These cross-border interactions were not mediated by a state; rather they were centered on social networks that transcended imperial or national allegiances.

A routine of interactions between subjects of different Atlantic empires was an integral characteristic of Río de la Plata during the eighteenth century. These interactions had been commonplace in the region during the era of Portuguese Colônia. Yet even after the expulsion of the Portuguese from Colônia in 1777, some Portuguese subjects continued to live in the region, and commercial networks with Portuguese America were maintained. British merchants were also a common presence in the estuary, often in partnership with the Portuguese. By the late colonial period, the powerful transimperial networks of trade and politics that had previously operated in Colônia had taken root in Montevideo. The Bourbon reforms and warfare in the Atlantic reinforced such connections under the legal disposition of trade with neutral nations, the Spanish conquest of Portuguese Rio Grande and partial incorporation of its population, and the expanding imperial control over the region. The interactions among Spanish, the Portuguese, and, to a lesser extent, the British not only shaped the development of imperial institutions and the region's political culture but also influenced the political projects that surfaced during the revolutionary decades. These transimperial networks were instrumental in maintaining monarchist governments in the Banda Oriental, especially the incorporation of the area into the Luso-Brazilian empire (1816–25), as well as the emergence of Uruguay as an autonomous country in 1828.

The countryside of the Banda Oriental was originally under the control of Buenos Aires. After 1777, however, Montevideo progressively increased its jurisdiction and status in the Spanish imperial system, gaining control over the territory and resources of the surrounding area previously controlled by Buenos Aires. By the first decade of the nineteenth century, the inhabitants of Montevideo and the Banda Oriental regarded themselves and were seen by others as their own community, not as part of Buenos Aires. In this process of increasing jurisdiction and the development of different political and economic agendas, control of transimperial trade and social networks within the Luso-Brazilian and British empires was a crucial element. Therefore, the social and economic developments examined in this book, although regional, are intimately tied to broader Atlantic processes.

ENTANGLED HISTORIES AND TRANSIMPERIAL NETWORKS

Historians of the twentieth century have created the general perception that early modern empires were independent, absolutist states, with strict mercantilist practices regarding their colonial possessions. In recent decades, however, scholars of the Atlantic World have shown that early modern Atlantic empires were porous and fluid (both in Europe and in African and American territories). As a result, economic, social, and cultural historians of the early modern period have increasingly realized the significance and consequence of processes unfolding in imperial peripheries for the political, economic, and social processes of the whole empire. The Atlantic World framework provides a new perspective on old topics by focusing on the practices and experiences of historical agents and their connections with other regions rather than exclusively on prescriptive political and commercial policies.[6]

The emergence of the Atlantic framework, and the subsequent decentering of European metropoles as exclusive agents of empire, does not obscure the imperial dimension of early modern historical processes. Atlantic societies were structured on principles of sovereignty and social networks that spanned Portuguese, Spanish, British, and French dominions in the Americas.[7] Writing about the integral role of the colonial territories in the very idea of empire, Tamar Herzog and Pedro Cardim suggest that a *polycentric monarchies* framework would provide a better understanding of early modern empires. Moving beyond the model of composite monarchies, where "clearly defined" centers (Madrid and Lisbon) controlled a "series of subjected, subaltern kingdoms, entities or cities," the concept of polycentric monarchies proposes that Iberian political entities were composed of "interlinked centers that interacted not only with the king, but also among themselves, thus actively participating in the forging of the polity."[8] In polycentric monarchies, colonial agents not only actively participated in the imperial venture in the pursuit of their own agendas, but their participation in imperial administration, trade, and politics eventually shaped the institutions of empires. It is in this social, political, and economic context that the processes and lives studied in this book unfolded.[9]

The idea of an Atlantic World of polycentric monarchies differs from the traditional history of empires in that it focuses on the mutual interactions and contributions among regions. Not forgetting the unequal relations of power between different social, ethnic, and religious groups, the Atlantic perspective gives more attention to the contributions of the colonies to their respective metropoles and empire building.[10] *Edge of Empire* advances this avenue of interpretation by including transimperial dynamics as an integral variable in the political culture, institutions, and colonial identity at the fringes of empires. In addition to the intracolonial spaces of polycentric monarchies, transimperial dynamics were crucial in shaping different regions of the empire differently, allowing for the emergence of intraimperial rivalries, transimperial alliances, and new political identities in the Atlantic.

Local elites built their political and social base on familial, religious, trade, and political networks. Fictive kinship, distribution of offices, marriage, and trade partnerships shaped colonial societies in general and Montevideo's in particular. I contend that the colonial state relied more on local subjects to build its authority and to assert its domain than previously thought. Nonetheless, the interests of these colonial groups did not always coincide with the prescribed norms dictated by metropolitan rulers. Quite the opposite: their position of power in the colonial setting was guaranteed by their ability to maneuver through and mobilize intricate webs of social, political, and economic agents. Often allegiance to social networks trumped imperial loyalties.

The earlier attention of scholars to processes unfolding within the confines of specific empires has resulted in a fictional subdivision of the Atlantic into three areas defined by their colonizing agents: northwestern European empires connected to North America, the Caribbean, and West Africa; the Spanish empire, including Central America, portions of North America, the Caribbean, and some areas on the Pacific coast of South America; and the dominions of the Portuguese empire, including the Atlantic islands, the Atlantic coast of South America, and West Central Africa and Mozambique.[11] My analysis of Río de la Plata shows that external dynamics were at the center of the emergence of colonial identities, of regional political institutions in the last decades of Spanish colonialism, and of the emergence of autonomist projects during the revolutionary decades. As a result, I argue for an understanding of one complex, interconnected, and interdependent Atlantic World instead of many separate Atlantic worlds.

Social networks were central to articulating early modern Iberian monarchies.[12] Although dynamically interconnected, networks differed in nature; they could be centered on family, religion, trade, or friendship. In colonial Latin America, different networks overlapped, allowing agents to belong to multiple groups, thus channeling resources from one to another in order to obtain better positions in these organizations and improve the group's performance. These interconnected relationships wove together the Iberian empires, and the case of late colonial Montevideo shows the endurance and complexity of these transimperial dynamics.

The analysis of Montevideo merchant elites' kinship networks reveals how the extended family had a central role in shaping the social dynamics and strategies of historical agents. The modern notion of individuals as autonomous agents does not match eighteenth-century Latin America reality. In these societies, the extended family (siblings, in-laws, relatives, and servants) constituted an economic unit under patriarchal control.[13]

Historians of Iberian empires have argued for the importance of incorporating foreigners through marriage in different cities in Iberia and in
Latin America within the merchant class.[14]

Among merchant families, marriage was a critical strategy to acquire
connections with bureaucrats, the military, and other geographic areas.
Marriage also allowed newcomer merchants to develop connections to
local aristocrats and bureaucrats. These practices influenced the political
and judicial system on all levels.[15] Familial networks were also important
in long-distance trade in that they created mechanisms of control to
ensure trust and to deal with bad behavior.[16] Through marriage, bureaucrats, *fidalgos* (noblemen), and merchants could participate in joint ventures centered on their family ties. In colonial settings, important families
constituted complex networks that exerted influence in different spheres
of colonial life. Having access to high bureaucrats and being able to obtain
licenses to operate could make all the difference in a noncompetitive market characterized by uneven privileges.

Shared experiences, previous knowledge of an individual's behavior
based on common acquaintances, and geographic origins played crucial
roles in structuring these networks. Shared experience on the battlefield
was a powerful bond between persons that could provide the basis for
partnerships, access to credit, and other relationships during periods of
peace.[17] These networks based on battlefield experiences affected elites
and subaltern groups horizontally and vertically. Due to the nature of military organization and recruitment, these networks could overlap with
networks centered on geographic origin. As a result, in this early modern
world dominated by empires, social networks structured communities
and shaped people's behavior and loyalties.

If an interconnected Atlantic World is the broad context in which
regional processes developed, the local space where these networks and
multiple interactions happened can be characterized as *interaction zones.*
Although transimperial networks could reach deep inside imperial
domains, transimperial interaction usually took place in port cities or borderlands. In this study the Atlantic is the main connector of peoples and
territories, and in the eighteenth century ports were crucial spaces for the
financing, regulation, and logistics of transatlantic traffic. Port cities such
as Rio de Janeiro, Luanda, Vera Cruz, Buenos Aires, Sacramento, Boston,

Charleston, and Montevideo were hot spots where an unlimited number of agents from diverse origins could interact. The communities that developed in these cities often counted on strategies to incorporate foreigners or on institutions that would bridge interactions. Examples are the incorporation of foreign merchants into local societies through marriage, religious brotherhoods that harbored foreign religious people, or a branch of bureaucracy that was entitled to bridge business and political agreements between two empires during peaceful times.

Transimperial interaction implies contacts between different social groups, European, indigenous, and African, as well as interaction between multiple cultures. Mary Louise Pratt has coined the term *contact zone* to define these non-European regions, usually colonial frontiers where unequal power relations developed. Using primarily travel literature from early encounters between Europeans and indigenous groups in Latin America, Pratt suggests that travelers exoticized the "other" and used European categories to describe non-European behaviors.[18] As a result, the narratives produced about colonial peoples and locations were not accurate reflections of the region being described. Because the imperial agents producing such narratives were "passive observers" and travelers, they were not able to capture colonial landscapes and the subtleties of colonial societies.[19] Pratt's concept, however, falls short when deployed to explain mature colonial settings and descriptions written by colonial subjects or imperial agents that were natives or lived in the areas for long periods and established familial and business roots.

Departing from the concept of contact zones, I suggest that the loci of transimperial interaction can be better understood as *interaction zones*. An interaction zone was a mature colonial region in which the elites were European or of European descent and agents of different geographic origins interacted. In interaction zones, normally port cities, subjects faced the differences of the "other" yet simultaneously shared most of the values, cultural codes, and political ideals of the host societies. Writers in interaction zones were integrated and constantly engaging with the societies they were writing about: they were more than "seeing" agents. In interaction zones, foreigners married local women, imperial agents established local roots, and natives used imperial discourses. Thus their descriptions were mediated primarily by their interactions with regional social groups and their place in the broader Atlantic scenario. It was in the Río de la Plata interaction zone where subjects from different empires, Africans, and indigenous agents interacted, crossed imperial borders, and shaped the very definition of empire and the new polities that emerged in the Atlantic.

ORGANIZATION OF THE BOOK

The first chapter details the social and economic significance of the Portuguese town of Colônia do Sacramento in Río de la Plata society of the eighteenth century, arguing that although contact between subjects of the Spanish and Portuguese empires was forbidden, enduring networks of family and trade connected subjects from Portuguese Colônia and Spanish Buenos Aires.

Chapter 2 examines the changes triggered by the Spanish conquest of Colônia and the end of the Portuguese imperial project in Río de la Plata. Although the Portuguese empire had to relinquish the region, Portuguese subjects remained in large numbers in Montevideo, in the countryside of the Banda Oriental, and in Buenos Aires. Most important, trade networks previously centered in Colônia do Sacramento were relocated to Montevideo. Finally, comparing census data, I suggest that Montevideo was more open to the participation of Luso-Brazilians and British traders than was Buenos Aires in the last decades of colonial rule.

Chapter 3 analyzes the reestablishment of transimperial trade networks between Río de la Plata and Portuguese America, paying special attention to the flow of ships between Rio de Janeiro and Montevideo, as well as the use of the Portuguese convoy system by Spanish ships during periods of war. These networks ensured the flow of silver, goods, information, and troops between Spain and its South Atlantic colonies during the turbulent decades of war.

Chapter 4 argues that colonial elites used reformist regulations to increase the jurisdiction of Montevideo authorities over territories and commercial and fiscal matters previously under the jurisdiction of Buenos Aires, especially control of contraband trade. This chapter relies on records detailing the confiscation of illicit goods to map the expansion of Montevideo's jurisdiction over the countryside of the Banda Oriental.

Using administrative records and travel literature, chapter 5 examines the evolving imagined geography of the region. Through analysis of the changes in descriptive and cartographic representations of Montevideo and its countryside during the period, this chapter tracks Montevideo and the Banda Oriental as it becomes an increasingly integrated space distinct from Buenos Aires.

Chapter 6 follows the life story and personal connections of don Manuel Cipriano de Melo, a Portuguese merchant who moved from Colônia do Sacramento to Montevideo, where he swore loyalty to the Spanish king and eventually was put in charge of repressing contraband trade, becoming the wealthiest merchant in the city. His life illuminates on a personal level the interplay of networks, regional identity, and transimperial interaction.

Chapter 7 examines how transimperial trade networks shaped the political projects that emerged after the crisis of the Spanish monarchy in 1808. During the 1810s the mercantile elites of Montevideo remained loyal to the Spanish monarchy and later sought to join the Luso-Brazilian empire. The maintenance of transimperial trade networks and the political status quo were crucial pillars of the political projects of the elites of Montevideo during the revolutionary period.

1 A Portuguese Town in Río de la Plata

In February 1680, don Manoel Lobo, governor of Rio de Janeiro, founded a Portuguese settlement on the northern bank of the Río de la Plata. This settlement, Colônia do Santíssimo Sacramento, located thirty miles and across the river from Buenos Aires, marked the southernmost commercial and territorial expansion of the Portuguese in the Americas. Colônia was created to reestablish profitable commercial routes between Río de la Plata and Luso-America that had flourished during the Iberian Union (1580–1640). From 1680 to 1777 it served as a profitable entrepôt for transimperial trade. Considered by many a nest of smugglers, it became a wealthy, populous port city and was a hot spot of powerful and longstanding networks of trade between Spanish and Portuguese merchants. From its founding, Colônia's transimperial commerce paved the way for the trade connections that characterized Montevideo's merchant community in the late eighteenth century.

In fact, Atlantic trade and transimperial connections between Luso-American and Spanish American merchants were the main forces behind the development of this Luso-Platine urban center.[1] The vitality of transimperial trade in Colônia allowed for consistent population growth, including free immigrants and a significant contingent of enslaved Africans. By developing a large slave trade, the town helped meet the demand for enslaved Africans in the Spanish territories across the estuary.[2] As a result, long-standing networks of trade, family, and religion connected Portuguese and Spanish subjects and shaped the region's development on both margins of the Río de la Plata.

In the eighteenth century Colônia do Sacramento, Buenos Aires, and Montevideo formed a port complex.[3] Rather than compete with one another, they played complementary roles. Merchants from Buenos Aires used connections in Colônia to obtain cheap Atlantic products and slaves and to export huge quantities of silver and hides. The growth and maintenance of these transimperial networks linked the region to the Atlantic World and constituted the emergence of an interaction zone, where agents from different empires engaged in multiple commercial, social, and political exchanges. The Portuguese presence in the region epitomizes how transimperial linkages shaped the emerging societies in the borderlands of América meridional.

As a hub of transimperial commerce, Colônia shaped the patterns of trade that characterized Río de la Plata for over a century. After the fall of Colônia in 1777, the agents and networks involved in transatlantic trade relocated to Montevideo. It is therefore crucial to examine Colônia as a center for Atlantic trade in order to understand the development of transimperial trade networks and late-eighteenth-century Spanish imperial policies in the region. Transimperial trade was an integral aspect of the historical process by which Río de la Plata became a port complex during the eighteenth century, and it influenced the social, political, and economic processes in the region both before and after the period of Portuguese dominion over Colônia came to an end in 1777.

THE GENESIS OF A TRANSIMPERIAL INTERACTION ZONE IN RÍO DE LA PLATA

During the nearly one hundred years of Portuguese control over Colônia do Sacramento, despite the flourishing transimperial commerce, the Luso-Brazilian presence was contested by the Spanish. The entangled development of Buenos Aires and Colônia in the Río de la Plata estuary

led to the formation of porous space where Spanish and Portuguese subjects interacted in many ways: they cooperated in commercial exchanges,
developed familial and religious connections, and competed for resources
in the countryside.

The founding of Colônia do Sacramento in 1680 was an expression of
the strong interest of the Portuguese Crown and merchants to gain access
to the profitable Río de Plata markets in silver and hides. Colônia, however,
was not the first place where Portuguese merchants explored trade opportunities in Río de la Plata. Since Buenos Aires's second foundation in 1580,
the city's inhabitants had been actively involved in direct trade, legal or
illegal, with foreign subjects, especially Portuguese traders. Because of its
marginal position vis-à-vis Lima, the official port of all Spanish South
America, Buenos Aires was always in need of European goods, as well as
sugar, tobacco, furniture, and even slaves. As a result, the city's inhabitants
were eager for legal and illegal trade with Luso-American, Dutch, British,
and French merchants. Foreign merchant ships used diverse strategies and
pretexts to land in the port in order to exchange European merchandise for
silver and hides. Silver from Potosí was the motor of the region's trade.
Merchants in Buenos Aires developed strong commercial networks that
covered an extended hinterland including the provinces of Río de la Plata,
Chile, and Alto Peru. The merchants of Buenos Aires drained silver from
the internal market and used it to participate in transatlantic commerce.[4]

During the Iberian Union, especially between 1580 and 1620, the Luso-
Brazilian presence in Buenos Aires shaped the city's merchant community. According to a contemporary observer, it was more important to
speak Portuguese than Spanish in order to conduct trade in the city,
because Portuguese was the main language of the merchant community.[5]
Furthermore, between 1580 and 1620 the Portuguese held the *asiento*, the
monopoly contract for supplying slaves to the Spanish empire. When
the union ended in 1640, Luso-Brazilian merchants lost legal access to the
Spanish commercial networks, but Dutch, French, and British traders
increased their direct contacts in the region.

The creation of Colônia in 1680 had important implications for Atlantic
trade and the regional economy. First and foremost, it marked the expansion of territorial disputes in the Americas between Spain and Portugal.
For the Portuguese, Colônia represented an opportunity to reopen access

to the Rio de la Plata market—a source of silver, which was always scarce in Portuguese America.[6] For the Spanish, the town was a Portuguese incursion into the Río de la Plata's North Bank (Banda Norte) and, most important, a dangerous and competing hub of Atlantic trade. In a regional context, the creation of Colônia meant that the Portuguese acquired a "monopoly" over one of the region's best natural harbor, which had been used by merchant ships, particularly Dutch, British, and French, involved in direct trade with the region.[7] The historian Zacarias Moutoukias argues that Buenos Aires and Colônia developed complementary rather than competitive roles in the commercial development of the region.[8] Despite the initial aggressive reaction from the elite of Buenos Aires, in the long term Colônia, Buenos Aires, and later Montevideo constituted a single port complex for Río de la Plata.[9]

The Luso-Brazilian presence in the region during the seventeenth century was characterized by intense commercial activities and limited territorial expansion. In the 1680s Colônia was basically a military-commercial factory with few civilian inhabitants. Commercial activities were limited to smuggling with Buenos Aires, an activity controlled by a handful of merchants via their connections with the governors of both regions.[10] However, in the beginning of the 1690s Colônia's population grew and expanded into the countryside (*campaña*). From the 1690s until 1705 official colonists (*casais*) were sent from Portugal and from the Portuguese Atlantic islands to develop agricultural production, to exploit feral cattle herds, and to support the commercial activities of the town. By the beginning of the eighteenth century Colônia was engaged in significant agricultural production, including wheat and hides for export.[11] Buenos Aires elites, however, regarded the Luso-Brazilian expansion as an illegitimate advance into Spanish territory. With the outbreak of the War of the Spanish Succession in 1705, imperial tensions turned to violence when Spaniards and allied Guarani Indians once more attacked and expelled the Luso-Brazilians from Colônia.

In 1716, after the second Treaty of Utrecht (1715), the Portuguese resettled Colônia with the intention of establishing a commercial entrepôt with a strong defensive military force and a population of permanent settlers to produce food and control the large cattle herds in the countryside. During the first years, the Luso-Brazilian settlement experienced steady growth based on diversified agricultural production, intense commerce, and exploitation of hides. In the 1720s and 1730s Colônia developed an urban structure and became an important regional market that attracted people from Buenos Aires and from the countryside. During this period, hides, wheat, and other foodstuffs were produced in the Colônia's countryside. The region's wheat and hides were not only sold locally but also transported for sale in Rio de Janeiro and occasionally in Buenos Aires. Within ten miles of the urban center there were at least thirty-one farms that belonged to the inhabitants of the city.[12]

Colônia also provided a safe haven for British vessels and traders. Although British ships were officially forbidden, they docked in Colônia under the pretext of undergoing repairs. Despite the commercial injunctions, Colônia merchants purportedly traded hides, tallow, and silver acquired through contraband trade with Buenos Aires in exchange for British goods. Moreover, four traders of British origin who had naturalized as Portuguese subjects were established permanently in Colônia.[13]

The strength and significance of transimperial trade fueled rapid urban growth in Colônia. A large number of free and coerced migrants arrived in the region, among them a large contingent of Portuguese subjects who progressively settled in Spanish territories on the North Bank and in Buenos Aires. Information regarding population numbers in Sacramento during the eighteenth century is scarce and scattered. I was able to find two "population maps" drawn up by the Portuguese governors in 1722 and 1760, a partial census taken in 1719, an official report of the governor from 1742, two estimations by on-site observers for the early 1730s, and a Spanish census from 1778.[14]

Table 1 shows the demographic changes that took place in Colônia for the whole period of analysis, based on all available data. The demographic data reveal that the pace of population growth in Sacramento in the eighteenth century can be divided into three periods. The first period, 1717–35, is characterized by intense population growth averaging 8 percent per year, reflecting the territorial expansion into the countryside and flourishing trade. The second period, 1737–42, experienced a shrinking population as a result of the great siege and the loss of unrestricted access to the countryside. The loss of the agrarian suburbs affected all Colônia's inhabitants, but it probably had a heavier impact on farmers whose properties

Table 1   Colônia do Sacramento Annual Growth Rate

Year	Population	Annual Growth Rate (%)
1722	1,388 *	
1732	3,000	8.00
1735	2,600	−4.66
1742	1,956	−4.19
1760	2,712	1.83
1783	290	−9.26

SOURCES: AHU, Colônia do Sacramento, Docs. 86, 513; AHU, Rio de Janeiro, Doc. 7286; Monteiro 1937; Silva 1993; Tula 1931.

were located on the outskirts of the town and outside the city wall. The loss of the agricultural hinterland brought two important consequences for Colônia's community: Luso-Brazilians became more dependent on the Buenos Aires trade for foodstuffs and hides; and the inhabitants of Buenos Aires could use hides, tallow, pigs, chicken, grain, and other agricultural products together with silver to pay for goods sold by Sacramento traders. The third period, 1742–77, was characterized by steady population growth (1.83 percent per year). The loss of the agricultural lands and the lack of access to the countryside of the Banda Oriental seemed to have been the major factors constraining the pace of Colônia's expansion. The loss of agricultural lands was in part balanced by the development of the slave trade. Although the town continued to attract immigrants and underwent population growth, many migrants were slaves to be sold in the regional market.

While the number of total inhabitants of the town in 1760 was similar to that of the population of the early eighteenth century, the demographics had radically changed. Figure 1 shows that the free population of Colônia now represented 42 percent, almost half of the approximately 80 percent in the 1720s. Race distribution also shifted dramatically. Whites made up only 36 percent of the population, while *pardos* (people of mixed race) and blacks constituted 64 percent. Colônia had changed from a predominantly white settlement to a predominantly black and pardo town.

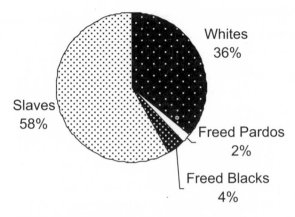

Figure 1. Colônia do Sacramento's Population
According to Race and Status, 1760.

Analysis of Colônia's baptismal records in the last years under Portuguese rule reveals that a large number of enslaved Africans bore children there. From November 1774 to January 1776, the priest of Colônia's Matriz Church recorded the baptisms of free persons and slaves in the Fifth Book of Baptisms, providing a rare glimpse of the demographic composition of Colônia in the last years under Portuguese rule. This snapshot into the family life of Colônia illuminates the diverse characteristics of society, which developed in tandem with the processes unfolding in Buenos Aires, thus revealing the intricate connections that crossed imperial boundaries in the region.

The place of origin of mothers bearing children in Colônia reveals a significant level of creolization of the population, an active inflow of Africans, and the existence of family networks connecting Buenos Aires to Colônia. Between November 1774 and January 1776, 43 percent (31 cases) of women bearing children in Colônia were free, 49 percent (35) were slaves, and 9 percent (6) were freed black and freed pardas. Half of all women bearing children between 1774 and 1776 were originally from Colônia. Women from West Central Africa (Angola, Congo, Benguela) constituted 28 percent of the baptisms, while Costa da Mina was the origin of 9 percent. Portuguese America was the origin of 9 percent of child-bearing women (Rio de Janeiro, Bahia, and Rio Grande), and 3 percent (2 cases) were from Buenos Aires.[15]

The high number of mothers born in Colônia attests to the creolization of Luso-Brazilian society in Rio de la Plata.[16] The prevalence of Colônia-born women in the parish records indicates the long-term presence and settled nature of Luso-Brazilian families in the town. Moreover, the records show that roughly 20 percent of the slaves giving birth in Colônia were residents of the city with long-standing connections in the community. The origin of godparents indicates clearly the rootedness of the African-descent community. Slaves owned by different Colônia residents were listed as godparents of each other's children. In one case, the mother was listed as the grand-daughter of an Angolan slave of Jeronimo de Ceuta Freyre, a merchant in town in the 1720s and 1730s.[17] The existence of the Brotherhood of Rosário and a freed-pardo militia battalion further attests to the significant presence of slaves in Colônia's social life in the second half of the eighteenth century.[18] In the majority of the baptismal records, there are no references to personal connections among slaves, and the godparents often are labeled simply as "witnesses." These data suggest that most slaves had arrived in Colônia recently or constituted a transient population. The role of Colônia as a regional slave-trade center had an impact on the demography of the entire Río de la Plata estuary.[19]

The high proportion of slaves suggests that Colônia's residents acquired slaves and reexported them to Spanish territories. Since the second quarter of the eighteenth century, slave ships from Rio de Janeiro, Bahia, and Africa entered Colônia's harbor. While Portuguese authorities established a tax to accrue on the slaves sold to Buenos Aires, Spanish authorities continuously confiscated slaves from the Portuguese vessels in the estuary under the guise of suppressing contraband. Thus Colônia's slave trade not only affected the demography of the Luso-Brazilian town but also shaped that of the region, including the Spanish colonies in South America. Furthermore, the trade in slaves shaped the institutional and commercial development of Colônia.

Because this Luso-Brazilian outpost in Río de la Plata did not include extensive agricultural territory after 1737, the large population of slaves lived in a relatively confined urban space. Administrative records indicate four main uses of slave labor in Colônia during the period: limited agricultural production, domestic service, artisanal and other wage labor, and port work as stevedores. Although the agricultural area available for agrarian production was reduced, the use of slaves in rural activities clearly developed. During the 1760s tithe records indicate significant production of *frutos do pais* (local goods, fruits, grain) and fish. The former usually amounted to around 50$000 reis (rs) (7 pesos) and the latter around 300$000 rs (400 pesos).[20] These values suggest that such products played an important role in providing the day-to-day food supply of Colônia. The use of domestic slaves was also important, especially considering that slave ownership accorded status. Skilled wage-earning slaves were also a source of income for families or widows in the town.[21] Finally, slaves performed the heavy work of unloading and loading cargo at the port's docks.[22] Nevertheless, domestic slavery, foodstuff production for the local market, and urban or port labor do not seem to explain why almost half of Colônia's inhabitants were enslaved in 1760. The commercially oriented community's strong connection with Rio de Janeiro—the largest slave port of South America—and the prevalence of slaves from Angola, Congo, and Benguela in the city suggest that it was a center of active slave trading networks. I suggest that the bulk of the slave population in Colônia was eventually sold to the Spanish American colonies.

Colonia's role as an outpost for the Atlantic slave trade had deep roots. In the 1740s Portugal collected a tax of 750$000 rs (10 pesos) per slave sold to Buenos Aires, an undeniable sign of the existence of an enduring and well-organized regional slave trade route.[23] For the year 1745, the total revenue produced by this tax amounted to 3:262$500 rs (4,293 pesos), which was equivalent to the sale of 435 slaves to the Spanish American dominions.[24] In 1746, on behalf of local merchants, Governor Antonio Pedro de Vasconcelos petitioned the king and the Overseas Council for the abolition of the tax, arguing that it was illegal since it was created without proper royal license. Furthermore, Vasconcelos lamented that the tax imposed on traders in Colônia undercut their competitiveness with the prices slave traders offered in Buenos Aires.[25] According to the Portuguese governor, the tax added 10 percent to the price of a slave in Colônia and drove Buenos Aires traders away from purchasing slaves there, which involved greater risk due to the trade's illegality. Based on these arguments, the tax was nullified.

There are records from the late 1740s of Colônia merchants operating directly in the slave trade from Africa or of slave vessels crossing the Atlantic from the African coast to Colônia In 1746, Manoel Pereira do

Table 2   Slaves Disembarked in Colônia from Africa

Year	Total Slaves	Children	Children %
1748	386	2	0.5
1749	409	77	18.8
1749	452	65	16.0
1749	407	61	15.0
Total	1,654	205	12.4

SOURCE: *Voyages–Online Slave Trade Database.*

Lago a prosperous merchant, a militia captain, and the *almoxarife da Fazenda Real* (royal treasurer), petitioned the king to send a slave vessel to the African coast to acquire slaves for Colônia.[26] Four slave vessels arrived in Colônia in 1748–49, and a total of 1,654 slaves disembarked.[27] These numbers suggest that the arrival of slave vessels would have had a strong influence on the town's demography, because the number of slaves arriving in this period roughly doubled the town's population.

The number of slaves that arrived from Bahia between 1760 and 1770 also suggests Colônia's role as a regional distribution center for the Luso-Brazilian slave trade. The town received 211 slaves from Bahia (208 Africans and 3 Creoles)—1.2 percent of the total number of slaves exported from Bahia in the period. Although the number is low, one must remember that the main commercial connection in Colônia was with Rio de Janeiro rather than Bahia. Furthermore, compared to other politically peripheral regions of Brazil, such as Rio Grande do Sul (0.3 percent), Colônia imported almost four times as many slaves from Bahia and close to the same number as the entire Mato Grosso region (1.2 percent) (table 2).[28]

Perhaps the most important slave trade carried out in Colônia was the one with Rio de Janeiro. Important information about the practice of Rio de Janeiro providing slaves to Colônia appears in a letter from the viceroy of Brazil to the king regarding the sale of slaves to the Spanish colonies in 1780. In this letter, Viceroy Luis de Vasconcelos (r. 1778–1790) justified the sale of ninety slaves to be shipped to Montevideo in 1780 by referring to the well-known slave trade to Colônia since the mid-eighteenth century.

A similar resolution [of selling slaves], in truth, went against the prohibition of selling slaves for areas that are not under the dominion of Your Majesty, passed on October 14, 1751. However, after the publication of this resolution, practices to the contrary had been common. From Colônia and other locations of this government, slaves always had been exported to Spanish dominions without any action against such trade by the authorities, and this is because such laws had been enacted only to satisfy Foreigners who complained about contraband of slaves.[29]

Colônia's last Portuguese governor, Francisco José da Rocha, offered more conclusive evidence of the scale and methods practiced in the Luso-Brazilian port. Rocha reported to the Overseas Council that Spanish Coast Guard vessels constantly attacked Portuguese boats in the Río de la Plata, "stealing" slaves under the pretext that they were being smuggled into Spanish dominions. According to the data gathered by the governor, the Spaniards confiscated more than a thousand slaves between 1765 and 1775. Usually the confiscations occurred while Portuguese boats were fishing in the River Plate. Each of these ships carried between six and fifteen slaves and between one and three free sailors.[30] Most of the confiscated "fishing" ships and slaves belonged to merchants and officers of Colônia.

Colônia's role as a regional center for the slave trade is also evidenced in a 1766 treatise on how to suppress contraband trade between that city and Buenos Aires.[31] According to the observations presented to the Council of the Indies, a slave in Colônia do Sacramento was sold for 100 to 120 pesos, a clandestine slave would sell in Buenos Aires for 180 to 200 pesos, and the cost of a "legal" slave in Buenos Aires could vary from 300 to 500 pesos.[32] The Spanish bureaucrat who wrote this "anti-contraband" memorial emphasized the need to eliminate taxes on all branches of trade as a means to curb the intense flow of contraband goods, silver, and enslaved people between the two towns. According to the anonymous Spanish bureaucrat, "All live off the clandestine commerce with the Province of Río de la Plata and the ones in the interior of Chile and Tucumán. From Colônia they obtain all products from Europe, food delicacies from Portugal, goods from Brazil, sugar, tobacco, *aguardiente de caña* (cane alcohol), and a large number of slaves."[33]

COLÔNIA'S MERCHANT ELITES

Colônia's mercantile community established familial and business connections with merchants and authorities from Buenos Aires.[34] In addition to kinship, business, and political networks, religious connections provided institutional stability for merchants to operate against mercantilist laws. The emergence of a regional elite with multilayered networks involving merchants and authorities from both empires during Colônia's era paved the way for the type of commercial arrangements that characterized Montevideo's role in the Río de la Plata port complex after 1777.

According to the Argentine historian Fernando Jumar, the development of Colônia as a commercial entrepôt in the Río de la Plata port complex had a profound impact on all sectors of Buenos Aires society. It allowed wealthy merchants and small traders to participate in transimperial trade.[35] Smuggling operations in Colônia were commonplace, often involving merchants and colonial authorities and varying from large transactions involving bribes and thousands of pesos to smaller deals worth as little as 700 pesos. The latter was the case of a transaction involving the Spanish petty trader Nicolas Carense and a Portuguese identified only as don Cristobal. The transaction was settled in Colônia and was worth 1,400 pesos. Carense paid the Portuguese don Cristobal 700 pesos in Colônia and arranged the delivery of the goods at night on the island of Martin Garcia, when he paid the remaining 700 pesos.[36]

The reestablishment of Colônia do Sacramento and the rapid development of a local Luso-Brazilian merchant community reveals the willingness of both communities to create trade connections beyond imperial limits. Between 1717 and 1722 only thirteen individuals identified themselves as merchants in the general census conducted by the local authorities. A few decades later 116 individuals were directly involved in trade.[37] Almost two-thirds of these individuals were identified as merchants (*homens de negócios*). Many of these merchants were also involved in the military under the Portuguese administration.

The deep connections between merchants and authorities in Colônia are exemplified by one of the most important families in the town during the eighteenth century, the Botelhos. Manuel Botelho de Lacerda was born in Vila de Murça, Portugal. In 1705 he served in the Portuguese army in Spain's borderlands. During the following years, Botelho carried out an exchange of prisoners with Spain and brought back more than six hundred freed soldiers to Portugal. In 1712 Botelho was in Portuguese America serving as *sargento-mor* (sergeant major) of the fort of Santa Cruz in Rio de Janeiro. Also in Rio de Janeiro, he earned the position of sargento-mor of an infantry garrison (*terço*). Botelho was redeployed to Colônia with this rank 1718. During his first two years in Colônia, Manuel Botelho supplied his garrison with 2,000 cruzados from his own estate to purchase food and pay salaries.

Botelho's position in Colônia's administration, responsible for official contacts with Buenos Aires, guaranteed him privileged channels to conduct trade with that city. In 1720 Botelho went to Buenos Aires for two months to negotiate the restitution of an amount of silver confiscated from the wreck of the Portuguese ship *Caravela* in the Río de la Plata. When Antonio Pedro de Vasconcelos (r. 1722–49) arrived in Colônia as the new governor in 1722, Botelho became one of his main advisers. Botelho was responsible for integrating the new governor into the legal and illegal local networks and advising him on the commercial dynamics of Río de la Plata. In 1725 Botelho traveled to Portugal via Rio de Janeiro to take care of personal business. While his interests were not restricted to the Río de la Plata port complex, his role in the Río de la Plata networks was precisely what allowed him to extend its business in other commercial centers in the Atlantic, such as Rio de Janeiro.

By the late 1720s Botelho accumulated key positions in the local power structure. In 1729 he was once again in Buenos Aires on an official mission under orders from Governor Vasconcelos. In the same year Botelho took office as Colônia's judge of customs. As a military and fiscal authority he earned social prestige, fiscal exemptions, and privileges that permitted him to act with more freedom in his own economic activities. As the official responsible for the contacts between the Buenos Aires and Colônia governments he had free access to Spanish American merchants. Further, as Colônia's judge of customs Botelho determined the legality of goods imported and exported from the Portuguese town. These positions granted him (and his partners) an extremely privileged position regarding commercial operations in the estuary.

The commercial advantages of holding offices in the colonial administration surfaced when a corruption scandal emerged. In 1734 Joseph Meira da

Rocha, a merchant resident in Colônia and an agent of the powerful Lisbon merchant house of Francisco Pinheiro, presented a series of denunciations against Botelho and the governor.[38] According to Meira da Rocha, the governor and his higher-ranking officers received bribes of around 4800$000 rs (6,315 pesos) to allow English ships to enter Colônia's harbor.[39] Meira da Rocha also denounced the "great scandal of the numerous dinners and banquets" where the principal merchants and authorities of Colônia socialized with Vasconcelos and British officers and merchants.

Portuguese authorities seemed to be aware of Vasconcelos's and Botelho's possible involvement in fraudulent activities. In a letter to the Overseas Council, Rio de Janeiro governor, Gomes Freire, to whom Colônia's authorities were subordinated, reported that "the Royal Treasury had suffered with great mismanagement by the Governor and by the Field Marshal, who is Judge of Customs [Manoel Botelho]."[40] Allegedly, the governor and his allies were not only involved in illegal activities, but had also sent "huge sums" to Europe through the Portuguese Jesuits of Colônia and Rio de Janeiro. Nevertheless, Rio de Janeiro's governor, Gomes Freire, advised the Overseas Council against prosecuting the governor or Botelho since their absence from Colônia's government would generate more drawbacks than benefits for the Crown. Vasconcelos and his officers were respected for leading the successful military resistance against the Spanish siege of 1735–37. Moreover, Gomes Freire considered it fundamental to maintain the current architecture of authority and commercial activities in the town because of the government's strong connections with mercantile factions in both Colônia and Buenos Aires.[41]

In fact, Colônia's merchants and authorities were deeply involved in legal as well as illegal commercial enterprises. For example, Manoel Pereira do Lago, who sent ships to Africa, and José Pereira da Costa, who exported goods to Buenos Aires and Chile, both held the office of Royal Treasurer.[42] The governor was the most central and visible participant in the scheme, followed by his loyal and wealthy mestre do campo and judge of customs, Manoel Botelho de Lacerda.[43]

Despite the conflict with Meira da Rocha, Botelho's rise to local prominence continued in the 1730s and 1740s. During the great siege of 1735–37 Botelho was interim governor of Colônia and provided loans to the Crown to pay for the costs of the war. And when ill health forced Vasconcelos to temporarily leave office in 1743, Botelho governed in his place. Botelho's reputation also granted him influence over larger institutional networks.[44] In the early 1740s Botelho's daughter, Rita Botelho Trindade, married an English businessman named João Burrish who resided in Colônia.[45] Botelho thus acquired ties to the British mercantile community in the region and overseas. This a connection was especially important given that the British had lost direct access to the region in 1737. After 1740 it became common for ships carrying both Portuguese and British flags to enter Colônia's harbor.

By the late 1740s Manoel Botelho was head of the most distinguished and powerful family in Colônia do Sacramento. His social and political position allowed him to obtain privileged positions for the members of his family in Colônia and elsewhere in Portuguese America. Manoel's son, Constantino Botelho, was named captain of the infantry terço in which Manoel was mestre de campo. It is noteworthy that military positions not only meant prestige and social status but also granted legal privileges and commercial exemptions. In the 1750s Constantino moved to Rio de Janeiro, where he eventually married the daughter of a wealthy merchant who had previously been Rio de Janeiro's *provedor* (superintendent) of the Royal Treasury. Four other relatives and siblings followed Constantino to Rio de Janeiro and also married into well-placed local families: his brother, Jose Botelho de Lacerda, as well as Ana Teresa da Felicidade and José Manuel Burrish, children of Rita Botelha and João Burrish. It is noteworthy that Constantino's daughter also married into an affluent family in Rio, attesting to the successful maintenance of the status his father acquired in Colônia.[46] Locally, Manoel Botelho's other son, Antonio, was excused from a subaltern position in the military service because of the influence and the merits of her father.

Botelho's privileged position also shaped his family's active participation in Colônia's religious life. In the late 1720s and early 1730s Botelho sponsored the construction of a chapel devoted to Santa Rita. The images, *alfaias* (ornaments), and silver objects used to decorate the chapel's interior were purchased in Buenos Aires.[47]

However, the Botelho family picture is not complete without mention of Manoel Botelho's brother, the captain Pedro Lobo Botelho, who also lived in Colônia. In the late 1740s the governor of Buenos Aires, Joseph de Andonaegui, referred to him as a "person of great character who deserves the most distinguished treatment."[48] Pedro Lobo acted as interlocutor between the governors of Colônia and Buenos Aires. This privileged position in the transimperial circuits of power continued at least until 1753. When the governor of Rio de Janeiro, Minas Gerais, and the captaincies of the south, Gomes Freire Andrade, count of Bobadela, visited Colônia, Pedro Lobo Botelho was mentioned as the "captain ambassador" of Colônia in Buenos Aires.

The wealth and status accumulated during the first half of the eighteenth century were enough to guarantee privileged social status in the decades that followed. Even after the change of governors and suffering from various physical ailments, Manoel Botelho continued to occupy positions of prestige in public and religious ceremonies. During the celebration of the inauguration of the king dom José I, Manoel Botelho sat beside Governor Luis Garcia of Bivar during all the public festivities.

Transimperial networks surpassed the mere involvement of isolated merchants and colonial authorities. The long-standing connections between Luso-Brazilians and Spanish Americans were not only based on commerce and governmental authority. The case of Botelho de Lacerda and family illustrates the deep connections between merchants and authorities in Colônia and Buenos Aires. The advantages offered by controlling key offices enabled the Botelho family to establish enduring commercial connections with Buenos Aires. Transimperial trade allowed the family to gain positions of influence and power in Colônia and to integrate the family into Rio de Janeiro society. This pattern of commerce, involving transimperial interactions and connections between merchants and authorities, continued in the following decades, even after the fall of Colônia, with its relocation to Montevideo.

This interlocked community of merchants on both margins of the Río de la Plata counted other institutional opportunities for socialization. If bureaucratic positions were instrumental in conducting trade in the region, religious institutions also provided an effective platform to support transimperial trade. Merchants from both urban centers were active members of the same lay confraternities, especially the Franciscan brotherhood. Participation in religious activities in general and in lay brotherhoods in specific not only provided an institutional avenue across the estuary but also ensured the existence of links of solidarity, trust, and trade among merchants.[49] Religious orders were actively involved in the long-distance financial transactions. Both Franciscans and Jesuits were charged, at different times by both Spanish and Portuguese authorities, with sending silver to Europe on behalf of local merchants.[50] The cross-border associations created by merchants illustrate the extent to which transimperial trade had come to define the mercantile communities of Río de la Plata.

The analysis of Colônia's urban life is especially revealing of the social relevance of participation in religious organizations. Formal property titles in the rural area surrounding the city were unavailable because of the official territorial limit, a *tiro de canhão* (cannonball shot). As a result, the traditional relation of landownership and status found in other parts of Portuguese America (e.g., Rio de Janeiro, Bahia) was not present in the region.[51] Therefore city life concentrated on the most important and prestigious activities, and the urban environment was the primary theater to display social status. In other words, the absence of formal titles of landownership meant more importance was attached to the representation of power through architecture, religious activities, officeholding, and participation in community life. Participation in religious brotherhoods was especially appealing to the mercantile elites, who could not only display their status and wealth but also enjoy the financial and commercial benefits of membership.[52] During the colonial period, these institutions were in charge of charity, poor relief, care for the sick, and burial of the dead. In addition, members of lay brotherhoods counted on mutual aid, and these institutions frequently supplied credit at the local level.[53]

In 1722, just five years after the reestablishment of Colônia by the Portuguese, seven religious brotherhoods had been created in the town, attesting to the importance of religious patronage and membership in religious orders.[54] Moreover, Colônia's principal authorities and merchants were patrons of the churches and chapels.[55] For example, Manoel Botelho de Lacerda's chapel dedicated to Santa Rita was constructed in the style of the chapel in Rio de Janeiro and was blessed by a priest from Rio de Janeiro the next year, 1723.[56] In the following decades Botelho bought several religious images and artifacts in Buenos Aires to display at his chapel. Those images were blessed by the bishop of Buenos Aires and were acquired from the Franciscans and from the Religiosos do Carmo in the same town.

The use of images in a Portuguese chapel blessed by a Spanish priest only became a fact of any consequence in 1748, when the bishop of Rio de Janeiro

threatened to excommunicate the residents who attended masses celebrated in the chapel in Colônia. The reason for such an extreme measure
was that the religious images and apparatus were blessed by religious men
from a bishopric outside the jurisdiction of the bishopric of Rio.

Public celebrations and religious festivals also provided opportunities
for sociability between Spanish and Portuguese elites. To celebrate the
marriage of Portuguese prince Don Joseph and the *infanta* Maria Anna in
the early 1730s, plays and parades took place in the streets of Colônia for
a whole week. Social status and hierarchy were rigidly reproduced, and
each person, authority, and corporation had its specific role to play.[57] The
participation of the Jesuits was also emphasized in the course of the pag-
eantry, highlighting the honors and distinctions that this order enjoyed.
During these occasions, authorities and merchants from Buenos Aires
participated in public festivities in Colônia and occupied honored positions.[58] The festivals allowed the elite of both cities to strengthen their
personal and commercial relationships while displaying a common understanding of social hierarchy.

Brotherhoods enjoyed an important role in the religious life of Colônia.
Between 1760 and 1777 there were a total of ten religious brotherhoods in
Colônia: three third orders and seven fraternities. In 1760 at least two
brotherhoods petitioned Lisbon to formalize a new altar and a new
chapel.[59] The Irmandade das Almas (Brotherhood of the Almas) petitioned for an altar in the Matriz church, and the Third Order of Carmo
asked to remodel a chapel for its use.[60]

In the second half of the eighteenth century the brotherhoods of São
Francisco and Carmo were the two most important in Colônia. Most of the
town's elites belonged to one of these third orders. Out of one hundred
death records examined, twenty-four people were buried in the Franciscan
habit, fifteen in the Carmo habit, and only one person in the Boa Morte
habit.[61] Brotherhoods also gained prominence in the community by
escorting the dead in processions prior to burial.[62] Of one hundred
records, only thirty-four people did not receive this honor: twenty-five
babies, three poor seamen who did not reside in town, two Indians born
in Spanish America, and one person simply listed as "poor."

In comparing data from other parts of Iberian America, Colônia's *cof-
radias* (lay brotherhoods) reflected the central role of commerce articulat-

ing society, attested by the importance of the Franciscans. Saint Francis was the patron saint of merchants. In Minas Gerais during the eighteenth century, São Francisco and Carmo were ranked in the sixth and thirteenth positions respectively.[63] In Buenos Aires merchant membership was most prominent in the brotherhood of São Francisco. Socolow found that 42 percent of the city's merchants belonged to the São Francisco brotherhood in the late eighteenth century.[64] Colônia do Sacramento's elites shared the same preference for religious brotherhoods.

The connections between Franciscans in Buenos Aires and Portuguese America is revealed in greater detail by a conflict opposing the governor of Buenos Aires, Pedro de Cevallos (r. 1757–66), and the superior Franciscan brother between 1761 and 1763. In the early 1760s, the arrival of Pedro de Cevallos as the new governor of the provinces of Rio de la Plata provoked changes in the political and social dynamics of the estuary. In 1761 the governor enacted a *bando* (decree) expelling all Portuguese Franciscan brothers from Buenos Aires and forbidding the Franciscan order from hosting Portuguese subjects. This measure was motivated by the "excesses" of the "large number of Portuguese from Colônia and Rio de Janeiro bearing the Franciscan habit."[65] The governor justified this measure as crucial to repressing contraband trade, stating that the Franciscans "were responsible for moving large quantities of silver for many merchants of Colônia, and from there exporting it to Rio and Lisbon."[66] Cevallos also cited specific cases of Franciscans involved with commercial enterprises in Colônia and Buenos Aires during the 1750s, emphasizing the losses caused to the Real Hacienda by the illegal export of silver.[67]

According to Cevallos, the Franciscans in Buenos Aires were "protectors" of Portuguese subjects and promoted the "intermingling of Spaniards and Portuguese," against the interest and regulations of the Spanish Crown. According to Cevallos, the Franciscan order counted approximately 350 members in Río de la Plata Province, and forty-five of them were Portuguese. As a result, in addition to their expulsion, the governor petitioned the Council of the Indies to forbid the membership of Portuguese subjects in the Franciscan brotherhood in Río de la Plata. This petition was denied, however; the Franciscan superior argued that the Franciscan order had a mandate to convert indigenous people and all other people in the *fronteras* according to the Council of Trent. Moreover, the superior reminded the council that expelling members of the order was "against the Laws of the Religion."[68]

Religious networks provided official pretexts for social and economic interactions across imperial limits. The participation of Spanish and Portuguese subjects in religious festivals and the acquisition of sacred art across formal imperial boundaries evinced the reality of intercultural fluidity and extensive cross-border interactions in Rio de la Plata. Often these transimperial connections persisted in violation of the regulations and interests of the colonial centers of power (namely Rio de Janeiro and Lima). Furthermore, religious orders and lay brotherhoods provided an institutional channel for transimperial interactions. The presence of Portuguese friars and lay brothers among the Franciscans in Buenos Aires and their involvement in commercial activities in Côlonia reveals the strength of transimperial networks connecting the merchant communities of Portuguese and Spanish America.

THE FINAL YEARS UNDER PORTUGUESE RULE

During the eighteenth century, transimperial trade fueled Colônia do Sacramento's demographic, economic, and social development. The town's growth was crucial in creating a space in which subjects of both Iberian empires interacted. The Portuguese colony played a crucial role in the incorporation of the Banda Norte into Atlantic circuits of trade. Moreover, the growth of the Luso-Brazilian urban center was intimately connected with the economic, political, and commercial development of Buenos Aires based on strong networks of trade, family, and authority that crossed imperial boundaries. In addition, the active slave trade in Colônia provided Spanish Americans with access to cheap labor and shaped the demographics of Buenos Aires and other regions in the interior of Spanish South America. Transimperial religious networks supported these commercial connections and provided additional legal pretexts for Spanish and Portuguese subjects to cross imperial borders. Religious festivals and the existence of third order chapters and brotherhoods provided relatively protected channels for transimperial interactions. Both Jesuits and Franciscans were deeply connected to merchants and authorities on both sides of the Rio de la Plata and used their privileged networks of communication and transportation to facilitate contacts and export silver.

By 1775 rumors of possible political changes in Rio de la Plata already informed Portugal's political strategies in the region. Between 1775 and 1777 Portuguese diplomats were increasingly aware of Spain's intentions to create the new viceroyalty of Rio de la Plata. As a result, when don Pedro de Cevallos attacked Colônia for the second time, the population was neither able to resist a military siege nor prepared to do so. Colônia's governor, Francisco José da Rocha (r. 1775–77), had instructions not to fight the viceroy's troops but instead to abandon the town. This time, unlike previous moments of distress, the Portuguese in Rio de la Plata could not count on strong British support. England was busy suppressing the revolution of its thirteen North American colonies and unwilling to engage in a conflict with the Spanish empire that could undermine British positions in North America. As a result, in the winter of 1777 the Portuguese population was expelled from Colônia for the last time.[69]

In 1778, one year after the destruction of the Portuguese imperial project in Río de la Plata, Spanish free trade laws opened the ports of Montevideo and Buenos Aires to the Atlantic market. These changes triggered a reconfiguration of the Río de la Plata port complex. In the following decades, Montevideo became the main Atlantic port in the estuary and the chief center of transimperial interaction. Although the Portuguese empire was expelled from the region, Portuguese subjects and transimperial networks endured. The logistics, methods, and networks developed in Colônia do Sacramento would shape the dynamics of trade unfolding in Montevideo. Although Buenos Aires was the main political and economic center of the region, Montevideo emerged as the main hub for transimperial trade, benefiting from the extensive connections, experience, and human resources provided by Luso-Brazilian traders who previously operated from Colônia. Despite the desire of Buenos Aires elites to have direct control over transatlantic shipping, Montevideo became the viceregal capital's principal deepwater port. Moreover, patterns of transimperial trade, which developed during the century-long Portuguese presence on the North Bank, eventually became the defining character of commerce in the Banda Oriental.

2 Departing without Leaving

LUSO-BRAZILIANS UNDER THE VICEROYALTY

In May 1777 more than ten thousand Spanish troops arrived in Río de la Plata under the leadership of the new administrative district's first viceroy, don Pedro de Cevallos. Cevallos had two missions: to establish the new viceroyalty with its capital in Buenos Aires and to conquer the Portuguese town of Colônia do Sacramento. By June Colônia was besieged by land and sea. On July 3 the Portuguese town fell.[1] Cevallos then ordered the demolition of fortifications and houses and sent the rock, tile, and wood to Buenos Aires. More than one thousand Luso-Brazilians were displaced from their homes. The defeated soldiers were allowed to return to Portuguese-held territory in America, but 540 Portuguese subjects remained in the area.[2] The latter were forcibly relocated to areas in the Spanish dominion, such as Córdoba, Tucumán, Buenos Aires, or Montevideo, and to the countryside of the Banda Oriental.

Following the conquest of Colônia, the transimperial networks that had existed before 1777 were reorganized. Concomitant with the creation of the viceroyalty of Río de la Plata, the city of Montevideo became the mandatory port of call for all vessels arriving or leaving Río de la Plata and the naval base for a newly created naval command in the region. These measures opened up opportunities for new social groups, mostly centered in

Montevideo, to enter the regional and transatlantic trade. Whereas political and economic elites were already established in Buenos Aires, upstarts in Montevideo found room to acquire power and wealth from the rearrangement of Río de la Plata's transimperial trade.

In this chapter I examine the relocation of Portuguese subjects and networks of trade that had existed in Colônia do Sacramento prior to 1777. Based on Portuguese and Spanish documentary evidence, I argue that although the Portuguese colonial project in the region was aborted after the fall of Côlonia, a significant contingent of Portuguese subjects remained in the region under Spanish rule and the city of Montevideo and the countryside of the Banda Oriental became a focal point for Luso-Brazilian inhabitants. Most important, the strong networks of trade linking Portuguese America and the Spanish population of Río de la Plata relocated to Montevideo. This process reflects the gap between official colonial policies and the social dynamics of colonial subjects at the edge of empire. Although the Portuguese state-sponsored enterprise had failed with the loss of Côlonia, the social, economic, and political networks connecting subjects of both Iberian empires were not destroyed. The long-standing Portuguese presence in Río de la Plata must be understood as an integral variable in shaping the region's historical process even after the expulsion of the Portuguese empire from the region.

Beginning in the seventeenth century, a large Portuguese mercantile community did business with Buenos Aires, but large-scale migration from Spain in the second half of the eighteenth century had effectively transferred that trade to Spanish hands by 1778. While Portuguese subjects in Buenos Aires were closely watched and controlled by the authorities (period restrictions on mobility, residence, and weapon and property ownership), in Montevideo and in the Banda Oriental relations between Luso-Brazilians and Spanish Americans were more fluid. A porous territorial border and the forced migration of Portuguese from Rio Grande to San Carlos in 1764 also facilitated the integration of the Portuguese into the society of the Banda Oriental to a higher degree than was common in Buenos Aires.

The difference between the Luso-Brazilian immigrant community in Montevideo and the one in Buenos Aires was more qualitative than quantitative; the Portuguese constituted 53.5 percent and 52 percent of the foreign population of each city respectively.[3] After the fall of Colônia, important sectors of the mercantile and seafaring communities that controlled logistic and social networks with Portuguese America relocated to Montevideo. By contrast, those who moved to Buenos Aires were mainly artisans and manual laborers. This difference, I suggest, is due to two factors: the elevation of Montevideo into an Atlantic port and the absence of a previously established mercantile and bureaucratic elite in that city. Montevideo's new administrative status not only allowed easier negotiations with the Luso-Brazilians from Colônia but also provided enhanced human and logistic resources for transatlantic commerce. By comparison, the large population and market of Buenos Aires suffered from a chronic lack of skilled manual and artisan labor. This attracted Luso-Brazilians from Colônia and also reflected the *porteño* (Buenos Aires) authorities' ability to integrate the foreign-born manual-skilled laborers.

Identifying the Luso-Brazilians in the Banda Oriental is not an easy task because authorities in Montevideo produced few documents on foreigners. Moreover, the Spanish military conquest of Colônia allowed Portuguese subjects to remain in the region if they swore an oath of loyalty to the king of Spain. The task of identifying the Portuguese inhabitants of Buenos Aires is much easier. After 1748, the porteño authorities conducted periodical surveys of the foreign population. More specifically, the authorities targeted the Portuguese and on more than one occasion limited their mobility and residence to certain areas of the city. Nonetheless, Buenos Aires's authorities expelled Luso-Brazilians from the city only in extraordinary circumstances.

LIVING BEYOND IMPERIAL LIMITS: LUSO-BRAZILIANS IN BUENOS AIRES BEFORE 1777

After the founding of Côlonia do Sacramento in 1680, the rivalry between Portugal and Spain took the form of sporadic armed conflicts in Río de la Plata. During most of this period, however, intense and enduring familial and commercial networks linked the town to Buenos Aires, despite being illegal in the eyes of Spanish imperial authorities. The existence of these networks never prevented conflict during periods of war between the two empires. Instead, local elites from Buenos Aires used war to renegotiate the balance of power in the estuary.[4] The population of Colônia frequently suffered the hardships of military sieges because of commercial and territorial disputes between the local elites on both sides of the Río de la Plata. In Buenos Aires, many resident Portuguese subjects during this period also suffered from restrictive actions and were kept under constant surveillance. Although the category "foreigner" was defined primarily by imperial origin, the policies governing foreigners affected different sectors of the Portuguese community in Buenos Aires differently.

The Portuguese presence in Buenos Aires had been significant since its second founding in 1580 and until the end of the colonial period (1808). During those two-hundred-plus years, the Portuguese population always accounted for more than 50 percent of all foreigners in Buenos Aires.[5]

During the first forty years of Buenos Aires's existence, the Portuguese mercantile community was crucial to the flow of trade in the region. Indeed, its individual traders benefited from their proximity to Portuguese America during the Iberian Union in the period 1580–1640 and established familial and commercial networks with the Luso-Brazilians that guaranteed the flow of trade outside the Spanish monopolistic system.[6] During this period, the Luso-Brazilian community in Buenos Aires enjoyed ample access to all societal groups.[7] According to Rodrigo Ceballos, at least 20 percent of the *vecinos* (neighbors) of the city were of Portuguese origin, and they not only enjoyed *vecindad*, or political rights of vecinos), but also had access to indigenous labor controlled by the Spanish officials.[8] The ability of the Portuguese to integrate with the elite shaped the political and economic conflicts that emerged in seventeenth-century Buenos Aires by acting as a pivotal element in the definition of the political and economic factions of the city.[9]

Nevertheless, Spanish authorities ordered the expulsion of Luso-Brazilians from the city and from Spanish domains during periodic wars between the two Iberian empires in 1641, 1749, 1763, 1801, and 1805. Even in these years, Luso-Brazilians were allowed to stay in the city if they were married to local women, well connected to both the authorities and Spanish American merchants, or made their living as artisans.[10] As a result, these policies never resulted in the removal of all Portuguese inhabitants from Buenos Aires. Rather, they expanded the scrutiny and control of the Luso-Brazilian population by Spanish authorities. Another important factor determining the control of Luso-Brazilians in Buenos Aires was their visible participation in the contraband trade, specifically during the eighteenth century.

The most visible Luso-Brazilian groups in Buenos Aires were artisans and merchants. In the seventeenth and eighteenth centuries the city was in constant shortage of manual laborers, and it became a welcoming haven to Portuguese artisans. As a result, Buenos Aires authorities allowed a large number of Portuguese artisans to settle in the city. Of the more than two hundred Luso-Brazilian artisans recorded as operating in Río de la Plata between 1580 and 1808, the majority resided in Buenos Aires.[11] In 1608 the lack of skilled labor in Buenos Aires caused the *cabildo* (municipal political body) to ask the Luso-Brazilian authorities in Rio de Janeiro to send blacksmiths and artisans who could repair weapons.[12] A royal decree of 1641 ordered the expulsion of Portuguese subjects from Spanish dominions. In Buenos Aires, Governor Cabrera ordered a survey of "suspicious" Portuguese inhabitants but did not expel those described as *oficiais mecanicos* (artisans) because of their "importance for the survival of the city."[13] The presence of Luso-Brazilian goldsmiths, silversmiths, blacksmiths, and painters persisted until the end of the colonial period.

In fact, the defection of artisans from Côlonia do Sacramento to Buenos Aires was a recurring problem for Portuguese officials.[14] According to the Portuguese authorities, Spanish officials readily welcomed artisans and oficiais mecanicos from Colônia, providing licenses for them to work or even to earn a salary as construction workers on public works. Similar assistance was not given to Portuguese traders in Buenos Aires.

The Portuguese merchants in Buenos Aires were also visible in the city, but their visibility was the result of conflicts over their often-controversial commercial activities. In the seventeenth century, active trade involving Luso-Brazilians from Colônia was common but still illegal under the laws of the Spanish Crown. Moreover, a large number of petty traders, storekeepers, and traders in Buenos Aires were of Portuguese origin. Although we have not been able to identify the total number of Portuguese involved in commercial activities before 1777, I have identified Portuguese subjects as owners of *pulperías* (general stores), street vendors, and small traders who also served as middle men between the commercial communities of Buenos Aires and Colônia.[15] Among the Portuguese charged with being illegal traders, the most noticeable characters in the documents are seafarers, who, according to the Spanish authorities, were *mercanchifles* disguised as sailors and seamen.[16]

In 1744 the Portuguese accounted for forty-seven (69.1 percent) of the sixty-eight foreigners living in the city. This number does not include the Portuguese who had settled in Buenos Aires in the previous century and already become vecinos or married local women. Nevertheless, in 1749 the governor of Buenos Aires ordered the expulsion of some of the Portuguese. According to the governor, the measure was accompanied by renewed efforts to suppress the contraband trade between Colônia and Buenos Aires because of the "scandal" and concern that such activities caused among some cabildo members.[17] However, in 1750 the Treaty of Madrid started a period of cooperation between the two Iberian powers in Río de la Plata.

Control of the Portuguese population by Buenos Aires authorities reached its apex in 1762 and 1763. Cevallos, then governor of the provinces of Río de la Plata, issued a series of bandos ordering the authorities to record the residence of all Portuguese subjects; the latter were not permitted to relocate, were required to observe curfews, and prohibited from owning weapons and from moving in certain areas of the city. Unmarried Portuguese without a legal occupation were considered suspicious and sent to other regions in the countryside, distant from ports and from the Portuguese domains. Moreover, Cevallos's regulations established capital punishment for Spanish subjects caught trading, selling weapons, furnishing food supplies, or harboring Portuguese subjects.[18] Although this ordinance was issued in a period of open warfare between Portugal and Spain, it affected populations that were not directly in the theater of war and had consequences that lasted beyond the end of hostilities.

Strict control of the Portuguese population in Buenos Aires continued in the following years. In a 1765 bando, Governor Cevallos ordered that a number of Portuguese subjects who were still residing in Buenos Aires be sent to the distant city of Córdoba. When many Portuguese failed to leave the city, Cevallos provided oxcarts to transport them out of Buenos Aires within four days. The order also provided that if any of the expelled subjects were found in the city, those who harbored or protected them were to be punished at the governor's discretion.[19] Such a decree suggests that previous efforts to remove the Portuguese were never entirely effective and that there were no effective mechanisms for population control.[20]

THE PORTUGUESE IN MONTEVIDEO BEFORE 1777

In summer 1723 a Portuguese expedition led by mestre de campo Manuel Freitas da Fonseca arrived in the bay of Montevideo and established a fort. This settlement went against the recommendations of Colônia do Sacramento's governor, who regarded the enterprise as competing for resources with his own town, located 150 miles north and refounded only seven years earlier. In 1724 a military expedition led by the governor of Buenos Aires, don Bruno Mauricio de Zabala, attacked the Portuguese in Montevideo and conquered this outpost. Zabala then founded the city of San Felipe de Montevideo, displacing Portuguese control of Montevideo's bay, the best natural port on the Río de la Plata. Curiously, the Portuguese authorities in Colônia provided no other aid than welcoming the displaced Portuguese refugees.

From the beginning Montevideo was intrinsically connected to the Portuguese presence on the North Bank of the Río de la Plata. If the very foundation of the city was a response to the Portuguese expansion into the Río de la Plata region, then the following decades of Montevideo's development were marked by the presence of the Portuguese town of Colônia do Sacramento. Geographic proximity, trade opportunities, the need for supplies, and the threat of hostile indigenous groups were factors that fostered the contacts between the subjects of Spain and Portugal in the region.

No laws directly prohibited contact between the populations of Montevideo and Colônia until 1730, when Spanish officials in Buenos Aires forbade Portuguese subjects from settling in Montevideo. The involvement of the Portuguese Domingo Martínez in the assassination of a Minuane Indian provoked the order. After the murder, Martínez fled to Colônia to avoid punishment.[21] As a result of the incident, the Minuane raided the suburbs of Montevideo. The porteño authorities issued the bando of 1730 to prevent such incidents in the future. Nevertheless, routine contacts between the inhabitants of both cities were common. The arrest of a Spanish subject charged with contraband for introducing cattle into Colônia reveals that such interactions were commonplace during the period. The smuggler alleged that he "did not know" about the unlawfulness of commercial and social contacts with the Portuguese of Colônia.[22] The need for supplies led the Cabildo of Montevideo to allow Spanish subjects in Montevideo to

acquire foodstuffs and other basic goods in Colônia.[23] This measure created
an official route between the two cities, allowing goods and people to flow in
greater numbers across imperial boundaries. The new route could, of
course, be used for illegal exchanges as well.

The presence of Portuguese subjects residing in Montevideo was also
notable. In the magisterial work *Genesis de la familia uruguaya*, the
Uruguayan historian Alejandro Apoland recorded that between 1726 and
1753, 27 of the 260 men who married (10.4 percent) in Montevideo were
resident Portuguese subjects. Most of these Portuguese subjects married
Spanish subjects, including official settlers from the Canary Islands.[24]
There was only one recorded case in which both groom and bride were
Portuguese subjects born in Portuguese America. More important, six
Portuguese subjects were married to settlers and received plots of urban
land distributed by the Spanish Crown.[25] Not only did the Spanish authorities officially acknowledge the Portuguese subjects' presence in town
through these actions, but these Portuguese were among the elite urban
landowners of Montevideo. As such, these early settlers were also granted
the status of *pobladores,* ensuring both their political participation and
their right to privileges regarding land use in the community.

The integration of Portuguese subjects into Montevideo's society was a
long-standing social and demographic phenomenon. In addition to the
Portuguese subjects married to Spanish women, patterns of property ownership attest to the successful insertion of the Portuguese in Montevidean
society.[26] For example, by 1754 the Portuguese tailor Joseph de Melo owned
a number of plots of land in the suburbs and a building in the city in which
he rented out rooms.[27] Unlike in Buenos Aires, in Montevideo Luso-
Brazilian subjects not only were able to become affluent members of the
community but also were loosely regulated regarding property ownership,
spatial distribution, and occupation.

The most revealing evidence of the strength of Portuguese social, political, and economic networks in Montevideo appeared during the 1762–63
war between Portugal and Spain. In 1762, the governor of Buenos Aires,
don Pedro de Cevallos, issued a bando ordering the expulsion of all
Portuguese from Río de la Plata. However, Montevideo's governor, Joaquín
José Joaquín de Viana (r. 1750–64, 1771–73), canceled the order. Viana
refused to expel the Portuguese because they were "useful and active in the

defense of the city" and had contributed their private resources to the war effort.[28] The governor was not alone in defending the Portuguese. The cabildo of Montevideo and the six Portuguese *benemeritos pobladores* (meritorious settlers) of the city also approved the petition to cancel the expulsion order.[29] Although the resolution did not include single, nonresident Portuguese, no Portuguese were actually expelled from the city.[30] The failure to expel the Portuguese in 1763 is symptomatic of the high level of integration of Portuguese subjects into Montevideo's elites. Governor Viana defied Cevallos's superior authority to defend the Portuguese, and the cabildo supported the decision. These two events reveal the significance of the Luso-Portuguese connections in local society and their ability to influence institutions and colonial policies.

The refusal of Governor Viana to expel the Portuguese had a political cost. In defying Cevallos, Viana gained a powerful enemy. In 1766 Cevallos wrote a series of letters to don Julian de Arriaga, a minister in the Council of the Indies, denouncing Viana's insubordination and involvement with the Portuguese. According to Cevallos, Viana was "un hombre de los mas perniciosos que jamas han venido a la América [among the most pernicious men who have ever come to America]" because he refused to obey orders and also incited officials and others in Montevideo to defy Cevallos's authority.[31]

The rivalry between the governors of Buenos Aires and Montevideo was also expressed in a dispute over who would conduct Viana's *residencia* (audit) at the end of his term in office in 1764. The governor of Buenos Aires pushed to have one of his political allies, don Joseph de Villanueva Pico, appointed judge. However, the appointment went to Manuel de Achucarro, who was "a relative" of Viana and a "vecino de Montevideo" according to Cevallos.[32] In an effort to discredit Viana, Cevallos and his allies argued that Viana was controlled by the Portuguese and pointed out that his sister was married to the Portuguese Manuel José Melo Pereira. Viana himself was married to dona Maria Alzaybar, the sister of Francisco de Alzaybar, the first *latifundia* owner on the North Bank and a powerful merchant who was involved in a plot to engage in contraband trade through the ports of Colônia and Montevideo in the 1730s and 1740s.[33] Interestingly, Francisco de Villanueva Pico, Cevallos's ally, had also been involved in a Buenos Aires company that traded illegally with Colônia in the 1740s. Nonetheless, Villanueva Pico also wrote letters denouncing

Viana and his allies for facilitating the exchange of correspondence and the flow of cattle and goods between Colônia and Montevideo.[34]

While it is clear that both Montevideo and Buenos Aires had strong commercial ties to Colônia, the rivalry that divided the political and mercantile factions in the cities was centered on the nature of relationships that each city had with the Portuguese. Viana and his partners in Montevideo were accused of being more lenient and permissive with their Luso-Brazilian neighbors in Montevideo and of having constant social and trade interactions with the settlers of Colônia. Such charges were followed by denouncements of contraband involving Montevidean inhabitants and authorities. Buenos Aires authorities, on the other hand, presented themselves as guardians of the Crown's interests in repressing contraband in the region. After all, the control of contraband was supposed to result in a stricter policy toward the Portuguese in Buenos Aires as well as against Colônia. Nevertheless, the active involvement of Villanueva Pico in these episodes suggests that extirpating contraband was not the source of the problem. Rather, the factional conflict concerned an effort to determine who would control the contraband networks and the terms of trade involved in such deals. While Buenos Aires elites used Cevallos's military campaigns against the Portuguese to obtain more advantageous terms in the commerce with Colônia, they also tried to minimize the participation of the elites from Montevideo.

In being more permissive and open to the presence of Luso-Brazilians settlers, Montevideans progressively strengthened their social and commercial networks with Portuguese America. If Montevideo lacked the powerful commercial community of Buenos Aires, the city was a safer environment for Luso-Brazilians in many respects. Montevideo's permissive policies toward Luso-Brazilians were visible by the existence of a group of Portuguese benemeritos in the city and the lack of control over the mobility of the Portuguese population. Furthermore, Montevideo's authorities canceled expulsion orders issued by Buenos Aires' authorities against the Luso-Brazilians. Also, Montevideo's governor and cabildo refused to engage in military campaigns against Colônia. As a result, Montevideo became a hub for familial and commercial networks that crossed imperial limits.

In 1777, however, Cevallos returned to Río de la Plata as its first viceroy and the leader of an expedition of ten thousand troops. No regional support was needed or capable of interfering with his intent to overtake and destroy the Portuguese town of Colônia. And by June the Portuguese population was expelled from Colônia and its urban structure obliterated.

WARFARE AND RELOCATION IN THE BANDA ORIENTAL

There is evidence of a substantial Luso-Brazilian presence and social involvement in the local communities of at least two regions in the interior of the Banda Oriental. San Carlos received more than one hundred Luso-Brazilian refugee families following the Spanish invasion of Rio Grande in 1764. In addition, Soriano and Nueva Mercedes, areas close to Colônia do Sacramento, were home to farmers and rural workers of Portuguese origin. In both cases warfare seemed to have been an important reason for relocation to Spanish dominions. Nonetheless, the social, economic, and political impact of the Luso-Brazilian contingent in the Banda Oriental extended beyond periods of war.

In 1763 Governor Cevallos launched an expedition to conquer all Portuguese territory east of the old Tordesillas Treaty line. With the nullification of the Madrid Treaty, which had replaced the Portuguese and Spanish diplomatic conventions regarding the imperial limits in America, the Spanish Crown reinvoked the 1494 treaty. In December 1763 the governor invaded Colônia do Sacramento and early in 1764 took possession of the Portuguese forts of Santa Tereza and San Miguel and the town of Rio Grande. The military campaign resulted in the Spanish invasion by sea of the island of Santa Catarina. The campaign had a serious demographic effect on the Luso-Brazilians in Colônia but an even greater one on the Portuguese settlers in Rio Grande.

The military invasion of Colônia did not produce an exodus of the population, and by December 1764 the town was returned to the Portuguese Crown. Rio Grande, however, remained under Spanish rule for twelve years. The military siege of Colônia probably provoked the flight of some of the town's inhabitants to the safety of neighboring areas. But considering the lack of serious military engagement and the absence of any official reports of population relocation, the number of emigrants was probably inconsequential. On the other hand, after the conquest of Rio Grande, Cevallos removed 173 Azorean immigrant families to Spanish dominions.

The casais from the Azores were state-sponsored immigrants brought to America by the Portuguese Crown to populate the borderlands.

The coerced migrants from Rio Grande were accommodated in the town of San Carlos, a few miles away from the Spanish settlement of Maldonado. In these cases, Portuguese subjects were legally required to swear loyalty to the king of Spain. In exchange, they enjoyed legal rights and privileges otherwise granted only to Spaniards.[35]

According to the Brazilian historian Moacyr Domingues, many of these settlers married into Spanish American families. At least fifty-two of the families were Portuguese settlers or composed of individuals of mixed Portuguese-Spanish descent.[36] If we assume the average size of the Azorean immigrant's household was similar to the one recorded for Rio Grande and Colônia in previous decades, the total number of Portuguese settlers in San Carlos would be somewhere between 553 and 657.

The Luso-Brazilian presence was also significant in the northeastern portion of the Banda Oriental, a region close to Colônia. Rural Soriano and Mercedes received many immigrants because of intermittent desertions of people from Colônia and sporadic military conflicts. Of an estimated total of 133 inhabitants in Soriano, the Argentine historian Jorge Gelman identified twenty-two Portuguese living in the area in 1771.[37] These Portuguese subjects were members of all social strata and included elites who owned property and more than two thousand head of cattle, medium-sized property owners, petty traders (*pulperos*), and rural wage laborers (*peones conchavados*). Gelman emphasizes the role of the Portuguese settlers as wheat producers not only in the countryside of Colônia but also in Soriano.[38] Among the twenty-two Portuguese mentioned above, fourteen were married and two were widows. Seven individuals owned farms, and only four did not own cattle. The wealthiest was Francisco Magallanes, owner of rural properties and more than two thousand head of cattle. A member of the local elite, Magallanes was living in the pueblo of Santo Domingo Soriano. That the Portuguese were landowners and property owners shows their integration into the social and economic patterns of the general population. There are no signs of extra control or coercive policies directed at the Portuguese. The Luso-Brazilian presence in the countryside of the Banda Oriental not only grew during the second half of the eighteenth century but also became deeply integrated into the region's Spanish population.[39]

THE PORTUGUESE IN RÍO DE LA PLATA
UNDER THE VICEROYALTY

The violence deployed by Cevallos's troops during the conquest of Colônia does not reflect the possibilities open to Luso-Brazilians. According to the Jesuit priest Pedro Pereira Mesquita, Governor Cevallos did not spare the elderly or women and children. Reporting from Buenos Aires, Mesquita provided a vivid image of the burdens faced by the Luso-Brazilians, "It is almost unbelievable that such things were done by a Catholic nation. . . . Castilians think that Portuguese are [nonhuman] species."[40] Such accounts cannot be taken at face value, however. Not all the Portuguese were treated in the same way. Moreover, remote locations were not the final destination for all the Portuguese subjects that remained in the region. Important merchants and seafarers from Colônia do Sacramento were found in the city of Montevideo in the following years. Several factors contributed to the different opportunities open to Luso-Brazilians in Montevideo and Buenos Aires: the absence of a deep-rooted merchant elite before the creation of the viceroyalty and the existence of trade, family, and friendship networks connecting the elites of Montevideo to Colônia and to Portuguese America.[41]

The most visible Portuguese who remained in Montevideo was don Manuel Cipriano de Melo and his wife, dona Ana Joaquina. Cipriano de Melo was a ship's pilot who switched allegiances before the attack on Colônia and participated actively in the Spanish conquest. By 1785 among the well-known Colônia merchants recorded as being resident in Montevideo and involved in trade were Manuel da Cunha Neves, Mamede João, Nicolao Vieira, Faustino and Antonio Dantas and the ship captains Gonçalves Cação (Cazón), Leonardo Perdigão, and Manoel José da Silva.[42] For these agents involved in transimperial trade, Montevideo was a safe haven. The city's newly acquired status as an official Atlantic port, its lack of a large established bureaucracy, and, most important, the preexisting yet incipient mercantile elite with strong ties to Luso-Brazilians from Côlonia represented distinct advantages.

The fall of Côlonia do Sacramento demonstrates that the end of official presence of an imperial state does not necessarily result in the end of previously established social, economic, and political networks. The perma-

nence of Portuguese subjects in the region and their subsequent integration into the local society show that networks of interaction were not
dependent on the state. Moreover, it exposes the difference between imperial politics and the interests and actual conduct of their subjects, who
simultaneously acted as the authorities of the Crown.

After 1777 Montevideo was the main port for arriving Portuguese vessels. It also emerged as the hub for official communications between the
Portuguese and Spanish Americas. In 1779, although the Portuguese representative in charge of negotiating the restitution of property and the
return of the Portuguese subjects from Colônia resided in Buenos Aires, it
was in Montevideo that Luso-Brazilians returning to Portuguese America
gathered. That year, seventy-nine Portuguese subjects were awaiting the
departure of the corvette *São Bento* for Rio de Janeiro.[43]

Unlike the Buenos Aires case, Montevideo's leaders never enforced
extensive policies to expel Luso-Brazilians and never engaged in war directly
against the Portuguese. The brief War of the Oranges between Spain and
Portugal in 1801 reveals the different opportunities Luso-Brazilians found
in Buenos Aires and in Montevideo. Locally, the Portuguese invaded and
conquered the Siete Pueblos missions. The Spanish military response originated from Buenos Aires. The porteño authorities not only sent troops to
the Siete Pueblos; they also quickly enacted regulation to control, disarm,
and expel the Luso-Brazilian population from Buenos Aires. All Portuguese
subjects who were not married or not residents of the city for at least ten
years were forbidden to remain within fifty miles of the city. They were also
forbidden from crossing to the North Bank of the River Plate.

The authorities in Montevideo reacted differently. They offered all
Portuguese subjects the option of swearing loyalty to the king of Spain. In
1801 a total of 129 male foreigners took the oath to become Spanish subjects: 98 Portuguese, 30 Frenchmen, and one Spaniard.[44] Although this
opportunity was given to all foreigners, the prevalence of Luso-Brazilians
suggests that they were the target population of this legal action. Moreover,
the registry containing the nationalizations was identified simply as
"Fidelidad de los Portugueses" and does not mention other foreign groups,
even though the French represented one quarter of those nationalized.
The fact that all the individuals were male, attests to the military purpose
of the legal procedure, but many of these men were heads of households.

Among the 98 Portuguese who took an oath of loyalty to Spain, 48 (37.3 percent) were from Portuguese America, 28 (22.8 percent) from Portugal, 15 (11.6 percent) from the Atlantic islands, and one from Angola. Of the Portuguese, 16 individuals were born in Rio de Janeiro and 12 were born in Colônia, cities that had historically strong social and commercial networks with Montevideo. Bahia and other cities in the neighboring region of Rio Grande recorded three subjects each, São Paulo two. Place of origin of the remaining subjects was listed generically as "Portuguese America." Thus geographic proximity was not the most important factor in the pattern of immigration. Furthermore, the relatively low number of Luso-Brazilians from the neighboring captaincy of Rio Grande de São Pedro shows that overland immigration from the state of Brazil was not significant within this group.

Of the Luso-Brazilians who swore loyalty to the king of Spain, the majority (58) were residents of Montevideo and its surroundings. Fifty-four lived in the city itself, two lived in the *extra-muros* of Montevideo, and two others lived in the nearby countryside. Of the residents of Montevideo, thirteen were also vecinos, which indicates they belonged to the political elite of the city, with full political rights. The four residents of the suburbs of Montevideo were also vecinos, which again suggests their incorporation into the community. It is noteworthy that vecindad was an index of belonging to the political elite even for Spanish subjects. By contrast, of the thirty French persons swearing loyalty, only six were recorded as living in Montevideo and only three were reported as vecinos. These data suggest a high level of political integration of the Luso-Brazilian community in Montevidean society. The high number of Luso-Brazilians residing in Montevideo also speaks to the community's urban concentration.

The general urban character of the Luso-Brazilian group is confirmed by occupational data in the register. Sixty-four percent (49 individuals) engaged in an urban activity, and the remaining 35.5 percent (27 persons) worked in agrarian activities. Among the urban-based group the vast majority were artisans (50 percent of the total), merchants (10.5 percent), and seafarers (3 percent). The large number of artisans can be explained by the need for manually skilled labor, and, most important, by the labor demand of the maritime industry of Montevideo. The relatively small number of traders and seafarers is noteworthy. A possible explanation might be that some merchants had migrated from Colônia thirty-three years earlier and had already sworn loyalty to the king of Spain. Transient seafarers probably saw little need to become Spanish subjects. The agrarian workers presented the higher number of married individuals, fourteen of the sixteen individuals for whom we have information. For the artisan group we have information for eighteen people, who are evenly divided between married and single.

It is striking that 92.5 percent of naturalized Luso-Brazilians were already enrolled in militia battalions. Moreover, 98.2 percent of them presented a militia captain as a witness to their loyalty. Among these supporters, the appearance of men like Cipriano de Melo and the merchants Manuel Diago, Francisco Antonio Maciel, and Melchor de Viana is noteworthy. After all, each of these witnesses enjoyed strong connections with Portuguese America.

The age analysis of the group reveals that those Luso-Brazilians who sought to become Spanish subjects in Montevideo and its jurisdictions were not young, unlike typical immigrant populations. The mean age of the group was 38.6 years, the median 39. Almost half (48.9 percent) of the Luso-Brazilians were forty or older, 20.5 percent were between thirty and forty, and 29.7 percent were under the age of thirty. This pattern suggests that many were long time inhabitants of the region and reinforces the conclusion that Luso-Brazilians were able to integrate into the Montevidean community with relative ease. The war of 1801 had provoked the formal integration of almost one hundred Portuguese and their families into the society of Montevideo and its hinterland.

The ease with which the Portuguese became incorporated into Montevideo's society is symptomatic of the authorities' lack of concern about the foreign population of the city. In Buenos Aires the same episode produced displacement and increased the authorities' control over the Luso-Brazilian population. In 1804, because of the continued European tension, a census of foreigners was taken in Buenos Aires and selected individuals were expelled in 1805. No similar action took place in Montevideo at the same time. In fact, British authorities undertook the first census of foreigners in Montevideo during the British invasion of 1807. British behavior contrasted greatly with the conduct of Buenos Aires's authorities. Nonetheless, the existence of these two censuses of foreigners taken in a relatively short time span in both cities permits a comparison between the foreign populations of Buenos Aires and Montevideo and the Luso-Brazilian population in particular.

The 1804 census of foreigners of Buenos Aires is the most complete survey of foreign subjects living in an urban environment in Río de la Plata.[45] The porteño authorities collected information on the origin, occupation, residence, and civil status of the city's inhabitants, including their property, capital, slaves, family information, and, in some cases, monthly salary. Depending on the census taker, the comprehensiveness of the information varied. However, it is clear that the census was intended to establish control over the large foreign population. In 1804 there were 481 foreigners residing in Buenos Aires, or approximately 1.05 percent of the city's population.[46] The Luso-Brazilians accounted for 51.9 percent (251 individuals) of the foreign population. In addition to the Portuguese, there were 146 inhabitants from Italian regions (21.5 percent), 26 U.S. citizens (3.9 percent), 19 British (2.8 percent), and 9 Irish (1.3 percent). All other places of origin accounted for less than one percent and included places as diverse as "Esclavonia," Iceland, and Sweden.[47] Luso-Brazilians accounted for one of every two foreigners living in the city, and many of them had been in the city for several years if not decades. Although listed as foreigners, the Luso-Brazilian population had deep roots in the region.

In 1806 a British naval expedition attacked the Spanish possessions in Río de la Plata. After a quick initial victory, the British were expelled by militias from Buenos Aires and Montevideo. In the following year, a new offensive was launched. British troops occupied Buenos Aires and Montevideo for several months, and, after their defeat in Buenos Aires, they stayed in Montevideo for almost four months regrouping and selling their merchandise before leaving the region.[48] During their occupation, the British governor ordered a survey of all foreigners living in Montevideo.[49] The census registered 165 foreigners, comprising 1.45 percent of the estimated population of Montevideo.[50] Of the foreigners for whom data on origin are available (157), 53.5 percent were Portuguese subjects, 29.3 percent were Italian, 14 percent were from France, and 3.2 percent were from the United States.

Montevideo, although counting a much smaller population than Buenos Aires, had a higher ratio of foreigners to Spanish subjects. In Montevideo as well as in Buenos Aires, Luso-Brazilians made up more than half of the foreigners present in the city. It should be mentioned that the Montevideo census did not count the Luso-Brazilians who were previously listed as swearing loyalty to Spain in 1801.[51] Thus the Luso-Brazilians listed in the census as recent arrivals were probably persons who were not fully integrated into Montevidean society. Moreover, the discrepancy between the 1801 and 1807 censuses suggests that the actual number of people of Luso-Brazilian origin residing in Montevideo could have been at least twice as large as the 1807 census indicates. Although the percentage of Luso-Brazilians listed in 1807 is similar to the percentage of Luso-Brazilians in Buenos Aires in 1804, their actual demographic and social presence was probably much higher.

In Buenos Aires, the occupations of Luso-Brazilians reflected the same pattern as the foreign population as a whole. Among the Luso-Brazilians, 44 percent (91) were artisans, while artisans constituted 47.9 percent of the general foreign population in the city. Twenty-two percent (47) of the Portuguese subjects were involved in commercial activity, slightly more than the 21.3 percent in the general foreign population. Slightly under 15 percent of Luso-Brazilians (31) were listed as seafarers, as compared to 11.5 percent of the general foreign population, and 11.6 percent (24) were rural workers. Thus although there was a prevalence of artisans among the Luso-Brazilian community, there was also a high concentration of traders and seafarers, reflecting both the city's constant need for skilled manual labor and the significance of commercial networks within Portuguese America.

Among the Portuguese subjects listed in 1807 in Montevideo, the occupational distribution shows a higher concentration of urban professionals. Here, the Luso-Brazilians artisans comprised the larger group, with 46.25 percent (37), compared to 45.5 percent of the general foreign population. Thirty-five percent (28) of Portuguese subjects were involved in trade, compared to only 29.7 percent of the general foreign population. Among foreigners, only 7.3 percent (12) were seafarers, but 50 percent of them (6) were Luso-Brazilians. Finally, three foreigners were listed as agrarian workers, two of whom were Portuguese subjects, one Genoese.

The occupational distribution in Montevideo was more concentrated than in Buenos Aires, and there was higher participation among Luso-Brazilians in commerce. This difference was not only quantitative but also qualitative. Among the twenty-eight Portuguese subjects who had established businesses in Montevideo, fifteen were merchants (*comerciantes*), seven were traders (*negociantes*), four were general store keepers (pulperos), and one was a *mercader* (wholesale merchant). For Buenos Aires, the occupational distribution of the Luso-Brazilians in commerce was as follows: ten merchants, two "comerciante en negros" (slave traders) one "merchant from Porto Alegre," one "merchant from Bahia," and one "merchant from Angola"; this suggests that these three individuals were not permanent residents in the city. In addition, there were seven traders (*tratantes*), two retailers, and eight pulperos.[52]

The data on the occupational distribution of the Luso-Brazilians involved in commercial activities in Montevideo and in Buenos Aires show that in Montevideo the percentage of Luso-Brazilians active in the field was relatively larger. The number of Portuguese subjects of high status in the merchant community was higher in Montevideo than in Buenos Aires in both relative and absolute terms. The number of negociantes was also higher. The number of tratantes was, however, significant in Buenos Aires, while this category did not appear in the Luso-Brazilian community in Montevideo.

The role of Montevideo as a friendlier environment than Buenos Aires for Luso-Brazilians is also reflected in the 1805 procedures to expel a number of foreigners from Buenos Aires. It is important to emphasize that this was the second expulsion of Portuguese from Buenos Aires in less than four years. Of the 129 foreigners forced to leave the city, 55.03 percent (71) were Luso-Brazilians. The others who were targeted principally included 16 Americans, 14 Genoese, 9 British, 9 Frenchmen, 6 Italians, 2 Irishmen, one Swede, one native of Bremen, and one British Asian. Among the Luso-Brazilians, 55 of the expelled individuals were from Portugal and the Atlantic islands, 8 from Rio de Janeiro, 2 from Minas Gerais and Rio Grande, and one from São Paulo, Santa Catarina, Luanda, and Bahia, respectively.

The absence of people from Colônia on this list is noteworthy. On the one hand, it suggests that the military conquest of Colônia enabled Luso-Brazilians to better integrate into the local society because of their right to remain in the Spanish possessions. On the other hand, two individuals originally from Colônia refused to surrender information on their properties, arguing that they should not be considered foreigners. Since they had sworn loyalty to Spain, they enjoyed the same status and legal rights as all subjects of Spanish domains. We do not know the outcome of this case, but it shows that not all people from Colônia were fully integrated into porteño society.

Buenos Aires authorities were specially interested in regulating the presence of Luso-Brazilians involved in commerce and seafaring. The occupational distribution of expelled Portuguese subjects shows the prevalence of individuals involved in commercial activities (34), followed by 9 seafarers, 9 artisans, and only 3 rural workers. These data suggest that Luso-Brazilians working in commerce had weaker ties to the authorities. In early-nineteenth-century Buenos Aires, Luso-Brazilians were the target of regulations, but it was those involved in trade who received most attention from local authorities.

The procedure to expel the Portuguese from Buenos Aires also reveals the role of Montevideo as a safe haven for foreigners in general and for Luso-Brazilians in particular. The same law that expelled the Portuguese from Buenos Aires also prohibited them from moving across the river to Montevideo. Nevertheless, at least four Portuguese were already in Montevideo by the time authorities tried to reach them, and some had fled Buenos Aires.

Both the Buenos Aires and Montevideo censuses of foreigners provide information on place of residence. Marcela Tejerina has shown that the Portuguese population of Buenos Aires in 1804 was concentrated in four blocks in the city (map 2). She argues that this pattern reflected some level of prejudice against these individuals within porteño society.

The pattern of residence of the Portuguese in Buenos Aires was concentrated in five quarters (2, 3, 5, 6, 7 on map 2), suggesting that their neighborhood networks tended to stay encapsulated within their community of origin. The existence of clusters of immigrants also may have created an image of a collective identity identified with the locale of residence. Finally, the distribution of the Luso-Brazilians in pockets of the city shows a tendency for endogamy regarding informal social relations, and this implies their absence in the community life of large areas.

Using the information of the British census of foreigners of 1807, I mapped the approximate distribution of foreigners, Luso-Brazilians in particular, in Montevideo (map 3). The Luso-Brazilian population of Montevideo did not form defined pockets or clusters in specific blocks of

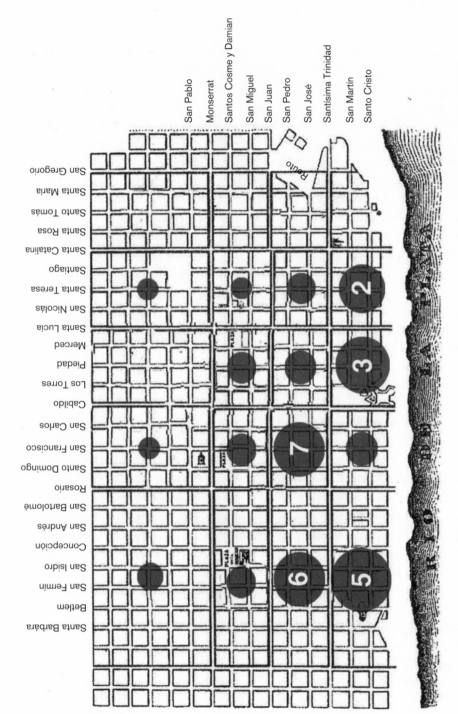

Map 2. Distribution of Portuguese Living in Buenos Aires, 1807. Map based on Marcela Tejerina's *Luso-Brasileños en la Plaza Mercantil de Buenos Ayres.*

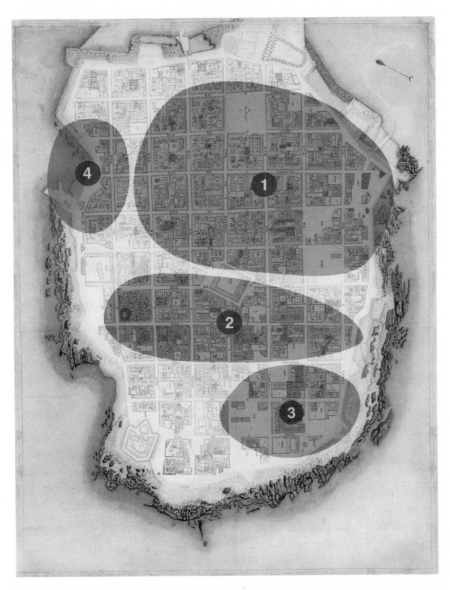

Map 3. Distribution of Portuguese Living in Montevideo, 1807. Original base map courtesy of the John Carter Brown Library at Brown University.

the city. Although some occupational concentration in certain areas is noticeable, Portuguese subjects were present in virtually all sectors of the city, with the exception of the northwestern corner, near the navy fort and headquarters, a relatively newly occupied zone.

In Montevideo, the overall distribution of the Luso-Brazilian population shows that they were spread out throughout the city. This pattern implies that on almost every block there was a Luso-Brazilian inhabitant, making him or her visible in community life but also allowing him or her to blend in with the rest of the population. The lack of clear clusters of Portuguese subjects also suggests that there was no formal or informal control by authorities or possible ethnic prejudice regarding where they could live. Moreover, Luso-Brazilians did not feel the need to live geographically close to each other for economic, social, or political reasons.

Occupational patterns, however, are noticeable in map 3. The concentration of Luso-Brazilians involved in commerce on São Benito Street is clear (zone 2), as well as the concentration of artisans close to the square on San Felipe Street (zone 1). Well-known merchants and authorities of Luso-Brazilian origin, such as dona Ana Joaquina Melo and don José Fernandes, lived on the same street, neighboring the powerful merchants Francisco Berro and Pedro José Irrazquin (zone 2). Other areas of Portuguese artisan and merchant concentration were near the port (zone 4) and near the Plaza Mayor and the cabildo (zone 1).

The end of the Portuguese colonial project with the fall of Colônia do Sacramento did not represent the end of the Portuguese demographic presence in Río de la Plata. Luso-Brazilians and their commercial and social networks relocated to other cities and to the countryside of the Banda Oriental. Some went to Buenos Aires; some were forcibly relocated to interior provinces of the viceroyalty. Another significant portion of the Luso-Brazilians from Colônia relocated to Montevideo and the North Bank of the River Plate. Montevideo and the Banda Oriental presented not only a higher concentration of subjects of Luso-Brazilian origin, but better political and social opportunities for social integration. Montevidean authorities passed laws offering opportunities for Luso-Brazilians to swear loyalty to the Spanish crown and did not enforce expulsion laws or exert any type of control over the residence and mobility of the Luso-Brazilians inhabiting the city. This did not hold true in Buenos Aires, where authorities intermittently issued orders to expel the Portuguese and imposed restrictions on mobility, property, and residence. In addition, in the countryside, Luso-Brazilians not only were present, but they also participated in political and social life.

The process of relocation of the Portuguese in Río de la Plata after the end of the Portuguese colonial presence in the region is an example of how social, commercial, and political dynamics in the late eighteenth century were not determined by imperial states. Strong networks of family, trade, politics, and friendship proved more enduring and malleable than state-sponsored ties. Despite the failure of the Portuguese colonial project in the region, several Portuguese social groups used relocation to and integration in Montevideo and the Banda Oriental as a successful survival strategy. The porous nature of the border between Portuguese American and the Spanish dominions in Río de la Plata and the fluid social networks between subjects of both Iberian empires deeply influenced the social and economic characteristics of Montevideo and the Banda Oriental.

3 Transimperial Cooperation

COMMERCE AND WAR IN THE SOUTH ATLANTIC

In the last quarter of the eighteenth century, a series of profound changes occasioned by revolutionary wars and imperial disputes shook the Atlantic World. In particular, the Spanish empire faced multiple crises, which many historians regard as having paved the way for the Spanish American independence movements after 1808. Spain's involvement in intermittent warfare in Europe weakened the Spanish economy and loosened the Castilian Crown's control over commerce and governance in many regions of its American empire. Military conflicts, especially the French invasion of Iberia in 1808, severed the commercial flow between the Peninsula and the colonies and, subsequently, opened the colonial economies to foreigners in the early 1800s. These processes have been considered crucial to the collapse of the Spanish colonial system.[1] However, such explanations are mainly based on evidence found in official records of the Spanish Empire deposited in the metropolitan archives. The analysis of historical sources generated by the Portuguese empire, and records generated in peripheral areas of the Spanish empire indicate the growing significance of commercial transactions between these areas and other Atlantic empires.

Trade between Spanish Americans and merchants in neutral foreign countries did not mean the interruption of trade routes with Spain.

Moreover, neutral trade could involve Spanish American merchants, foreign merchants, and peninsular merchants as well. As a result, during periods of war, trade involving neutral agents, especially Luso-Brazilians, assured communication and the flow of goods and people between Cádiz and the River Plate. Thus Spanish American merchants were able to profit from commercial intercourse with foreigners and to shape imperial dynamics in the South Atlantic during the last decades of the eighteenth century.

Since the 1780s colonial subjects throughout Spanish America had actively engaged in trade with the colonies of other Atlantic empires. Colonial merchants made full use of the laws promulgated by the Spanish Crown allowing colonies to trade with foreigners (neutral nations) during periods of war. In addition, Spanish American subjects used legal pretexts to carry on a semilegal trade with the subjects of other Atlantic empires. In the Caribbean and the North Atlantic, commercial intercourse between Spanish, British, and North American traders became commonplace. Either by using neutral trade licenses or excuses for ransoming confiscated prizes in British ports, Spanish subjects found ways to actively conduct trade beyond imperial limits in the Caribbean.[2] Although the period was marked by a crisis affecting traditional Spanish commercial routes, the volume of transimperial trade grew substantially. Several authors have examined the growth in neutral trade, often considering it as contributing to the decline of Spanish colonial commercial and political control in the Americas and to a process that was a precursor of free trade and independence.[3] Furthermore, these authors have understood transimperial trade as disconnected from peninsular trade routes. Nevertheless, a close analysis of the changing patterns of trade in the Río de la Plata region based on interimperial sources shows a different picture.

In the 1780s and 1790s the flow of trade between Spain and its southernmost viceroyalty was not interrupted by war. A close analysis of the trade patterns in Río de la Plata suggests that, since the 1780s, Río de la Plata merchants used Portuguese routes to ship goods and information to Spain. Between 1780 and 1806, Río de la Plata's merchants and some of their peninsular counterparts used previously existing networks of trade (legal and illegal) to the Portuguese empire—mainly Rio de Janeiro and Lisbon—to avoid the dangerous crossing of the Atlantic under the Spanish flag. As a result, neutral trade routes enabled the movement of goods, people, silver, and information (including military, administrative, commercial, agricultural, financial, sociopolitical, and geopolitical intelligence) between Río de la Plata and Spain via Portuguese America. Despite the sharp decline in commerce between Spain and its Spanish American colonies, the deep involvement of colonial subjects in neutral trade contributed to the maintenance of imperial dominion in the colonies.

War against England undoubtedly disrupted traditional Spanish trade routes, but a significant number of ships and goods found their way to the Peninsula using the Portuguese route. Consequently, the expansion of commercial connections between Montevideo, Rio de Janeiro, and Lisbon proved crucial in maintaining the flow of administrative, military and commercial information between Spain and its colonies in the South Atlantic. Furthermore, these transimperial routes allowed the export of silver and goods to Spain. Spanish merchants and traders employed Portuguese vessels and relied on merchants and ports in other parts of the Americas. By utilizing the language of empire and reforms, by presenting trade with foreign colonies as fundamental to the growth and maintenance of the Spanish possessions in the region, Río de la Plata merchants justified and pursued transimperial trade. Specifically, Montevidean merchants enjoyed new opportunities for trade with foreigners to enhance their city's role as an imperial commercial center.

Neutral trade regulations opened new possibilities not only for trade but also for shipping routes via Luso-Brazilian and Anglo-American ports. They also encouraged the acquisition of slaves and ships from neutral powers. The scale of neutral trade provoked changes in the balance of power within the mercantile communities of the Spanish empire. I argue that neutral trade and other forms of transimperial interactions did not represent the interruption of commerce and the flow of information between Spain and the South Atlantic colonies. Instead, new legal routes and connections linking Río de la Plata and Brazil in general and Montevideo and Rio de Janeiro specifically acquired strength and significance. Because of the centrality of its port and the existing connections with Rio de Janeiro, Montevideo profited most among the Río de la Plata ports after 1777. As a result, transimperial networks between colonial subjects were responsible for the maintenance of Spanish dominion in Río de la Plata in the late eighteenth century rather than its debilitation.

TRANSIMPERIAL TRADE IN RÍO DE LA PLATA

The Spanish conquest of Colônia do Sacramento in 1777 ended almost one hundred years of direct trade between Portuguese and Spanish American subjects in the Río de la Plata port complex. It represented the empowerment of Buenos Aires elites in commercial matters affecting the entire region and forced Rio de Janeiro's mercantile elites to negotiate new ways to access the silver and hides of the Río de la Plata markets.[4]

By the end of the eighteenth century, Buenos Aires had become a thriving commercial center, in part because of the ease with which colonial merchants could acquire foreign goods from foreign traders. Since Buenos Aires's second founding in 1580, the city was supposed to be supplied with goods via the Spanish commercial system from Lima. But direct and extralegal trade with merchants from other Atlantic empires proved more profitable and soon became a characteristic of the region's commerce. Between 1580 and 1620 Portuguese merchants held the contract for introduction of slaves in Spanish dominions, and they were prominent players in the Buenos Aires commercial community. During the seventeenth century, Dutch, British, French, and Portuguese traders regularly arrived in Río de la Plata using different excuses for trade. After 1680 up to the late 1700s, Portuguese Colônia was the entrepôt for what Spanish authorities considered contraband trade. The regular presence of foreign traders in the region was in sharp contrast to the dearth of official Spanish vessels arriving in Buenos Aires, averaging less than two ships per decade in the eighteenth century. In Buenos Aires a powerful merchant community emerged, which derived its wealth from acquiring cheap European and American goods as well as slaves from Portuguese and other European traders. By the mid-1750s, Buenos Aires merchants controlled commercial networks that spanned the interior of the region to Alto Peru. As a result, Buenos Aires merchants were able to tap huge amounts of silver from Alto Peru and the countryside. Access to silver was one of the main attractions of the region's commerce for foreigners. Because of the close connections between Luso-Brazilian and British traders, Colônia was a hub not only for Portuguese but also Anglo merchants, providing easy access to cheap Atlantic goods. The creation of the viceroyalty and subsequent expulsion of the Portuguese from the region brought about a rearrangement of ports and logistics within the estuary.

When the Spanish empire's proclamation of free trade included Río de la Plata in 1778, Montevideo joined Buenos Aires as an authorized Atlantic port. Endowed with an excellent natural harbor at the entrance of the River Plate, Montevideo became the region's Spanish naval base. Furthermore, the North Bank port became the mandatory port of call for Atlantic trading vessels and the administrative seat of the Resguardo, the office in charge of repressing contraband trade. Practically, Montevideo became the port of Buenos Aires and the seat of naval, customs, and additional port logistics authorities.

In the last quarter of the eighteenth century, the Río de la Plata region was the fastest growing area in Spanish America. The bureaucratic reform that created the viceroyalty and the economic policy that opened both Buenos Aires and Montevideo to Atlantic trade contributed to demographic and economic development. Although Buenos Aires became the seat of the viceroyalty and the Audiencia (High Court) and was home to the wealthiest merchants who controlled the commercial networks to the interior, Montevideo's status as the designated regional port of call for all transatlantic vessels, as well as the only one authorized to disembark slaves, ensured relative advantages in relation to the capital city.

As a result, Montevideo merchants and authorities occupied a strategic position regarding Atlantic commercial networks: a hub for transimperial trade and the port of the viceregal capital. Merchants in Montevideo served as proxies to ensure the logistics, payment of legal fees, and additional commercial agencies necessary for the merchants of Buenos Aires to conduct long-distance trade.

Montevideo's emerging merchant community derived extensive economic and political benefits from being the Atlantic harbor for Buenos Aires's trade. After 1778 Montevideo became the primary exporter of hides in the region. The Argentine historian Juan Carlos Garavaglia has shown that between 1779 and 1784 Montevideo accounted for 53 percent of all hide exports of Río de la Plata.[5] In 1790 Montevideo's share of total hide exports was 56 percent, compared to Buenos Aires's 44 percent, of the total hides export from Río de la Plata.[6] Garavaglia has also demonstrated, based on tax records, that both Montevideo and Buenos Aires experienced fast-paced economic growth, with the total wealth collected by the Crown jumping from 3,000 pesos and 16,000 pesos respectively in 1761–65 to 21,000 pesos and 35,000 in 1798.[7]

Montevideo's inhabitants benefited extensively from outfitting ships at the port. Local merchants, artisans, urban plebeians, and peasants found new opportunities in supplying the mercantile trade and professions. The costs entailed in loading a ship and outfitting it included port fees, food supplies, labor, and warehouses, as well as interpreters and divers and other human resources. To load a vessel at Montevideo, a merchant would invest nearly a month and around 7,000 pesos while his ship was at dock.[8] Furthermore, most Buenos Aires merchants who were involved in transatlantic trade, either with Spain or other foreign countries, had to maintain agents in Montevideo.

Buenos Aires merchants relied on local agents acting as proxies for all logistical and legal procedures involved in sending and receiving goods because Montevideo's deep-water port hosted its own independent customs and port authorities. Local *apoderados* (attorneys) were responsible for paying customs, posting bail for ships, acting on legal disputes, reporting prices and other commercial information, and storing and moving the merchandise, including contraband. Between 1778 and the British invasions of 1806–7, of approximately seventy-seven Montevideo merchants, twenty-one were agents or attorneys for more than twenty-six Buenos Aires merchants and commercial houses.[9] Prominent and successful merchants from all branches of trade employed proxies in Montevideo, including Tomás Antonio Romero, Martin de Alzaga, Casimiro Necochea, and Gaspar de Santa Coloma.[10] Montevideo merchants such as Pasqual Parodi and Juan de Aguirre operated commercial houses in partnership with Buenos Aires merchants. Montevidean merchants also profited from their connections with porteño traders to obtain access to credit and commercial networks in Buenos Aires and in the interior. By the turn of the nineteenth century, five Buenos Aires merchant houses had loaned more than 25,000 pesos to Montevidean merchants.[11] The growth of Montevideo as an Atlantic port was therefore intimately connected with the growth of the Buenos Aires merchant community. By 1803 Montevideo's port was responsible for 73 percent of all transatlantic shipping in the Río de la Plata estuary[12]

Imperial wars encouraged the region's merchants and traders to adapt their commercial strategies in order to make transimperial trade viable during wartime. In the 1780s and 1790s, merchants and ship captains manipulated colonial law to engage in transimperial trade by pushing the limits legality in using licenses for trade with neutral nations and by profiting from public auctions selling confiscated vessels and confiscated cargo. As a result, even the repression of smuggling could benefit specific merchants and stimulated the local market. These transactions ultimately allowed transimperial trade to acquire semilegal status within the Spanish empire. Rather than paralyze colonial trade, war fostered colonial subjects' participation in transimperial commerce afforded by the new Atlantic conjuncture.[13]

Merchants in Río de la Plata used neutral trade laws and also appealed to the traditional right to emergency landing, referred to as *arribada forzoza* in Spanish law, as a pretext to admit foreign vessels in their ports and to enter foreign ports, mostly on the Brazilian coast.[14] Ship captains and merchants were well practiced in this commercial strategy, and customs authorities and Coast Guard officers cooperated in the corruption. In Río de la Plata such tactics were commonplace, and Dutch, French, British, and Portuguese captains had employed them to enter the port of Buenos Aires since the early seventeenth century.[15] The tactic of maritime distress became less common during the eighteenth century when Portuguese Colônia provided a safe haven for Portuguese and British vessels. However, after 1777 Portuguese and other foreign vessels began to appear off the port of Montevideo and to request the right of emergency landing.[16] Under Spanish regulations of *arribadas*, only goods necessary to repair and supply the distressed ship were permitted to be sold.[17] In practice, this law was largely ignored, and vast quantities of merchandise were disembarked in the port of call. The use of this ploy allowed merchants from different empires to engage in commercial intercourse, even during periods of war.[18] Such was the case of the Portuguese ship *Nossa Senhora de Belen y San Josef,* captained by Miguel Josef de Fleytas. The ship left Rio de Janeiro in 1782 bound for Rio Grande, a southern Brazilian port, but bad weather forced the ship to dock in Montevideo. After the ship was in the harbor, authorities authorized the captain to disembark sugar, textiles, and timber, as well as 130 slaves, eventually sold in Montevideo and Buenos Aires.[19] In the following years, operations like this became commonplace.

Transimperial trade took different forms. Many ships that engaged in trade with neutrals did not have a foreign port as the final destination for its cargo, and on occasion the foreign port was not the final port of call of the vessel itself. Making use of well-known routes in the South Atlantic, Río de la Plata merchants and their associates in Cádiz were able not only to trade with neutrals but also to transship merchandise to Europe from Spanish to Portuguese ships using the Brazilian route. On other occasions, Spanish vessels departing from Montevideo would seek the protection of the Rio de Janeiro convoy to cross the Atlantic with the Portuguese flag on their masts. Sometimes the Portuguese flag was deployed for navigation between the Fluminense and Platine ports as well.[20] These strategies sometimes bordered on illegality, and they were not regulated by imperial authorities. Consequently, colonial merchants found the ways and means to conduct their business regardless of whether metropolitan imperial officers had authorized their commerce.

In practice, regulations that authorized only Spanish vessels to engage in trade with foreigners did not constrain "neutral trade." In fact, commercial data indicate that a high degree of intercolonial trade and contact took place between both mercantile communities utilizing the ships of many different nations. Between 1778 and 1806 a minimum of 231 ships were involved in transimperial trade with Río de la Plata (Montevideo). Of these, 116 were Portuguese ships (50.2 percent), 81 were Spanish (35.1 percent), 14 were Anglo-American (6.1 percent), 8 were British (3.3 percent), 3 were French (1.2 percent), and one was Danish. In 18 cases (7.8 percent) there was no information or the documents were damaged in a way that the flag of origin was not legible.[21] The ships arrived in the ports of Montevideo (85), Rio de Janeiro (47), Santa Catarina (3), and Lisbon (4).[22] This pattern shows the strength of the connection between Montevideo and Rio de Janeiro mercantile elites during this period. Among the 81 Spanish vessels, 32 arrived in Montevideo, having passed through Portuguese ports, and 44 declared Rio de Janeiro as a port of call when leaving the port. Three ships arrived in Santa Catarina, and only one ship stopped at the port of Lisbon on its passage to Montevideo. As the distribution of the vessels' ports of origin and flags shows, transimperial trade was not only carried out by Spanish vessels sailing to foreign ports but also concentrated heavily at Montevideo, where a considerable number of Portuguese merchant ships delivered cargos belonging to Spanish, Montevidean, Portuguese, and Buenos Aires merchants. The majority of Spanish vessels that arrived in Montevideo stopped at Portuguese ports before entering Montevideo. By 1804, 78 percent of all transatlantic shipping in Río de la Plata was concentrated at Montevideo.

The ships' itineraries were extremely varied, involving navigation via South American, European, North American, Caribbean, Pacific, West and East African, and Atlantic island ports. From Montevideo, Spanish ships most frequently declared Cádiz or other ports in Spain (Santander) as their final destination, but these vessels commonly docked in Rio de Janeiro. Other regular destinations included Spanish ports in the Americas such as Havana and Callao or foreign ports such as Islas Mauricio, Manila, the coast of Africa, Cayenne, Providence, Boston, or simply "Foreign Colonies." Discrepancies between the official destinations and the actual routes trading vessels at Montevideo sailed reveal that colonial subjects enjoyed a level of autonomy and confidence in conducting transimperial trade.

Spanish officials in Sevilla were aware that sending information, people, and goods via the Portuguese route, Rio de Janeiro–Lisbon, was the safest way across the Atlantic. Conversely, Portuguese authorities saw in this system of cooperation the possibility to obtain Spanish silver and hides, which had not arrived on a regular basis since the fall of Colônia. Nonetheless, a series of restrictions applied to such trade, but during periods of war new opportunities and regulations could be deployed. As a result, colonial subjects adapted imperial law to suit local elites' interests.

The records of foreign ships entering the ports of Rio de Janeiro and Montevideo provide evidence of the higher number of vessels admitted in the ports beyond imperial boundaries. For the period between 1778 and 1792, based on all the available data, sixty-seven official arrivals of Portuguese vessels in Río de la Plata were recorded.[23] For the same period, customs' officials inspected fifteen Spanish vessels that entered Rio de Janeiro's harbor. From 1793 to 1802 a total of fifty-three Portuguese ships arrived in Montevideo (sixty-four counting the arrivals in Buenos Aires's

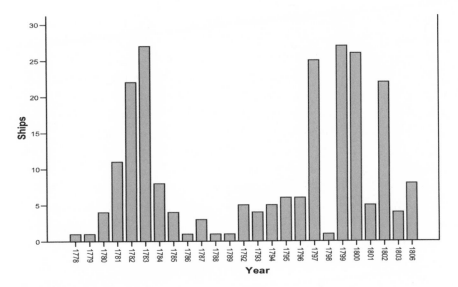

Figure 2. Foreign Vessel Arrivals in Montevideo.

ports).[24] Between 1793 and 1802, fifty-seven Spanish ships arrived in Rio de Janeiro. The historian Ernst Pijning estimates that the coastal trade between Rio de Janeiro and Río de la Plata in the early nineteenth century involved from thirty to forty ships of varied sizes annually.[25] Data show the active role of Portuguese merchants in sending ships to Montevideo in the first half of the 1780s (figure 2). These arrivals were favored by lax regulations during periods of war but also the lenience of Montevideo's port authorities.

Montevideo merchants and authorities benefited from the new trade arrangements. According to the Uruguayan historian Arturo Bentancur, the merchants acted as "intermediaries," "attorneys," and "agents" for their counterparts in Buenos Aires, Cádiz, and Brazil.[26] A significant part of the naval movement of Montevideo was derived from commercial operations conducted by Buenos Aires merchants. Moreover, merchants from Montevideo, such as Matteo Magariños, Francisco de Medina, Manuel Diago, Francisco Berro, José Irrasquin, and Francisco Viana, were able to acquire ships and dispatch their own vessels in Atlantic enterprises.[27] By the early 1790s traders from Buenos Aires would comment on the "increasing number of merchants" located in Montevideo and the need to pay attorneys there to conduct business.[28]

The 1790s were a turning point, a moment when trade between Portuguese American ports and Río de la Plata grew in scale and became more regular. It is noteworthy that the number of Spanish vessels arriving in Rio de Janeiro reached its peak during the 1790s, especially from 1797 to 1799. During the 1790s Spain experienced intermittent warfare, and the laws for trade with neutrals were renewed constantly. These laws and decrees allowed trade between Spanish colonists and foreign colonies— including Rio de Janeiro—during moments of warfare. However, the justifications recorded for such arrivals evince that European ports rather than Rio de Janeiro were the final destination for many of those ships and/or their cargo. During this period, at least forty vessels used Portuguese routes to reach Spanish ports. In other cases, although the final destination was not Europe, transshipment of merchandise to the Peninsula occurred. Thus, the notion that the Atlantic was closed to Spanish commerce must be reconsidered. Foreign shipping allowed for the maintenance of 20 to 40 percent of the regular transatlantic movement during peacetime.[29]

The importance of the route connecting Rio de Janeiro and Río de la Plata had grown to such an extent that in 1799 a petition of merchants and farmers on the "road to Minas Gerais" presented a list of more than two hundred products to export to Río de la Plata, with information on prices and rates of profitability. The list included Luso-Brazilian and European goods.[30] Ernst Pijning has made clear the integration of the Río de la Plata trade into Rio de Janeiro's mercantile circuit via contraband trade and/or semilegal operations.[31] Under ambiguous regulations, local mercantile elites connected with local authorities could use the gray areas of Portuguese law to control transimperial trade.

The trade data for the earlier period 1778–92 reveals the new arrangements and strategies for commerce between Montevideo and Rio de Janeiro. These years followed immediately after the fall of Colônia and reflect the new diplomatic moment between both Iberian empires in 1777.[32] By the early 1780s Spanish Montevideo had replaced Portuguese Colônia as the main Atlantic port for transimperial trade in Río de la Plata.

RECONNECTING RÍO DE LA PLATA TO RIO DE JANEIRO

While the Bourbon reforms may have elevated Montevideo's political and economic stature by turning it into the principal Atlantic port of the viceroyalty of Río de la Plata, it was trade with the Portuguese after 1777 that contributed most to enriching the city and its merchant class. Montevideo benefited more than other Platine ports from the Spanish conquest of Colônia and subsequent decline of Portuguese arrivals upriver and the relocation of merchants and ship captains to the city.[33] Since the 1750s the city was already a safe haven for Portuguese settlers, deserters, and artisans.[34] After 1777 Portuguese traders who resettled in Spanish possessions brought their families, capital, and Brazilian connections with them. In 1778 Manuel Cipriano de Melo, a Lisbon-born Portuguese previously established in Colônia, was appointed a commandant of the Reguardo, the new office created to repress contraband trade. Cipriano de Melo naturalized as a Spaniard and rapidly became one of the wealthiest merchants in Montevideo.[35] Possessing many connections in the local community as well as in Brazil, he was able to convert his family's real estate from Colônia into credit in Montevideo, and in the following years he asked permission to bring back another 30,000 pesos from Brazil.[36] Montevideo's merchants and authorities profited economically and politically from the expulsion of the Portuguese from Colônia by reconnecting the trade routes between Brazil and Río de la Plata.

Merchants and authorities in Montevideo developed commercial and political networks to ensure the viability of transimperial trade. Local authorities, such as Cipriano de Melo, played a crucial role in controlling and participating in smuggling activities since they had the power to determine whether or not the entrance of ships.[37] Therefore, Cipriano de Melo's allies, the Montevideo merchants Francisco de Medina, Melchor de Viana, Francisco Maciel, Francisco Joanico, together with other traders interested in the business of Brazil, enjoyed a pivotal role in restructuring the connections between Río de la Plata and Portuguese America. These merchants were supported by important Buenos Aires merchants, including Tomás Antonio Romero, Manuel de Aguirre, and Domingo Belgrano Perez, who could assure access to the trade networks to the interior of the viceroyalty.[38]

In 1778 the port authorities of Rio de Janeiro recorded the arrival of the Spanish ship *Nossa Senhora—Begonha* from Montevideo under the pretext of arribada forzoza. The *Begonha* was carrying soldiers and correspondence to Cádiz.[39] This was the beginning of the restoration of a route that would become well established in the following decades. It was also the beginning of the route in which Rio de Janeiro functioned as a dominant port of call between Río de la Plata and Spain. A few months later, Vasconcelos, viceroy of Brazil, in a letter to the Overseas Council, detailed part of the new arrangements in order to keep the trade going, even if it went against previous regulations.

In January 1780, the Spanish ship *San Juan e San Jose* docked in Rio de Janeiro under the pretext of arribada. Although it did not unload its official cargo, Vasconcelos reported to the Overseas Council in Lisbon that the officers of this vessel came prepared with silver to acquire tobacco, iron, sugar, and also slaves from Brazil. The viceroy also stated that he wanted to keep as much silver as possible in Rio.[40] Therefore, he made arrangements to supply the Spanish crew with all the goods that they demanded, including slaves. The total value of the operation exceeded 22,000$000 rs (28,947 pesos).

> The amount of silver that remained here could have been much larger if I could had provided more tobacco than the 365 *arrobas* and 28 *arreteis*, which was the product of their (Spaniards') biggest interest. They also took much timber, goldsmith's tools, some wine, 30 *arrobas* of sweets, textiles, iron, wire, and, finally, 93 slaves. Regarding the slave transaction, in the first place I tried to create difficulties, but I ended up allowing such transaction as a big favor. Similar resolution, in truth, went against the prohibition of selling slaves for areas that are not under the dominion of Your Majesty, passed on October 14, 1751. However, after the publication of this resolution, practices to the contrary had been common; from Colônia and other locations of this Government, slaves always had been exported to Spanish dominions without any action against such trade by the Authorities, and this is because such laws had been passed only to satisfy Foreigners who complained about contraband slave trade.[41]

In this letter Vasconcelos reveals the methods deployed by Spanish captains and officials to acquire goods without involving official cargo in order to avoid charges of smuggling. Moreover, these practices were not new but rather an adaptation of already tested methods. Although the ship's destination was another port in the Spanish empire, the captains arrived "prepared" with silver to acquire goods and buy slaves. All these signs suggest that in 1780 old networks of trade were being reestablished. The portfolio of products purchased also reveals the clear knowledge of Spanish traders about what they needed to acquire in Rio—tobacco, timber, and iron—all products typically exported to Río de la Plata via Colônia do Sacramento prior to 1777. Additionally, Platine merchants' acquisition of slaves in Rio de Janeiro revealed the continuity of transimperial trade networks between Río de la Plata and Brazil, an old practice employed since the days of Colônia.

After the 1780s Montevideo became the main hub of transimperial trade in the region and the gateway for the introduction of slaves from Brazil. In 1783 the powerful merchant Domingo Belgrano Perez owed Montevideo customs around 20,000 pesos for taxes on his slave trade operation.[42] This illustrates the strategic situation of Montevideo for profiting from transatlantic commerce and exposes the relationship between the Montevideo's port activity and Buenos Aires's merchant community.

The Brazilian viceroy Vasconcelos's communication evidenced the Portuguese interest in retaining silver and the high level of autonomy local authorities and merchants enjoyed. The viceroy boldly stated that his main goal in welcoming the Spanish arribadas was to obtain the maximum amount of silver possible from those transactions, even though the transaction contradicted imperial laws. Tobacco, wood, iron, and tools were not supplies strictly necessary for the vessel to continue its voyage or to return to its port of origin. Most noticeable, however, was the sale of ninety-three slaves to the Spaniards. The viceroy's correspondence shows that the 1751 royal ordinance forbidding trafficking of slaves was never observed, and many Portuguese authorities thought that the ordinance was in fact intended to divert the attention of foreign powers. Furthermore, Vasconcelos mentioned that the slave trade in Colônia had been conducted without official impediments.[43] In his assessment of the benefits of the trade, Vasconcelos emphasized the recovery of the flow of silver, the incorporation of the Spanish market into economic routes of Rio de Janeiro, and the increased tax income that would result for the Crown.

Although trade with foreigners was specifically regulated, the authorities and merchants of Rio de Janeiro and their partners in Río de la Plata did enjoy a relative level of autonomy in their transactions. With the formal support of local authorities, no previous authorizations were needed from metropolitan powers. On the contrary, the viceroy only informed authorities in Lisbon after the fact. Colonial subjects made decisions about trade with foreigners in the colonial space.

Less than a year later, in 1781, when the same subject was again brought to the attention of the Overseas Council in Lisbon, the viceroy reported in greater detail about the growth of trade with Río de la Plata. He reported that the number of Spanish vessels arriving in Rio and other Brazilian ports had increased because of the war between Spain and Britain. If in the past the Spaniards were willing to come to Rio, now they were also willing to harbor Portuguese vessels in the La Plata estuary.[44] Moreover, Río de la Plata authorities wanted to make clear to the merchants in Rio that Portuguese vessels would be welcomed in Montevideo.

The Spanish envoy assured Rio de Janeiro authorities that Montevideo's port commandant would welcome Portuguese ships seeking to enter the port under the pretext of arribada but in fact wanting to trade. In order to emphasize Montevideo merchants' interest, he brought from Montevideo more than one hundred thousand pesos to show their willingness to spend large sums on trade. Such evidence was enough to convince some ship owners to send their ships officially to Santa Catarina, Rio Grande, and other southern ports, but the vessels would instead sail to Montevideo under the pretext of arribada. In addition, the Spanish envoy promised Rio de Janeiro authorities that such ships would return "loaded with hides and silver, since the Spaniards would facilitate that with abundance."[45]

The traders arriving in Rio from Río de la Plata also wanted to establish partnerships with Rio merchants because the Atlantic was becoming progressively more dangerous for Spanish vessels. The merchant emissaries from Río de la Plata wanted to ensure that traders from Montevideo and Buenos Aires could ship large quantities of hides, silver, and other products from the River Plate to Europe using Portuguese ships.[46] The viceroy confirmed that some merchants from Rio had already sent a ship to Montevideo a couple of months earlier and had been welcomed by port authorities.

The authorities in Brazil, however, were somewhat suspicious of the "good faith" of Río de la Plata merchants. Vasconcelos mentioned to the Overseas Council that the Spaniards could use such excuses to make cheaper shipments to Europe, since the difference in prices between Rio de Janeiro and Río de la Plata could be as much as 60 percent of the total cargo price to Europe.[47] Moreover, Vasconcelos broached his concern about possible smuggling activities; the increasing number of Spanish vessels arriving in Rio would make the control of illegal interactions more difficult. Nevertheless, the viceroy himself was in favor of the trade and attached to his memorandum documents supporting his view. Among these documents was a letter from the powerful and respected merchant of Rio de Janeiro, Brás Carneiro Leão.

Carneiro Leão supported partnerships for transshipping Río de la Plata products to Europe, as well as sending Portuguese vessels to Montevideo. According to Carneiro Leão, the war had made the ocean crossing too risky for Spanish ships, and some Cádiz merchants had authorizations to send capital and information via Portugal. Moreover, the circuitous route offered several advantages to the merchants of Rio: namely, almost all the silver transported would remain in Rio de Janeiro because silver was not shipped but sent via *letras de cambio*. Finally, the existence of friendly and trustworthy merchants in Cádiz and Montevideo would be an advantage.

Carneiro Leão, one of the wealthiest merchants in Rio, had experience with the Platine market dating to Colônia. In 1775 he had a partnership with the Colônia-based merchant João de Azevedo Souza, and together they had advanced to the Colônia administration more than 1,315 pesos. Between 1778 and 1786, Carneiro Leão appeared repeatedly as a trade partner of Cipriano de Melo, commandant of Montevideo's Reguardo. He attested that Cipriano de Melo had credits in Rio de Janeiro amounting to 30,000 pesos and that he had traded slaves and other goods in partnership with him. Carneiro Leão was also involved with captains and merchants that were commonly seen in Río de la Plata, such as João da Cunha and the popular contrabandist known as Captain Barriga (Belly), who was a close friend of Cipriano de Melo.[48]

The justifications used to legitimize disobedience of imperial regulations emphasized the benefits of the Río de la Plata trade and its relative legality. The growth of commerce and the access to silver would be highly significant for the Rio de Janeiro economy. Brazilian viceroy Vasconcelos mentioned the fake licenses given by Spanish authorities, namely, the viceroy of La Plata and the superintendent, permitting Spanish ships and traders to dock in Rio de Janeiro. Given Portugal's neutral status, Portuguese authorities could not deny help or admittance to Spanish ships. Viceroy Vasconcelos also mentioned the possible advantages of such trade: "as for the intended purpose of these shipments, [it seems to me] the merchants can make great use of the neutrality of our flag and of the liberties assured by the agreements between Portugal and Great Britain that declare free and exempt, the merchandise of enemies on board our ships."[49]

According to the viceroy, warfare could be profitable to the Portuguese, because they would benefit from the legal treaties between the Atlantic empires. Without undermining Portugal's position of neutrality and as a primary partner of Britain, transshipment of Spanish cargo allowed Portuguese ship owners and merchants to profit and also reinforced trade and political alliances with Spanish subjects. It is important to recall that in Portugal some politicians were still able to remember the lack of support and protection given by Britain in 1777. At that moment, Portuguese intelligence reports were clear about the Spanish expedition to Río de la Plata that culminated in the fall of Colônia; however, British authorities denied the veracity of the Portuguese information.[50]

Finally, at the end of his long memorandum to the Overseas Council, Vasconcelos reminded metropolitan agents of the commitment of local authorities in Río de la Plata. With the goal of trading and transshipping merchandise, Platine officials were already authorizing Spanish subjects to sail from Montevideo under many different pretexts to Brazilian ports. An example was the 1781 arrival of don Francisco de Medina, one of the merchants in charge of negotiating informal agreements with merchants in Rio. Medina, who was also a trading partner of Cipriano de Melo, was sent by Montevidean merchants to research tobacco cultivation and to buy slaves skilled in it. Medina returned with large amounts of tobacco and slaves to Río de la Plata. However, he brought back neither a single slave able to produce tobacco nor plans or information about tobacco factories.[51]

A memorandum of 1783 indicates that transshipment and incorporation of Spanish ships into the Brazilian fleet were already a fact of commercial life in Río de la Plata. On March 19, 1783, the Portuguese viceroy reported to the Overseas Council that he would not allow ships to sail from Rio de Janeiro straight to Cádiz, nor would he accept Spanish ships coming straight from Spanish ports in the Peninsula to Rio de Janeiro.

Such itineraries would be extremely suspicious if those ships were intercepted en route; thus Spanish ships leaving Europe should only sail to Rio de Janeiro from Portuguese ports. Nonetheless, the viceroy was afraid that the direct trade would facilitate contraband and the avoidance of payment of the transshipment fees in Portuguese ports.[52]

During the early 1780s, war between Spain and England allowed colonial subjects of the Iberian empires to deepen transimperial cooperation. In helping Spanish authorities and merchants, Portuguese traders could have privileged access to Spanish territories and markets. In 1782, while transporting the Spanish surveyors to establish the boundary limits stipulated in 1777, the ship *Carlota* was caught by British privateers close to the Madeira Islands. The *Carlota*'s crew, officers, and astronomers and some of its cargo were transported in Portuguese ships to Rio, where Domingos Mendes da Viana, the powerful director of the whaling contract in Rio, offered help. Viana provided loans and cash advances to be collected in Montevideo, as well as transportation for the crew and passengers to the same port.[53]

Similar acts of explicit cooperation were recorded in Montevideo almost two decades later, when French corsairs arrived with Portuguese ships they had intercepted in the Atlantic. Authorities in Rio soon reported on the important help provided by the "Spanish friend Francisco de Medina." In 1799 Medina not only housed and provided loans to the officers of the three ships overtaken by the privateers but also helped the Portuguese officer in charge of liberating the confiscated ships. Medina interceded with local authorities in order to reinforce the Portuguese claim of illegal apprehension of the ships and the legal implications for the Spanish authorities in allowing such transactions to happen.[54]

The exchange of information on prices, markets, political developments, naval movement, and social unrest was another important form of transimperial cooperation, which also revealed the overlapping interests of Luso-Brazilians and Spanish American subjects. In 1799 when the French privateers arrived in Montevideo, the authorities and merchants of Río de la Plata were vigilant of the foreign crews. On the one hand, the French provided confiscated ships and goods and new business opportunities. On the other hand, Portuguese ships entering the estuary were potentially endangered by the French warships. Without losing time, Río de la Plata's authorities and merchants sent fast-sailing boats to Santa Catarina and Rio de Janeiro to warn Luso-Brazilian authorities and merchants about the French presence in the region.

The acting viceroy of Río de la Plata, a former governor of Montevideo, Antonio Olaguer Feliú (r. 1797–99), was explicit in saying that he had no idea about the plans and strategies of the French ships and that consequently he was sending this warning message in a fast ship with an experienced crew to spread the news. The Spanish viceroy also asked the Luso-Brazilians to use caution when sending ships to Río de la Plata:

> I cannot avoid asking V. Ex. to be sensitive to the repercussions of such news; because I am only in charge of executing orders that I have sworn to protect, I would be delighted in helping the Vassals of *S. Mag. Fidelissima* if it was an option to me without sacrificing our respective responsibilities.[55]

The Río de la Plata viceroy wanted to be clear that he and the Río de la Plata merchants were unable to protect and harbor Portuguese merchant ships at that time.

The war between Britain and Spain was both an important element of and a pretext for trade interactions in the early 1780s, but the end of hostilities after 1783 did not stop the commercial traffic between the Portuguese and Spanish possessions through Río de la Plata. To ship silver and hides via the Portuguese fleet and to acquire slaves and other goods in Rio de Janeiro after 1783, Spanish ships continued to sail into the Fluminense port on their way to Cádiz. The most frequently used excuse for the forced arrivals was that the ships had encountered storms in the Atlantic, and Rio was the nearest port for repairs.[56] After they entered the port, they would be granted time to perform repairs that could vary from fifteen days to six months. In many cases, Spanish captains would manage to transfer their cargo to Portuguese ships in order to reach their final destination in Cádiz via Lisbon. The fees of 4 percent for transshipment and 3 percent for port use were normally applied in Rio de Janeiro. The existence of such procedures and fees shows the everyday character of such interactions.

The use of arribadas as a pretext for trade was a preconceived and predictable commercial strategy. On one occasion in 1785, Captain Ignacio Sestiaga declared it necessary to sell his cargo of hides, copper, and silver in order to pay for repairs and acquire other necessary goods. In fact, however, the captain carried this cargo precisely to pay for services and goods in Rio de Janeiro.[57]

These interactions reveal that semilegal commercial transactions that were permitted during war were continued in peacetime. The patterns of arribadas, transshipment of merchandise, and acquisition of goods remained the same. Moreover, the cargo transported was virtually the same as that transported in the previous years. Once again, imperial laws against trade with foreigners did not impede the cooperation between merchant communities of Río de la Plata and Rio de Janeiro.

Another important factor in allowing such interactions was the new laws favoring the slave trade in the Spanish empire enacted from 1791 on. Based on physiocratic ideas, Spanish reformers aimed to increase Spanish participation in the slave trade. Thus the Crown granted licenses to Spanish colonial subjects to acquire slaves from Africa and even from neutral powers.[58] Such licenses, however, explicitly forbade any other type of trade between Spanish subjects and foreigners. During the 1780s merchants from Río de la Plata obtained licenses to bring significant number of slaves from the coast of Brazil. Nevertheless, as Alex Borucki shows, it was in the 1790s that such traffic increased substantially.[59] However, if the slave trade alone was authorized, it did not prevent merchants from conducting other types of trade.

In the early 1790s, contacts between Spanish and Portuguese subjects intensified. During this period commercial trends observed in the 1780s developed even further. The combination of imperial laws liberalizing the slave trade and trade with neutrals during periods of war enabled colonists to further pursue their own commercial interests.[60] By the turn of the century, direct trade between Rio de Janeiro and Río de la Plata as well as the use of Portuguese ships to transport merchandise across the Atlantic became commonplace. Cooperation between colonial subjects allowed the maintenance of the connections between Spain and its colonies in South America, as the empire progressively depended more on the resources of the colonists.

In the 1790s the number of ships from Río de la Plata entering the port of Rio de Janeiro rose significantly. The stated reasons presented for the arrival of Spanish ships in Rio de Janeiro were of three types: to seek protection to cross the Atlantic with the Portuguese convoy or to transfer goods to Portuguese ships to be sent to Europe; forced arrival due to storms in the Atlantic that would allow Spanish captains to transfer merchandise to Portuguese ships or to sell their goods in Rio de Janeiro; and to use official licenses to undertake commerce with neutrals and to acquire slaves and even ships in order to "nationalize" them in Río de la Plata.

The means by which ships sought protection on the Atlantic crossing could involve the substitution of the Spanish flag for the Portuguese one or the transfer of merchandise from Spanish ships to Portuguese ships. In this last case, Spanish ships normally returned to La Plata loaded with Brazilian and European products and slaves. Such pretexts were normally used during periods of war, when British ships would prevent Spanish ships from sailing to Europe.[61] Nevertheless, in 1796, during a brief interregnum in warfare, such excuses were also used by captains, who claimed to have licenses granted prior to the cessation of hostilities. This strategy was also used to ship merchandise from Cádiz to Río de la Plata via Lisbon and Rio de Janeiro, either using transshipment of merchandise or substituting flags.[62] Both methods proved effective. As the captain of *La Judit* reported, his ship sailed from Lisbon to Rio de Janeiro with a cargo from Cádiz owned by Buenos Aires merchants, with Montevideo as its final destination. *La Judit* crossed the Atlantic in a convoy of 136 ships. At 5°N the convoy was approached by two British privateers, but Portuguese officers made sure that none of the Spanish ships were confiscated.[63]

The use of Portuguese ports, ships, and intermediaries became commonplace. In 1802 the Buenos Aires merchant Francisco de Necochea presented a petition in Brazil and in Lisbon asking that Spanish merchants should not pay port and transshipment fees twice, in Brazil and in Portugal. Necochea asked for a standard regulation for Spaniards to use the Portuguese routes and mentioned that this would benefit their Portuguese associates from Rio and Lisbon. Nechochea proposed a total fee of 7 percent, arguing that the existing fees—two port fees of 3 percent and a 4 percent fee for transshipment—made the cost of doing business prohibitive.[64] Although we do not know the outcome of this case, it shows the importance and regular usage of the Portuguese route by Spanish merchants. Although merchants from Río de la Plata were officially using their prerogative for neutral trade, their transactions did not end in Rio de

Janeiro or other Brazilian ports. They used their knowledge and networks in Brazil to maintain the flow of goods and information between Río de la Plata and the Iberian Peninsula during the 1790s and early 1800s.

The most frequently used pretext by Spanish captains to enter Luso-Brazilian ports was to claim they needed repairs due to storms encountered in the South Atlantic. Even during periods of war, this excuse was used by a large number of captains.[65] In 1796, for example, a Spanish ship owned by an influential Buenos Aires merchant, Tomás Antonio Romero, faced problems while trying to enter Rio de Janeiro. Local authorities initially considered the arrival of his ship, *Jesus Maria José,* illegitimate. Captain José Antonio Sarzetea was originally bound for the Cape of Good Hope, but he entered Rio de Janeiro seeking protection. His ship was permitted into Rio's harbor after the captain and the senior officers—who were Luso-Brazilians—explained the need for repairs to the ship's sails and rigging. This also gave the ship the potential to sell part of its cargo.[66] It is noteworthy that Portuguese ships would deploy the same excuse when docking in Río de la Plata ports. As ship captains used the weather as a pretext to enter foreign ports, this also afforded the benefits to which trade with neutrals' regulations entitled them. Nevertheless, storms were a pretext that would never go out of fashion. From 1800 to 1806, 70 percent of the Spanish ships that arrived in Rio de Janeiro claimed to need repairs because of damage caused by storms.[67]

The first couple of years of the nineteenth century were marked by war between Spain and Portugal. During periods of war, in addition to use storms as a pretext, captains also deployed the rights of emergency landing due to warfare in the Atlantic. In 1800, when a large number of Spanish vessels arrived in Rio de Janeiro, some asked for protection from British corsairs, others sought repairs after naval conflicts, and still others used the weather as the pretext. Interestingly enough, the war waged over the territories in southern Brazil apparently did not prevent trade between Spanish and Portuguese subjects. Because licenses for neutral trade were granted and revoked periodically, I believe that by the 1800s Spanish American subjects had acquired enough experience to know that the arribada conventions were more reliable.

Merchants from Río de la Plata used licenses to acquire slaves in foreign ports to arrive in Rio de Janeiro (as an arribada or not). In doing so, they bought slaves and goods like tobacco, *cachaça* (distilled sugarcane liquor), sugar, and textiles and transshipped merchandise to Europe. Although Spanish laws explicitly forbade the introduction of any other goods together with slaves, they were widely ignored.[68] In many cases, the number of slaves transported on these voyages was relatively small, sometimes fewer than a dozen.[69] The main difference in the use of this pretext as compared to the other two patterns previously analyzed is that these ships did not cross the Atlantic, nor were they officially sending cargo to Europe.

The slave trade route between Brazil and Río de la Plata also attests to the high level of cooperation between Iberian subjects in the South Atlantic. In the 1790s new Portuguese regulations forbidding the export of slaves to foreign regions were enforced. According to Luso-Brazilian authorities, the large numbers of slaves sent to Río de la Plata had provoked an increase in slave prices in Rio de Janeiro from 50$000 rs (66 pesos) to 100$000 (132 pesos), damaging rural producers, since slaves were "the arms of the farmers in this land."[70] Nevertheless, contraband trade involving slaves was extremely hard to stop. Authorities continuously complained that they could not patrol the harbor properly, since Rio de Janeiro merchants would send small boats with slaves to other areas along the nearby coast and then embark slaves directly onto Spanish ships after they had left the harbor.[71] The importance of preexisting networks of trade proved important for the logistics of such operations. In war and in peace colonial subjects were able to find legal excuses to cross imperial boundaries, as well as to find illegal ways of doing so.

Another important opportunity provided by the liberalization of trade in slaves for Río de la Plata merchants involved the possibility of acquiring ships from foreign nations and "nationalizing" them in a Spanish port. Often, the ship to be "nationalized" would arrive in Río de la Plata with a cargo of slaves and other products.[72] The acquisition of ships represented another level of transimperial cooperation, since Spanish American subjects were expanding their trade and naval capacity with the aid of foreign suppliers. These transactions also depended on stable networks of trade, since credit was a crucial element. I have identified transactions that varied from 3,000 to 38,000 pesos.[73] Although such transactions often involved a great amount of silver as the method of payment, traders also purchased on credit and through consignments of merchandise, revealing the dynamic role of transimperial networks of trade.[74]

CONCLUSION

In the late eighteenth century, intermittent warfare between European empires provoked a profound change in the Atlantic patterns of trade. After experiencing an impressive growth in the commerce with its colonies after the reforms of free trade in the late 1770s, the Spanish trade system was disrupted by wars in the last decades of the century. Historians have argued that Spanish ships were impeded from crossing the Atlantic in the 1790s and that Spain was left without control over trade and communication with its colonies. In order to allow the colonies to obtain supplies, imperial officials allowed trade with neutral powers and permitted Spanish subjects to acquire goods in other regions of the Americas. However, analysis of both Portuguese and Spanish sources demonstrates that Spanish colonists from Río de la Plata used Portuguese ships to send silver, goods, commercial and administrative information, and people to Spain. Moreover, on many occasions Spanish ships crossed the Atlantic in Portuguese convoys.

The Río de la Plata was one of the most dynamic regions of the Spanish empire in the last decades of the eighteenth century. After expelling the Portuguese and securing both banks of the estuary, the Spanish empire opened the ports of Buenos Aires and Montevideo for Atlantic trade within the Spanish empire. During this process, Montevideo became the principal deep-water port of the region. The centrality of Montevideo as the port practically made Buenos Aires merchants dependent on agents and authorities located on the port of the North Bank. The requirement that most legal and logistical procedures for shipping across the Atlantic had to be conducted in Montevideo coupled with the renewed connections with Portuguese America gave the city's merchants relative advantages in relation to Buenos Aires. Between 1778 and 1806 more than two hundred ships sailed between Brazil and Río de la Plata. Montevideo became the hub for transimperial trade. The merchants and ship captains who relocated to Montevideo from Colônia brought not only their capital but also their commercial connections. The result was the rapid growth of Montevideo's merchant community and institutions.

Benefiting from laws on trade with neutrals and previously existing networks of trade, Spanish subjects in Río de la Plata were able to keep at least a partial flow of goods between Spain and its southern Atlantic colonies. Such commercial routes involved stable partnerships, credit, and cooperation between Luso-Brazilian and Spanish American merchants and authorities. Such interactions were not always legal, and a variety of legal excuses were used in an attempt to legitimize this route. Despite the extralegality of these transimperial networks, they allowed the Spanish empire to maintain contact with its colonies to a greater degree than the historiography has previously suggested. The agency of colonial subjects in establishing these connections with foreign merchants shaped Spanish colonialism in the last decades of the eighteenth century and into the early nineteenth century.

4 · The Making of Montevideo

CONTRABAND, REFORMS, AND AUTHORITY

In the second half of the eighteenth century, Spain enacted important political, administrative, and fiscal reforms in its American territories. The so-called Bourbon reforms aimed to make imperial administration more efficient and to increase metropolitan control over the vast American dominions. The new regulations had disparate consequences in different parts of the empire and provoked different reactions within the colonies. In colonial centers of power, elites felt that the reforms undermined their authority. In peripheral areas, local elites were able to use the reforms to enhance their position within the empire.[1] In imperial borderlands, the reforms affected not only the way in which local groups related to the metropole but also the way in which they interacted with the local center of power. In Río de la Plata, the creation of the viceroyalty (1776), with its capital in Buenos Aires, empowered the city's political and commercial elites. Nevertheless, the establishment of Montevideo as the region's main Atlantic port allowed the elites of Montevideo to build their own power niche in the region.

Montevideo evolved from a small colonial city dependent on Buenos Aires into a provincial capital in the last half of the eighteenth century, expanding its influence over the territory of the Banda Oriental. In this process the city gained jurisdiction over territories and commercial routes that were previously under the control of Buenos Aires or contested by the Portuguese. Networks connecting Montevideo to Luso-Brazilian merchants enhanced Montevideo's control of transimperial trade routes. Moreover, the knowledge acquired by groups centered in Montevideo about the borderlands during the decade Rio Grande was under Spanish rule (1764–77) played a crucial role in the process. As a result, although economically dependent on Buenos Aires mercantile community and capital, Montevideo merchants and authorities managed to use their privileged port, newly created institutions, and networks to progressively improve their status and enhance their autonomy within the estuary.

This chapter investigates the ways local elites interpreted imperial law in order to expand the jurisdiction of authorities based in Montevideo. It pays special attention to the attempts of Montevideo's elites to use the imperial reforms to secure control over transimperial trade, to guarantee access to resources in the countryside, and to elevate the status of the city within the viceroyalty. The proliferation of new administrative offices with overlapping jurisdictions within the viceroyalty of Río de la Plata led to conflicts that exposed regional tensions and reflected new commerical and political opportunities for regional elites.[2] The analysis of administrative and judicial records reveals how the elites of Montevideo used the newly created Bourbon institutions to control transimperial trade and to repress contraband. Montevideo's administrative officials progressively aggregated authority while the city's merchants developed a higher level of commercial and political autonomy from the viceregal capital. Consequently, commercial and political factions from both sides of the Río de la Plata came into conflict over the control of trade, contraband, and administrative jurisdiction in the Banda Oriental.[3]

Platine merchants and imperial officials in Buenos Aires and Montevideo belonged to interconnected communities, but, beginning in the 1780s, increasing competition between them played out in a series of legal disputes over property, natural resources, and commerce in the Río de la Plata estuary and borderlands. The formation of the Consulado de Comercio de Buenos Aires (Merchant's Guild of Buenos Aires) in the mid-1790s drove the wedge between the interdependent mercantile communities of the Río de la Plata ever deeper. Specifically, Montevidean merchants and authorities complained that the porteño institution did not represent their interests and protested the collection of a new port tax (*averia*) to be charged in Montevideo and credited to the Buenos Aires Consulado.[4] Meanwhile, the merchants and authorities of Buenos Aires questioned Montevideo's exclusive right to dock ships involved in transatlantic trade and attempted to undermine the power of Montevideo's authorities by accusing them of engaging in smuggling, by emphasizing the "second rank" of the city, and by proposing the licensing of a third port in the region at Ensenada de Barragan to serve as an extension of the port of Buenos Aires and bypass Montevideo. Despite these conflicts, Montevideo's primacy in Río de la Plata's transatlantic trade was already well established—a fact that the Crown reaffirmed in 1804.[5]

JOCKEYING FOR JURISDICTION

By using the Bourbon reforms to gain commercial and political autonomy from Buenos Aires, the elites of Montevideo profited from the creation of new offices and the expansion of the duties of existing administrative agencies. They took advantage of the reformist impetus that created additional administrative and political powers to expand Montevideo's jurisdiction over a territory that had previously encompassed multiple cabildos or areas that had been under the jurisdiction of Buenos Aires.[6] This process was legally based on manipulating the competing jurisdictions of the newly reformed fiscal system in the region. Although dependent on the capital and growing economy of Buenos Aires, Montevideo merchants and authorities managed to use their position as a main port and hub of transimperial trade to improve their status and expand their jurisdiction over the Banda Oriental. They justified this expansion of jurisdiction by appealing to the imperial desire to assert sovereignty over the borderlands and to curb contraband trade. In doing so, Montevideo's elites secured control of and access to natural resources and networks of trade in the countryside.

Following the institutionalization of the intendancy system in Río de la Plata in 1776, Montevideo's elites used the legal ambiguities of the Spanish concept of jurisdiction to gradually aggregate increasing political authority over commercial matters and natural resources within the territorial limits of the Banda Oriental. In doing so, they concentrated not on gaining power through the exercise of a single administrative office but on proliferating their authority through multiple branches of the colonial state structure and bureaucracy.

One of the key reasons Montevideo's elites were able to use the Bourbon reforms to gain more autonomy and enhance their status vis-à-vis Buenos Aires was that the term *jurisdiction* was open to multiple legal interpretations and claims. The ambiguities of the term left it open to dispute between competing authorities. In the late eighteenth-century Spanish empire, *jurisdiction* meant the right to govern specific matters and specific territories. The 1780 edition of the *Diccionario de la Real Academia Española* defined term as the "faculty or power conceded to the government to decide over causes" and also as the public *potestad* (power) over legal matters. Furthermore, this power of authorities to rule over civil, criminal, and economic matters was connected to a "place," a territory defined "from one Province to the other."[7] As a result, the disputes over jurisdictions in eighteenth-century Río de la Plata involved different groups claiming the power of the Spanish state over defined territories. Specifically, elites in charge of the new offices created in Montevideo claimed potestad over the regulation of commerce (legal and illegal) and the exploitation of resources in the Banda Oriental.

The jurisdictional powers of the colonial cabildo offered Montevideo's elites the means to gain authority and influence in the region. The cabildo of Montevideo was created in 1729 by the governor of Buenos Aires, Bruno Mauricio de Zavala. Its first officials were elected in 1730. Following the pattern established by cabildos of other dependent cities in the Spanish empire, it had six officials (regidor and alcaldes) plus one alcalde of Santa Hermandad de Buenos Aires.[8] During the initial phase, most of the members of the cabildo of Montevideo were either immigrants from the Canary Islands, Spaniards, or porteños. In these years, the jurisdiction of the cabildo was limited to local affairs, having for its limits the undefined area that could be disputed by neighboring Portuguese of Colônia, the Missions' estancias, and indigenous groups.

Historians tend to consider the cabildo the main institution controlling the jurisdiction of colonial cities and the principal source of local author-

ity. During the seventeenth century and most of the eighteenth, the colonial cabildo was in charge of justice, public works, the distribution of
urban land plots, the construction and maintenance of urban infrastructure, and the regulation of local commerce in the area of its jurisdiction.[9]
It had jurisdiction over food prices, local taxes, local police, and public
works. Neighboring cabildos often clashed over their respective areas of
jurisdiction.[10] The cabildo usually reflected the interests of the vecinos,
residents with full political rights. As the colonies grew, however, more
cabildos were created, and disputes over jurisdiction of territories between
old and new cabildos increased.[11] Often disputes between cabildos
reflected disputes among different groups within a region over the control
of local resources.

Throughout the eighteenth century, however, cabildos were progressively disempowered by the fragmentation of their jurisdictions. The
reforms of the late eighteenth century further diminished their authority.
The emergence of new regional groups that claimed authority over local
affairs as good subjects of the king fostered the creation of new cabildos.
With the exception of newly settled frontiers, the new cabildos governed
areas previously under the control of "older" cabildos. This process was
contradictory. On the one hand, it empowered local groups that found in
the regional cabildos a fortress to defend their local interests. On the other
hand, the fragmentation of jurisdictions weakened the influence of the
institution.[12] Nevertheless, the cabildo maintained the right to directly
petition authorities in Spain, including the king himself, about local matters. Moreover, because the Bourbon reforms created new offices with
jurisdictions that overlapped with those of previous administrative agencies such as governors and intendants, the cabildo became the locus of
regional disputes over local affairs. Montevideo's cabildo proved no
exception.[13]

The office of the provincial governor provided local elites in Montevideo
with another kind of instrument to assert jurisdiction over local and
regional affairs. Governors and viceroys held key authority over fiscal,
military, and political matters that encompassed the area of multiple
cabildos. The governors oversaw customs, military and frontier matters,
and foreign trade. The branches of the Royal Treasury and Customs
House, as well as many officials and clerks, were under the authority of the

governor or the viceroy, where one existed. During most of the eighteenth century, there was a strong connection between imperial authorities and the local elites. That kind of symbiosis between provincial and metropolitan interests was also facilitated by the office of the royal governor in Montevideo, a position first established there in 1751. The governorship of Montevideo extended approximately one hundred miles, from the center of the city in the east, roughly defined by the Cerro Pan de Azucar, and in the north by the San Jose creek. Nevertheless, the region's intermittent warfare enabled Montevideo to extend its jurisdiction in the interest of restraining the Portuguese expansion. In 1757 the governor of Montevideo founded the town of Maldonado in order to promote Spanish control of the port and counterbalance the Portuguese presence in the region. Although given formal jurisdiction over fiscal, military and political matters in the area, Montevideo's governor was still dependent on Buenos Aires; Montevideo had neither a branch of the Royal Treasury nor a customs house. Thus the suppression of contraband trade in Río de la Plata was directed from Buenos Aires, although the officer in charge, Francisco de Alzaybar, had strong interests on the North Bank.[14]

Moreover, the long tenure of Montevideo's governors suggests that the city's elites enjoyed good relations with the Crown's local representatives. On average, a governor served in office in Montevideo for approximately ten and a half years. Five men were appointed governor of Montevideo between 1751 and 1804, and one of them, José Joaquín de Viana, held office twice. Viana is especially notable because he was Montevideo's first political and military governor and because he held the position the longest during his two terms in office. As an officer who led the joint armies of the Spanish and the Portuguese against the rebellious Siete Pueblos Missions during the Guaraní War of 1754–56, Viana gained extensive experience with the Portuguese. During his first thirteen-year term (1751–64) as governor of Montevideo, he maintained good relations with Portuguese authorities and merchants from Colônia. Furthermore, during war between Spain and Portugal , Governor Viana refused to expel the Portuguese population from the Spanish domains. Viana's successor, Joaquin del Pino, also governed Montevideo for more than one decade. Del Pino (r. 1764–77) and subsequently Governor Olaguer Feliú (r. 1790–97) would climb the bureaucratic ladder and become viceroys of La Plata;

they demonstrated their administrative skill at harmonizing local and imperial interests on behalf of the city and the Crown.

The proliferation of new branches of imperial military, fiscal, and commercial administration in Montevideo in the 1760s and 1770s only added to the growing jurisdictional powers of the city. In the late 1760s the Spanish Crown established regular postal service between Montevideo and the Atlantic coast of Spain, and shortly thereafter the port of Montevideo was chosen as the location for a naval base in the region. The year 1772 brought the creation of a branch of the Royal Treasury in Montevideo, giving the region more autonomy in fiscal matters. The following year, a royal ordinance established Montevideo as the official port of entrance in the region, but it was only after the expulsion of the Portuguese from Colônia in 1777 that Montevideo, like Buenos Aires, became a licensed Atlantic port.[15] In 1778, the new Reglamento de Comercio Libre (Regulation on Free Trade) made Montevideo the mandatory port of call at the entrance of the Río de la Plata estuary. In the following years, a customs agency and the Comandancia del Resguardo, in charge of repressing contraband trade, expanded the jurisdiction of Montevideo over transimperial trade routes and the resources of the countryside. The Resguardo initially employed thirty-four people, including officers, mariners, soldiers and clerks.[16] This agency gained more autonomy in 1781, when, for all intents and purposes, Montevideo became the port of Buenos Aires.[17]

The creation of the office of intendant and later that of superintendent also empowered some governors (*gobernadores intendentes*). Thus regional governors gained authority over fiscal and political matters that had previously been exclusively the viceroy's purview. Between 1782 and 1788 the Office of the Superintendent had jurisdiction over the Comandancia de Resguardos and Customs; in addition, it oversaw Real Hacienda matters. In Río de la Plata, Superintendent Sanz claimed jurisdiction over transimperiall trade and, although located in Buenos Aires, supported Montevidean authorities and interests. Between 1785 and 1789 a conflict developed between superintendent Sanz and the viceroy marquis of Loreto (r. 1784–89) over jurisdiction over the slave trade, navigation, and the territories bordering Brazil. The conflict not only exposed the difficulties generated by overlapping jurisdictions but also between Buenos Aires and Montevideo. Sanz was a fervent advocate of expanding the power of the newly created agencies located on the North Bank, especially the Resguardo, giving it legal and de facto jurisdiction over emergency landings of ships, the local branch of the Real Hacienda, the Customs House, and the port.[18] Buenos Aires contested the validity of such measures and accused the superintendent, merchants, and authorities of Montevideo of facilitating contraband trade.

The creation of the viceroyalty of Río de la Plata in 1777 changed the institutional arrangements in the region, and the correspondence between the viceroys in Buenos Aires and the governors of Montevideo illustrate how Montevideo's merchants and colonial elites gained increasing political, administrative, and fiscal autonomy as their city became the principal Atlantic port in the region. As Montevideo became a transimperial hub, its governing authorities assumed more and more control over commercial matters in Río de la Plata and enhanced the prosperity and power of the city's elites.[19] In addition, the founding of cities and villages in the borderlands (e.g., Maldonado and Minas) attested to the further expansion of Montevideo's influence.[20]

In the 1770s, before the creation of the viceroyalty, when the Portuguese were still in Colônia do Sacramento, documents sent from Montevideo to Buenos Aires show a strong pattern of administrative and economic dependency of the former on the latter. The correspondence exchanged between the authorities of the two cities included monthly lists of the amounts of money spent on housing and supplying troops, salaries paid to the troops, and hospitalized soldiers.[21] There were also directives on the creation of *quadrilleros* (police forces) in the interior region of Rio Negro and Yi with the specific instruction to send the people and the goods seized to Buenos Aires (map 4). During this period, contraband apprehended via land or sea was handled by Buenos Aires authorities. Furthermore, reports from Montevideo authorities justifying the actions taken after the emergency landing of a Portuguese ship and handling of prisoners reveal the city's subordinated and dependent role in relation to Buenos Aires for payments and administration of justice.[22]

This institutional arrangement changed drastically with the founding of the viceroyalty in 1777. While Buenos Aires became the seat of the viceroy and the Audiencia, Montevideo benefited from the creation of a customs house and the Comandancia del Resguardo. The enhanced status and power of Buenos Aires as a viceregal capital was accompanied by the increased status and autonomy of Montevideo. The correspondence shows that Montevideo's authorities started informing and reporting on administrative and executive actions already carried out by local authorities rather than requesting authorization and funds. The documents produced in Montevideo were lists of colonizers being dispatched to the new colonies of Malvinas, Santa Lucia, and Maldonado. These colonies were under the direct administration and jurisdiction of Montevideo. Despite the enhanced autonomy, however, the governor of Montevideo still submitted lists of tools and supplies provided to the colonists in order to get reimbursed by the Reales Cajas (Royal Exchequer) de Buenos Aires.

Analysis of this administrative correspondence also shows the growing role of Montevideo authorities in repressing inland and maritime contraband. Illicit commercial activities in the region of the Yi and Negro Rivers were under the jurisdiction of the Real Hacienda of Buenos Aires in the 1770s, but in the 1780s they were under the jurisdiction of Montevideo's Resguardo. The commandant was Don Antonio Pereira, an officer in Montevideo's militia batallion (map 5). Confiscation of contraband goods by a Resguardo officer occurred not only in the Yi and Negro Rivers, but also in Santa Lucia and various areas of the Montevideo port. The confiscated goods were sent to Montevideo, where authorities conducted the legal procedures and the local branch of the Royal Treasury collected taxes and fees.

The suppression of smuggling was one of the chief jurisdictional responsibilities Montevideo assumed following the creation of the viceroyalty of Rio de la Plata. Both the presence of a large number of foreign ships at the port of Montevideo and its authorities' role in suppressing the contraband trade reflected the city's growing commercial preeminence. The Montevidean Aduana (customs) and Resguardo confiscated and auctioned goods, thus laundering the merchandise and then sending it into the legal market.[23] Such operations regarding confiscation and auctioning of smuggled goods not only empowered local authorities and institutions by increasing local institutional revenue but also offered a relative advantage to local merchants, who had privileged access to the confiscated (and often cheap) goods.

By the 1790s Montevideo had emerged from under the shadow of Buenos Aires and had begun to assert a higher degree of administrative and legal autonomy. That such an evolution took place is further evident in Montevideo's dealings with foreign subjects and settlers and in its management and maintenance of the Malvinas and Patagonia colonies.[24] Montevideo's administrative correspondence included reports of the total number of hides exported via Montevideo's port, a list of Portuguese settlers asking permission to live in the Spanish dominions, and lists of prisoners being sent to the Malvinas.[25]

The appearance of multiple requests from Portuguese to emigrate to areas under Montevideo's jurisdiction in the 1790s suggests the fluidity of relations in the borderlands and the relatively easy integration of the Portuguese into the Banda Oriental society. In 1792 Montevideo's government received petitions from seventeen former inhabitants of the Rio Grande, including a physician, who were willing to settle in the Banda Oriental.[26] Most interesting is the petition of a contrabandist, Manuel Pereira. After finishing a three-and-a-half-year jail term in Montevideo, Pereira asked to become a Spanish subject because he had "a brother and relatives[who were] living in the jurisdiction,"and he had been born and "raised in this Province."[27] Although the outcome of Pereira's request is unknown, the episode reveals the fluidity of the borderlands and the normality of contraband trade in this society.

The administrative correspondence also reflects the geographic expansion of the jurisdiction of Montevideo during the 1870s. The regions bordering the Yi and Negro Rivers; Santa Lucia; the forts of Santa Tereza, Santa Tecla, and Maldonado; the Merin Lagoon; and even the regions of Herval and Piratini, in the southernmost Brazilian captaincy of Rio Grande, were now held by the governor and Resguardo of Montevideo (map 6).[28] Outposts controlling the extraction of hides and cattle and preventing the entry of runaway slaves and illegal Portuguese settlers were also charged with suppressing contraband trade along the border and throughout the inland routes.[29] Prisoners arrested for trafficking in contraband and the goods confiscated from them were transported to Montevideo as the above regions were under the jurisdiction of the Real Hacienda of Montevideo.[30]

The correspondence between authorities in Montevideo and Buenos Aires reflects a significant increase in interaction with Portuguese subjects and authorities in the period between the late 1770s and mid-1790s. Documents reporting confiscations in the countryside of dark tobacco and sugar (both of Brazilian origin), and hides, as well as slaves, appear repeatedly.[31] The routine nature of contraband trade is also seen in documents

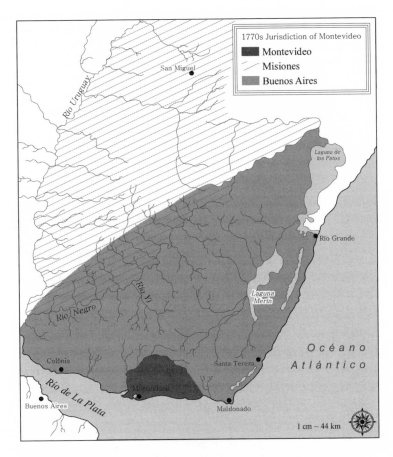

Map 4. Multiple Jurisdictions over the Banda Norte in the 1770s: Montevideo, Misiones, and Buenos Aires.

SOURCE: Alonso Pacheco. Plano en que se demuestra la demarcación ejecutada por las primeras partidas de España y Portugal. 1757. Agustín Ybañez. Mapa del Territorio ocupado por los portugueses. 1804.

about the smuggling of hides, the arrival of Portuguese ships, and the confiscation of contraband goods and slaves in Montevideo's port.[32] The increase in the jurisdictional area together with the expansion of trade registered in the period led Governor Olaguer Feliú to complain about the urgent need for more government officials to perform the duties of customs and to control the routes in the countryside.

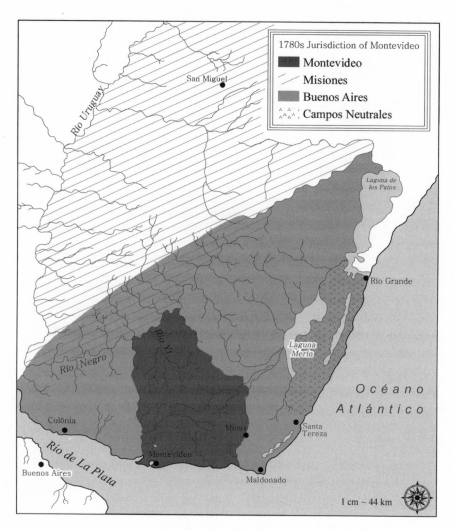

Map 5. Jurisdiction of Montevideo, 1780s.

SOURCE: Alonso Pacheco. Plano en que se demuestra la demarcación ejecutada por las primeras partidas de España y Portugal. 1757. Agustín Ybañez. Mapa del Territorio ocupado por los portugueses. 1804.

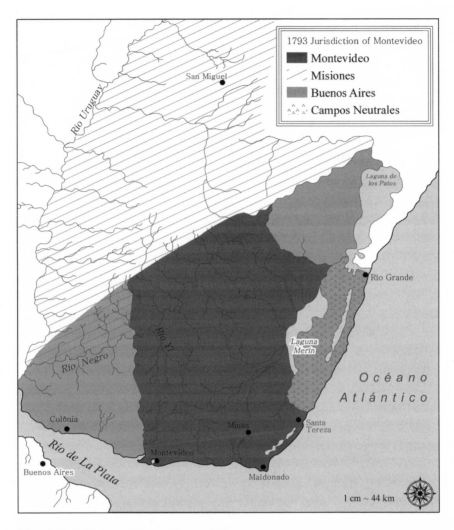

Map 6. Jurisdiction of Montevideo, c.1793.

SOURCE: Alonso Pacheco. Plano en que se demuestra la demarcación ejecutada por las primeras partidas de España y Portugal. 1757. Agustín Ybañez. Mapa del Territorio ocupado por los portugueses. 1804.

The administrative correspondence between Montevideo and Buenos Aires in the 1780s and 1790s shows the expansion of Montevideo's jurisdiction and administrative autonomy. However, this was not an uncontested process. While Montevideo was able to concentrate authority over transimperial trade routes and the exploitation of the resources of the countryside, Buenos Aires—the main political and commercial center in Río de la Plata—was losing its sovereignty over the same region and increasing its dependence on the port of Montevideo.

THE CONTESTED EXPANSION OF THE JURISDICTION OF MONTEVIDEO

In the aftermath of the Bourbon reforms in the late 1770s and early 1780s, jurisdictional conflicts in Río de la Plata focused on the countryside of the North Bank. After the expulsion of the Portuguese from Colônia do Sacramento, the Spanish divided the North Bank of Río de la Plata into three jurisdictions: the region of Colônia and Soriano, controlled by Buenos Aires; the jurisdiction of Montevideo extending toward Maldonado and Brazil; and Misiones, whose jurisdiction was the estancias (open range) south to the Siete Pueblos (see map 4). In addition to these areas, the Treaty of Santo Ildefonso (1777) created the Campos Neutrales, or Neutral Fields, a hundred-kilometer-wide buffer zone between both empires in the Americas that included the regions of Chuy and the Merin Lagoon. In theory, this area was supposed to be evacuated and remain unpopulated.[33] In practice, however, these were vaguely defined jurisdictional limits, and opposing factions in Montevideo and Buenos Aires jockeyed for control over the contested region, including its contraband trade, valuable cattle herds, and territory.

In 1781 and 1782 a heated correspondence between Viceroy Loreto (r. 1784–89) and the commandant of the Resguardo, Antonio Pereira, signaled the emergence of a legal conflict opposing Buenos Aires and Montevideo authorities over policing and repressing contraband in the Banda Oriental's countryside.[34] The viceroy reminded Commandant Pereira of his duty to repress smuggling along the border and prevent the Portuguese *changadores* (cowboys who produced hides) from processing cattle hides close to the Campos Neutrales. After repeated requests were ignored, the viceroy sent a squad of *blandengues* (cavalry) to patrol the region close to the Yi and Negro Rivers, adjacent to the Campos Neutrales. In addition to the Portuguese, Spanish agents exploited the herds of wild cattle and claimed their traditional right to do so.[35] At the same time, inhabitants of the Eastern Missions region also claimed the right to exploit the herds based on the Jesuits' prior agricultural activities in the region.

Viceroy Loreto took legal action to undermine the authority over contraband and cattle herds in the region of both officials who sought to expand Montevideo's jurisdiction: Montevideo's Resguardo captain, Antonio Pereira, and Río de la Plata's intendant, Francisco de Paula Sanz. Loreto denounced the actions of Commandant Pereira, charging him with trading in contraband, and successfully removed him from office. In addition, viceregal authorities attempted to nullify the right of the vecinos of Montevideo to claim the herds that grazed along the Yi and Negro Rivers near the borderlands. Although Sanz's office was based in Buenos Aires, he advocated for the empowerment of officers in Montevideo who were under his direct supervision, not under the immediate control of the viceroy.

The removal of Antonio Pereira from office triggered a furious response from Intendant Sanz, who accused the viceroy of abusing his powers as "if his authority has no limits," especially regarding his dismissal of the Intendant Statute.[36] Sanz also mentioned that jurisdiction over the herds and lands of the Banda Oriental already had been settled by Loreto's predecessor, Viceroy Vertiz (r. 1778–84). Three imperial officials—Vertiz, Sanz, and Pereira—had agreed on the distribution of estancias along the borderland to the *hacendados* (landowners) of Montevideo. Moreover, settlers under Montevideo's jurisdiction had been populating the region since the 1760s. Sanz also mentioned that the commandant of the Misiones had not protested these practices. Most important, the actual distribution of the hinterlands around Montevideo had been based on the most accurate information about the region—information provided by authorities and agents who were present in the region and knew how to repress contraband and exploit the herds without Portuguese interference. As proof of the success of this policy, Sanz pointed out the large number of confiscations by the Resguardo officers.[37] His rhetoric suggests that he believed it was in the best interest of the empire to keep the region in the hands of the authorities of Montevideo. Moreover, the large landowners of Montevideo were also portrayed as responsibly converting the region's natural resources into royal revenue. According to the Arreglo de los Campos, there were no northern limits to the estancias of Montevideo. This allowed the hacendados to penetrate into the Campos Neutrales.

Eventually, Sanz's legal arguments convinced the Council of the Indies to rule in favor of the supremacy of Montevidean authorities to regulate and prosecute contraband in the region. The council also ruled that Montevideo's large landowners' rights to the herds of the region should be respected by Spanish subjects from other jurisdictions (i.e., Buenos Aires and Misiones). Although the Council called for a future limit to the region's extension, Montevideo was to regulate the branding of cattle in the area and patrol for Portuguese interlopers.[38]

In late 1786 a royal order was signed confirming the jurisdiction of the Resguardo officers and Montevideo's branch of the Royal Treasury, both under the direct control of the superintendent. The Crown established that "the countryside's jurisdiction over suppressing contraband trade is under the intendant's authority (and its dependent agencies), as well as other goods produced in the Portuguese domains, such as the smuggling of tobacco from Brazil and other illicit trade goods."[39] Moreover, all the confiscated merchandise, *sumarias del proceso* (first reports of charges), and prisoners originating in the Campos Neutrales were to be sent to Montevideo. Even if a Buenos Aires military patrol caught a smuggler, all the materials were to be handled in Montevideo. The viceroy's jurisdiction in the Banda Oriental was, thus, restricted to defending the borders with military force, preserving the safety of the population against "robberies and acts of violence," and protecting the borderland against the Portuguese and other foreigners.[40]

The effectiveness of such regulations can be seen in the general correspondence between the viceroyalty and the governor intendant of Montevideo. Although the office of superintendent was extinguished in 1788, the duties of the governor intendant remained in force.[41] In 1792 officials in Buenos Aires received frequent reports from the governor of Montevideo of confiscations of contraband goods and slaves and the arrival or immigration of Portuguese subjects. By then, Montevideo controlled regions disputed in the 1780s as well as Herval and Piratini, areas claimed by the Portuguese.[42] In 1797 the Cuerpo de Blandengues of

Montevideo was created to patrol the region of Colônia. Although Colônia was under the jurisdiction of Buenos Aires, the Gremio de Hacendados (Landowners Guild) of Montevideo was responsible for funding this company. This suggests that, in practice, groups located in Montevideo controlled parts of the area under the jurisdiction of Buenos Aires.

Control of contraband and transimperial trade allowed the authorities of Montevideo to collect taxes, control legal processes related to smuggling, and auction embargoed goods.[43] The evolution of the city's jurisdiction was intimately related to its claim that it was successfully controlling the borderland while preventing Portuguese expansion and contraband. However, the expansion of Montevideo's jurisdiction favored existent transimperial trade and familial networks. Indeed, these networks tied illegal trade to local authorities who protected the large-scale introduction and circulation of contraband goods.

THE ATLANTIC PORT OF RÍO DE LA PLATA AND JURISDICTION OVER TRANSIMPERIAL TRADE

Beginning in the 1790s, a serious conflict took place over the jurisdiction of Atlantic commerce in Río de la Plata. The merchants of Buenos Aires bitterly complained that Montevideo's commercial role had increased ever since it became the mandatory first port of call in Río de la Plata in 1778.[44] The merchant guild of Buenos Aires protested against the rising importance of Montevideo, complaining that "to want to distinguish a dependent city [Montevideo] more than the Capital is the cause of annoying actions . . . of which the harmful results we have seen."[45] The result of that conflict was the polarization of the regional merchant community into two increasingly separate factions tied to either Buenos Aires or Montevideo. Although the two merchant communities were intrinsically connected (Buenos Aires merchants depended on the port of Montevideo, and Montevideo merchants depended on the capital and naval movement generated by porteño merchants), they grew divided by competition, jealousy, and jurisdictional and institutional disputes in the 1790s and 1800s. This conflict represented the increasing political empowerment of Montevideo's elites in affirming their authority and power in the logistics of transatlantic trade.

The mercantile correspondence of the Buenos Aires merchant Martin de Alzaga, a strong supporter of peninsular trade, reveals the deep logistical and bureaucratic dependence between Buenos Aires merchants and Montevidean authorities and local agents. Although the wealthier and more powerful commercial houses were located in Buenos Aires, porteño merchants had to channel a large part of their trade through Montevideo. While Alzaga developed commercial networks that spanned Mozambique, Hamburg, Madrid, Chile, Lima, Alto Peru, Córdoba, and Bahia in Brazil, most of his correspondence was exchanged with Montevideo merchants.[46] Between 1784 and 1806, Alzaga's main agent in Montevideo, Zacarias Pereira, was the primary interlocutor. Nonetheless, Alzaga also exchanged letters regarding commercial operations with the main merchants in Montevideo, such as Francisco Joanico, Juan Francisco de Zuñiga, Francisco Antonio Maciel, and Carlos Camuso, in addition to less influential local traders.[47] These letters reveal a varied range of agencies that Montevideo's merchants had to carry out for their Buenos Aires partners, including the posting of bail for departing ships (normally stipulated as half of the ship's value), customs clearance, management and dispatch of legal documents, and the hiring of lawyers, paralegals, and interpreters. Furthermore, Montevideo agents were responsible for managing the warehousing of goods, hiring and paying workers, acquiring and shipping hides, and transportation in Río de la Plata. Montevideo merchants also informed their Buenos Aires associates on availability of goods, political news, and commodity prices.

The correspondence between Martin de Alzaga and Zacarias Pereira reveals that local agents were also in charge of receiving values (including those for silver) and collecting debts in Montevideo.[48] In 1803 alone, Pereira was in charge of collecting at least 4,210 pesos owed to Alzaga. In addition, local agents were in charge of acting at public auctions of confiscated goods (paying in silver) and liberating confiscated goods belonging to their porteño associates. Also in 1803, Pereira was in charge of conducting "all diligences in order to demonstrate the legitimacy, value, and product" of one of Alzaga's ships destined for transatlantic.

In Montevideo, local merchants enjoyed improved business opportunities as agents of porteño merchant houses. Because the legal procedures involved in transatlantic shipping required large sums of money to cover shipping costs and legal fees, local agents had to have enough capital, in both silver and credit, for operating costs. As a result, prominent Montevideo merchants concentrated the management of commercial agencies for large porteño merchants. The Montevideo merchant and slave trader Francisco Antonio Maciel represented the interests of four Buenos Aires merchants, Manuel Antonio Rosales, Manuel de Aguirre, Juan Santiago Barros, and M. A. Pinedo Arroyo. In 1803 Maciel paid 13,606 pesos just for posting bail on ships on behalf of Aguirre.[49] In the same year the total value of bail posted specifically for ships sailing on behalf of Buenos Aires merchants in Montevideo amounted to 45,064 pesos.[50] On occasion, Buenos Aires merchants relied on their Montevidean agents to obtain clearance for privateering expeditions. In 1805 Spanish privateers were allowed to sail against English vessels. In order to obtain clearance for the frigate *Neptuno*, the Montevideo merchant Antonio de San Vizente guaranteed up to 60,000 pesos as bail on behalf of the Buenos Aires merchant Benito de Olazabal. Serving as agents for Buenos Aires merchants proved an effective way of strengthening connections with powerful merchant houses and gaining access to capital and trade networks to the interior.

Maintaining strong connections with Buenos Aires merchants was crucial to the mercantile success of Montevideo merchants since the former controlled trade with the interior provinces. Furthermore, the viceregal capital was the seat of the viceroy and Audiencia and home to the wealthiest merchant community in the region. Buenos Aires merchants performed the same function for their Montevidean counterparts. All the prominent merchants established long-standing relationships with their associates on the western bank. As we have seen, earlier, in 1800, five porteño merchants had 25,000 pesos with Montevideo merchants.[51] Merchants like Francisco Maciel, Francisco Joanico, Jose de Silva, and Antonio de San Vicente benefited from having influential and trustworthy porteño partners to conduct commercial and legal services in Buenos Aires. Others, such as Pasqual Parodi and Juan de Aguirre, established companies with Buenos Aires merchants. In the case of Aguirre, his business partner was also his brother, Manuel de Aguirre.

This growing dependence of Buenos Aires merchants on commercial agents and authorities in Montevideo provoked growing tensions between the two Río de la Plata ports. The creation of the Consulado de Comercio de Buenos Aires in 1794, however, led to the escalation of the institutional conflict between the two interconnected mercantile communities, since Montevideo's merchants complained about their dependence on Buenos Aires's Consulado.[52] The Consulado was the Crown's answer to the old and recurring demand of the merchants of Buenos Aires for commercial autonomy from Lima, as well as recognition of the significant donation of 100,000 pesos by Buenos Aires merchants to help finance Spanish war expenditures.[53] The existence of a local consulado ensured rapid access to justice, local regulation of trade, and local resolution of commercial disputes. Montevideo's merchants were allowed to create a *junta de comercio* (merchants' association), which could send a delegate to represent the city's mercantile community in the Consulado. Between 1796 and 1812, a total of fifteen respected Montevideo merchants served in this office. Through the Junta de Comércio, Montevideo's merchants confronted the interests of the Buenos Aires Consulado and petitioned the Crown for their own autonomous merchant guild.

The main complaints of Montevideo's merchants against the Consulado regarded the authority for taxation and Montevideo's representation in the guild. The creation of the Buenos Aires Consulado was granted with the right to collect the *averia*, a shipping tax on imports and exports. Although it was to be collected at Montevideo, it was to be put at the disposal of the newly created merchants guild in Buenos Aires.[54] The payment of the *averia* (0.5 percent on silver and gold exports) was originally intended to finance port improvements, road construction, and other infrastructure projects to improve commerce.[55] Nevertheless, the Consulado used the new source of revenue to repay local merchants who had made loans to the Crown.[56]

In February 1794 eighty-one merchants congregated in the newly created Junta de Comércio of Montevideo to protest that the Buenos Aires Consulado did not represent their commercial interests. They argued that it was "illegal" for Buenos Aires merchants to collect a tax in Montevideo, and, most important, they complained that they had not been informed about either the creation of the Consulado or the new tax.[57] Moreover, Montevideo's merchants argued that the Montevideo and Buenos Aires trade was "completely independent from each other" and that Montevideo's commerce had "never been regulated or subordinated to deliberations carried out by Buenos Aires merchants and authorities."[58] The merchants of Montevideo were only allowed to create a local merchants' association, which was dependent on the Consulado, like the other interior provinces, Córdoba, Tucumán, and Salta. These provincial associations could send a delegate to express the local or municipal interests to the consulate in Buenos Aires. For the next decade, the commercial corporations of Buenos Aires and Montevideo would remain politically at odds, although both merchant communities remained mutually dependent. While Montevideo merchants sought increased local autonomy and increased control over port taxes and fees, Buenos Aires merchants sought to weakening Montevideo's authorities by making denunciations of corruption and contraband trade, as well as attempting to circumvent Montevideo's port.

In 1798 the Consulado of Buenos Aires announced that the city was suffering *"prejuicios"* (losses) due to Montevideo's port monopoly. The Consulado demanded the maintenance of the "primacy of the trade of Buenos Aires" over Montevideo, the termination of the mandatory stop of all transatlantic vessels in Montevideo, the end of Montevideo's exclusive right to receive slave ships, and the prosecution of Montevidean authorities on charges of contraband.[59] Furthermore, the Consulado argued that the port of Montevideo was geographically disadvantaged compared to Ensenada, that the losses to Buenos Aires merchants caused by port fees and the requirement that ships leaving Buenos Aires stop in Montevideo were detrimental to porteño commerce, and that corruption was rampant among Montevideo's "bad and unfaithful officials."[60]

In trying to bypass Montevideo's harbor, the Consulado focused on the harbor's "adverse" conditions. According to Manuel Belgrano, "nobody could deny the advantages of the port of Buenos Aires compared to Montevideo's port," since the former was, in the eyes of the merchant, better protected against foreign invasions.[61] The Consulado alleged that the slow procedures of the officials and, to a lesser degree, the fees collected from the *almojarifazgo*, a Montevideo import duty, were a source of losses in their commercial transactions.[62] As an example, the Consulado presented the case of Jose de Maria, whose ship waited for two months to be authorized for clearance, as a result of which he suffered a loss of 4,000 pesos.[63] In addition, it reported that ships from West Central Africa, Ile Bourbon, and Rio de Janeiro were forced to return to Montevideo if they arrived in Buenos Aires carrying slaves or in distress. In one case, they estimated that Pedro Duval lost 30 percent of his sugar cargo and 15 percent of the cachaça.

The Consulado of Buenos Aires accused the elites of Montevideo of try-ing to stifle their access to transatlantic trade. According to Maria, the interim viceroy and former governor of Montevideo, Olaguer Feliú, pre-vented him from sending ships to the coast of Mozambique to buy slaves. Maria also denounced Olaguer Feliú for not allowing two of his ships that came from Rio de Janeiro to enter Buenos Aires's harbor, forcing them to dock first at Montevideo.[64] The merchants of Buenos Aires were so inflamed by Olaguer Feliú's policy that they petitioned the court to remove the viceroy and institute a Residencia.

The Buenos Aires Consulado also denounced the loss of royal revenue because of smuggling in Montevideo. It reported that goods worth more than 40,000 pesos were carried by a French frigate. Moreover, the Consulado reported that Montevideo officials turned a blind eye to goods arriving on foreign ships. Illegal merchandise was rarely confiscated in Montevideo, while in Buenos Aires the Real Aduana seized large quantities of it.[65] The strongest denunciations of smuggling were reserved for the authorities and merchants involved in the trade with Brazil:

> The ships come [from Portuguese colonies] straight to our ports without slaves and loaded with aguardiente, rice, and other goods. Such is the case of the Portuguese ship named *S. Del Buen Fin y S. Antonio.* . . . [T]he day before another ship under the Portuguese captain D. Manuel José de Silva had entered the port transporting 58 barrels of *aguardiente* and 50 bags of rice. . . . Enough has been said in the previously mentioned documents, and it has been proven that the Resguardo officers have not done anything about the matter.[66]

Despite the charges of corruption and contraband trade, the merchants of Montevideo petitioned the Crown for their own independent consulate in 1799 and 1802. They reminded the Crown of their numerous acts of loyal service: protecting the borders, fighting hostile indigenous groups, and maintaining the port without any support from Buenos Aires.[67] Montevideo's delegates complained that although the *averia* was created for the mainte-nance and improvement of Montevideo's port, these funds were diverted from their original purpose.[68] Specifically, the merchants of Montevideo complained about the failure of the Buenos Aires Consulado to build light-houses (on the island of Flores and on Montevideo Hill), to construct rub-ble-mound breakwaters, and to outfit two boats to patrol the coast.[69] By

1802 Montevideo authorities demanded that the Consulado allocate the sum of 12,000 pesos that had been ordered by the Crown to build lighthouses and promote improvements in Montevideo's port. As a way of putting pressure on the merchants of Buenos Aires for prompt payment of this amount, Montevideo merchants refrained from sending naval and commercial intelligence (about port activity, the arrival of correspondence, and the public auction of embargoed goods).[70] Of more consequence was the creation of an almojarifazgo fee by Montevideo's junta that was applied to large and small vessels alike. This fee was collected and managed by Montevidean authorities.

The new fee triggered a strong reaction from Buenos Aires's Consulado. Since the porteño merchants were dependent on Montevideo's port for their transatlantic voyages and used small boats to transship merchandise from Montevideo to Buenos Aires, they complained to the Crown that the docking fee affected small shippers disproportionately. These disputes led the Consulado to construct a small lighthouse at the entrance of the port on Montevideo Hill. Nevertheless, the 12,000 pesos were never invested in Montevideo's port as the Crown had intended.

Tensions rose when Buenos Aires's merchants attempted to turn Ensenada into a licensed port for their Atlantic trade between 1801 and 1803 and for the docking of local ships after 1804. Between June 1803 and June 1804, Ensenada was responsible for 5 percent of the Atlantic trade, according to the local newspaper, *El Semanario de Comercio*. Montevideo accounted for 78 percent of the Atlantic shipping in the estuary, while Buenos Aires accounted for just 13 percent.[71] Thus Ensenada never challenged Montevideo's commercial supremacy, and this fact forced Buenos Aires merchants to maintain their agents in the Banda Oriental. If the opening of Ensenada's port as an extension of the port of Buenos Aires did not undermine Montevideo's importance in 1801, it did, however, provoke efforts to safeguard the competitive advantages of the Banda Oriental's port. In 1802 Montevideo's Junta de Comércio eliminated the almojarifazgo fee in order to remain competitive, since the fee was not charged in Ensenada. Nonetheless, transimperial trade remained based in Montevideo.

Even those porteño advocates who had supported the attempts to circumvent Montevideo by developing Ensenada recognized the preeminence of the former port and continued to conduct business on the North

Bank. Powerful Buenos Aires merchants who promoted the Ensenada port, such as Casimiro Necochea (and later his widow), Tomás Antonio Romero, Martín de Alzaga, Benito Olazabal, and Manuel de Aguirre, among others, continued to send shipments to and from Montevideo in the early 1800s and even after 1808.

Nonetheless, the long-standing networks between Buenos Aires's and Montevideo's merchant communities did not prevent the emergence of bitter institutional disputes. As one of the most vocal and vehement critics of Montevideo's port authorities, Martín de Alzaga demonstrated how resentment of Montevideo's ties to the Portuguese could inspire anger among porteño merchants. Alzaga refered to the majority of Montevideo shopkeepers and traders as "smugglers" who benefited from the illegal goods introduced by Brazilian and English merchants. According to Alzaga, viceroy marquis of Aviles, Gabriel de Aviles Itúrbide (r. 1796–1801), tolerated Portuguese contraband in Montevideo, in collusion with local authorities. He wrote, "Brazil never stops supplying us with abundant contraband."[72] Furthermore, Montevideo's harbor received British and Portuguese vessels "all the time, allowing local merchant to acquire textiles on the cheap," and send them to the market at very low prices.[73]

Despite the protests, Montevideo's elites kept their jurisdiction over Atlantic trade and continued to benefit from the existing commercial networks they enjoyed with Brazil. Montevidean authorities and merchants maintained transimperial networks that not only ensured the supply of goods and slaves for the region—even in periods of war—but also ensured that Spanish ships could cross the Atlantic under Portuguese protection in the Rio de Janeiro fleet.[74]

The end result was the increasing autonomy of Montevideo's merchants and authorities in matters of trade. The control of transimperial networks empowered local elites and allowed the authorities to strengthen their control over the countryside. The last two decades of the 1700s witnessed jurisdiction building in the region of Montevideo. Based on the reformist aim to control contraband and to promote administrative efficiency, the elites of Montevideo used their privileged insertion in transimperial networks to optimize new opportunities. In securing jurisdiction over transimperial Montevideo progressively reterritorialized the region previously under Buenos Aires's control or disputed by the Portuguese.

5 Changing Toponymy and the Emergence of the Banda Oriental

In the century between the founding of Montevideo (1724) and Uruguay's formal independence as an autonomous state (1828), the names by which people referred to the region of the North Bank of the Río de la Plata changed substantially.[1] It was described variously as the Banda Norte, Otra Banda, Province of Montevideo, Fields of Montevideo, or Banda Oriental. This evolution was not linear, and several of these terms were used interchangeably or as synonyms. Moreover, written accounts reveal the growing centrality of Montevideo to the region. Between 1777 and 1810, the representations of space and colonial populations in Río de la Plata became more complex and nuanced, and the North Bank of the Río de la Plata emerged as a distinct space.[2] As a result in the last half of the eighteenth century, the North Bank of the Río de la Plata was delineated as a discrete region and Montevideo appeared as the central urban space in that area, the Banda Oriental.

On the one hand, written descriptions simultaneously abandoned the application of the label "Spaniard" to describe all colonial residents of the region and began to distinguish between the inhabitants of the Banda Oriental and those of Buenos Aires. On the other hand, the Portuguese were redefined and connected to the Brazilian territory rather than

Colônia do Sacramento. These descriptions ultimately reflected the historical process of the late colonial period and how imperial competition, reform, and intracolonial disputes influenced the reconfiguration of space and the imagined geography of the region.

This chapter analyzes the changes that took place in written descriptions of Montevideo and its adjacent countryside. At the same time that Montevidean and porteño elites disputed jurisdiction over the Banda Oriental, the former shaped a spatial reconfiguration of the region by adopting a new toponymy and new representations of the region's inhabitants. Crucial to this process was the capacity of Montevideo's elites to manipulate networks of information and trade that crossed imperial borders. The process of regional reterritorialization that surfaces in written accounts was intimately tied to Atlantic networks of information, trade, and politics.

By the end of the eighteenth century, Montevideo had become a regional hub for trade with foreigners. Already by the end of the 1790s, Montevideo's merchant community had solidified its role as the chief intermediary between Buenos Aires and foreign traders. Much to the chagrin of the merchants of Buenos Aires who had attempted to bypass Montevideo completely, Montevideo could not be dislodged from its commercial preeminence.

The evolution of the region's toponymy suggests that, progressively, Montevideo was perceived, by locals and foreigners, as the main urban center of the adjacent territory. This process unfolded simultaneously with an effort by Montevideo's elites to foster their influence and control over larger areas of the borderlands that were previously claimed by the Portuguese or under the jurisdiction of Buenos Aires.[3] As the previous chapter argued, Montevideo's merchants and authorities occupied a strategic position regarding the legality and logistics of Atlantic trade in Río de la Plata. Once Montevideo became the region's mandatory port of call for transatlantic ships entering or leaving the estuary and acquired customs officers to oversee foreign trade and suppress contraband, Montevideo's authorities gained a kind of monopoly over regulating the region's oceanic trade.[4] Empowered with greater commercial authority, Montevideo's elites not only produced written accounts for administrative and commercial purposes but also hosted and informed travelers who then wrote about the region's landscape and resources.

In order to examine the changing spatial representations of Río de la Plata in written accounts about the region, this chapter is structured in two main sections. The first analyzes the methodological challenges, limits, and advantages of examining written descriptions as spatial representation. The second and main section of the chapter examines spatial representations and the changing toponymy in written accounts produced by Portuguese, Spanish, and British subjects.

Montevideo's rise as commercial hub occurred at the same time that the nomenclature used to describe the region and its inhabitants changed, a process that can be detected in written accounts of the region. The new names that were deployed were not neutral but instead loaded with multiple meanings, reflecting the way in which inhabitants constructed, experienced, and made use of space. The changing conceptualization of space implied the creation of a new imagined geography of roads, landscapes, and social and political links connecting the countryside with the urban center. Specifically, the period's changing toponymy reflects the centrality of Montevideo rather than Buenos Aires to the Banda Oriental.

THE RÍO DE LA PLATA INTERACTION ZONE

In the late eighteenth and early nineteenth century, the production of written reports on non-European regions increased substantially, a result of a wide-reaching change in Atlantic empires wrought by the crises of the Old Regime and mercantilism in the face of liberalism and a capital-oriented rationale. In Río de la Plata, economic, political, and social change motivated Spanish, Portuguese, British, and French agents to produce a large number of maps and written accounts of the region, including historical and geographic descriptions and commercial and military reports. The men who created these documents were of diverse backgrounds. Some were Spanish and Spanish American–born bureaucrats, military officers, merchants, and clergymen. Others were British military men, traders, seafarers, and naturalists. Still others were Portuguese merchants, military men, and bureaucrats. The information these agents produced and circulated contributed to imperial disputes in Río de la Plata. They were instrumental in policy making and constituted the available data that informed imperial designs and decisions. Most important, these descriptions share linguistic and categorical similarities that not only reveal the existence of a common European (or Europeanized) audience but also point to the importance of information networks in shaping the imagined geographies of the Atlantic World.

Sophisticated observers were able to identify and make direct comparisons between Río de la Plata and Europe or colonial cities in the Americas in terms of buildings, clothing, customs, and many aspects of daily life. They also interacted primarily with Europeans, or people of European descent, and, although reproducing European social hierarchy and prejudice, they considered the local elites interlocutors, friends, and even possible business partners. The *criollos,* in the words of one businessman were "very smart, and the more exchanges with affluent Europeans, the more their worldviews and immediate interest will contribute for the development of trade."[5] Specifically, some merchants and other elites became friends and guides of businessmen in the region, such as the merchant Francisco Joanico, who hosted several travelers in the early nineteenth century.[6] The possibility of comparison and the creation of social networks allowed continuous interaction as well as a significant role for local elites to shape the spatial and social representation produced about the region.

In these written descriptions, the authors routinely compared Río de la Plata to Europe. Observers described religious activities, architecture, clothing, cultural habits, marketplaces, and fauna and flora, always in relation to Europe. Accounts differ not in essence but in degree. Often, authors described church buildings as less opulent than those in Europe, yet we are told that religious parades displayed more ornaments and more luxurious garments.[7] Wheat was consumed in Europe and in the New World; as one British merchant noted, "Onions, lettuce, potatos and artichokes grow to good sizes and are not inferior in good taste."[8] The yield of harvests, though, were more abundant in the Americas.

The frequent description of marketplaces, postal services, and the prices and availability of inns in the region attests to the importance of the commercial and political agendas of the foreign travelers.[9] In addition to descriptions of lists of goods sold locally and their prices, foreigners enumerated port services and market prices of imports and exports.[10] One British merchant who traveled in Río de la Plata in 1826–27, J.A.

Beaumont, considered inns in Río de la Plata second- or third-rate as compared to similar establishments in London. And the author noticed that, unlike in England, mail was not delivered at home but was separated and handled at the post office.[11]

The urban-based local elites also borrowed most of their cultural and political ideas from Europe, allowing them to appropriate European cultural ideas without sacrificing their local identities and practices. In Río de la Plata, urban elites had a prominent role spreading colonial order and rationality from ordered and lettered cities to their hinterlands.[12] Although the colonial elites' discursive and political rhetoric emphasized comparisons to their European counterparts, their political practices and daily lives were distinct, specifically, because of the significant presence of indigenous and African inhabitants in the region. Nevertheless, through the written word and spatial representation, Latin American elites legitimized and reified power relations. By the eighteenth century, they used European-derived ideals, information, and symbols that were circulating in the Atlantic to claim control over space and people.

Nonetheless, the descriptions produced in eighteenth-century Río de la Plata were varied and had different goals. Written accounts could range from war narratives praising the authorities and others subjects for their actions, often aimed at obtaining rewards (*mercedes*) from the Crown, to private or bureaucratic letters and classified intelligence.[13] In addition, there were cartographic and natural history descriptions of the region. Eighteenth-century science, racial and commercial ideologies, and administrative reports shaped by Enlightenment ideals influenced these written accounts.[14] Though diverse and not necessarily connected, the accounts created through their circulation a transatlantic flow of information that was tied to imperial and regional dynamics and needs. Imperial agents and foreigners used them simultaneously as intelligence, and to represent regional interests revealing how local groups wanted to be perceived and integrated in the transimperial scenario.[15]

For European empires, written accounts were the most important format in which information about the overseas regions were presented and contributed to the integration and governance of colonial and non-European territories.[16] These narratives circulated in small yet influential elite circles throughout the Atlantic World. On the one hand, they informed large segments of the reading public, partially shaping mass opinions in the transimperial arena; on the other, they informed policy makers and business leaders in Europe and in the Americas.[17] More often than not, written accounts provided instrumental knowledge for empire, science, religion, and commerce.

The accounts of the historical agents—both locally born and foreigners—in the eighteenth and nineteenth centuries were shaped by specific agendas, place of origin, and economic, political, and cultural backgrounds. Both local inhabitants and foreigners benefited from the commercial, political, and geographic information contained in these accounts. Nevertheless, local agents, by selecting and prioritizing specific aspects of the region, actively influenced the written pieces that circulated in transimperial networks. They manipulated ongoing political and economic processes and influenced the flow of information according to their own designs.[18] Consequently, written descriptions, created by outsiders and insiders alike, influenced social agents' strategies in interacting in local, imperial, and transimperial settings.

The perspectives of observers always shaped their representations, and therefore they must be analyzed with care. In the contexts of colonial contacts between Europeans and other societies, written accounts were produced in what Mary Louise Pratt described as "contact zones."[19] These were spaces in which two different cultures encountered each other and social agents redefined themselves in relation to the other. Pratt's contact zones existed in frontiers or ports where European travelers tended to be passive observers and described the foreign society using European categories. Thus European writers made the "other" simultaneously familiar and exotic. In the colonial setting of eighteenth-century Río de la Plata, however, the spaces in which such encounters took place—especially its port cities—should be more accurately defined as interaction zones.[20]

Interaction zones encompass regions that were already colonized by Europeans and that hosted dealings between a variable number of agents from different empires and from different cultural backgrounds. Within these zones, I suggest, the nature of the interaction that shaped the writer's perspective was more important than his or her cultural origin. Unlike Pratt's contact zones, which focus on northwestern European encounters in Asia and Africa during the eighteenth and nineteenth centuries, the colo-

nial regions in the Americas were already transformed by European colonialism and trade and African and indigenous influences. The balance of
power between these influences, though, privileged European social and
political values (albeit not all values, and not equally). The authors of written accounts (colonial elites, local and foreign traders, clergymen, military,
and travelers) in eighteenth- and nineteenth-century Río de la Plata viewed
colonial urban centers that were in many aspects similar or at least comparable to Europe, with the exception of the significant African and mestizo
presence.

Observers in interaction zones were not passive; they had specific
projects that they wanted to implement, and those designs shaped their
accounts.[21] Thus an interaction zone is not merely a cultural and geographic space in which social agents define themselves in relation to each
other, or a space where two different cultures enter into contact for the
first time.[22] It is marked by long-standing social, political, and economic
interactions among diverse social groups that, albeit of different origin
and cultural background, experienced shared cultural, religious, institutional, and social practices. Moreover, the interaction zone constitutes a
hub, often a port city, where subjects of different polities (foreign empires,
native groups) sustain long-standing interactions. The significance of the
port condition and the multiple interactions with overseas agents also
makes interaction zones different from borderlands and frontier spaces.
The accounts that were produced in the interaction zone of Río de la Plata
informed readers about policy making, investments, and group alliances.
In interaction zones, imperial agents would marry local women, indigenous people would explore the limits of the imperial legal system, and
transimperial trade connected agents from many different polities. The
type of interaction each author experienced in the region (i.e., access to
networks, social insertion, interests and the length of time spent in the
area) determined the type and quality of the information gathered. Over
time, however, these accounts contributed to the changing toponymy of
the Río de la Plata interaction zone, specifically, the emergence of the
Banda Oriental as social, political, and economic space. That adjustment
to how the region was seen and described had serious repercussions for
the recalibration of power and sovereignty within the Spanish empire and
between Montevideo and Buenos Aires in particular.

THE SPANIARDS, THE PORTUGUESE FROM
COLÔNIA, AND THE EMERGENCE OF
THE BANDA NORTE (1727–1770s)

During the period of Côlonia do Sacramento's existence as a Portuguese town (1680–1777), the toponymy and words used in written accounts of Río de la Plata to describe its social groups brought to light the rivalry between the two Iberian empires. The Spanish were considered a some-what homogeneous category, as opposed to the Portuguese, who were principally the people from Colônia do Sacramento.

One of first accounts about the region after the founding of Montevideo dates to the late 1720s. In 1727 an anonymous Scottish naval officer stayed for more than a year in the Río de la Plata on board the *Saint Michael*, anchored close to Colônia's harbor.[23] During his stay, the officer registered his many impressions of the region. He described the buildings as lowly, in comparison with their European counterparts. He mentioned that the religious festivals and masses were quite similar to those celebrated in Portugal. He described the fauna and flora, mostly comparing them to those of Europe and using scientific names in Latin to describe species. The traveler's eyes did not have to wander far beyond his home continent to find comparisons for the reality that he was trying to explain.

This anonymous Scottish officer identified two main groups, the Portuguese from Colônia and the Spanish from Buenos Aires. In his nar-rative, Spaniards from Buenos Aires and Portuguese from Colônia appear as potential trading partners.[24] While visiting the region, the Scotsman socialized more with the Portuguese than with the Spanish and generally maintained commercial relations with the latter. Thus he described the Portuguese settlement as an urban, civilized, European-style environ-ment, a little backward in relation to England but still similar to Portugal.

Almost ten years later, in 1735–37, Colônia do Sacramento underwent a military siege by the Spaniards. This event resulted in the production of two printed accounts authored by Portuguese officials who were present in the town. The work of Simão Pereira de Sá, *História topographica e bélica da Colônia do Sacramento,* and that of Silvestre Ferreira da Silva, *Relação do sítio da nova colônia,* were printed in Portugal in the late 1740s and early 1750s. These books, although centered on military events, provided comprehensive accounts of the region from a Portuguese perspective.

Pereira de Sá and Ferreira da Silva described most of the geographic information and human interaction in relation to Buenos Aires and its inhabitants. Although both authors wrote their books to legitimize the Portuguese claim over the Banda Norte and, particularly, over Colônia do Sacramento, the description of the social groups in the region was clear: some inhabitants were the subjects of the Spanish Crown, while others were the subjects of the Portuguese monarchy. For the authors, the Spanish were synonymous with Castelhanos. The author used "Castellanos" as well as "Hespanhoes" to refer to as the Spaniards from Buenos Aires, but both terms could also be used to refer to the inhabitants of Montevideo.[25]

Naturally, the Spanish, or Castelhanos, were perceived in opposition to the Portuguese and also contrasted with two other groups, the Indians and the British. Indians were always differentiated from the Spanish in the region, including those labeled "Tapes" who were considered vassals of the Spanish Crown after the Jesuits had converted them.[26] The British were not settlers; rather, they appeared as commercial partners who enjoyed close ties to the Portuguese, although they traded with all Europeanized groups.[27]

The Portuguese authors Pereira de Sá and Ferreira da Silva derived their views through interaction with the region's people. As elites involved in imperial administration and commerce, both authors voiced Luso-Brazilian perceptions of the regional geography. Their main spatial references were Portuguese Colônia in opposition to Spanish Buenos Aires.

In the 1770s the reformist impetus of the Spanish Crown and the economic dynamism of the Río de la Plata region attracted more attention from imperial agents. During the 1770s, religious and administrative agents produced accounts about the area. From this moment on, the distinction between the two margins of the Río de la Plata become a common feature in describing the region. In addition to the term *Otra Banda*, writers started using *Banda Norte* or *Banda Oriental* to the describe the region, often in relation to Montevideo and in opposition to Buenos Aires.

In 1772 a Spanish geographer, Francisco Millau, and a clergyman, Bartolomé Cosme Bueno, produced detailed accounts of the Río de la Plata region. Their descriptions circulated within administrative, military, and religious circles across the Atlantic. Although they traveled separately and, perhaps, never met one another, both delineated a clear spatial difference within the Spanish domains in the region. Millau, who was traveling under a royal commission, distinguished between those Spanish dominions that comprised the Río de la Plata region of Buenos Aires and the "Banda Norte." Cosme Bueno described the countryside on the northern bank of the Río de la Plata as the hinterland of Montevideo. According to Cosme Bueno, "on the other margin, or 'banda' of the River, further to the East is located Montevideo."[28] He mentioned the existence of a Franciscan convent, continued to describe the other settlements and lagoons of the area, and used Montevideo as a reference point.[29] While Montevideo is the reference point for the spatial description of the "Otra Banda," Buenos Aires is the center of reference for the parishes of San Ysidro, Matanzas, and Magdalena and other locations in the western margin of the River Plate. Although they composed their accounts from different viewpoints, both authors described the region as comprising two areas and linked the "otra banda," or "Banda Norte," to Montevideo as its center.

Millau's *Descripción de la Provincia del Río de la Plata* encompasses the whole jurisdiction that was under the formal rule of Buenos Aires, from the eastern side of the Andes to the eastern bank of the Río de la Plata, with special attention to the latter. He dedicates three chapters exclusively to the Banda Norte, emphasizing the natural ports of the region, the city of Montevideo, and its campañas.[30] Although Millau did not differentiate between the Spaniards in Buenos Aires and those in Montevideo, his descriptions of the territory and its farms and human activities appear divided between two reference points: Buenos Aires as the provincial capital and trade partner for the Portuguese from Colônia and Montevideo as a small port city with its own distinct hinterland.[31]

Although Millau does not describe separate social groups, he articulates a representation of a region that was already territorialized in different ways. He portrays Montevideo as the center of economic and social life for the Banda Norte.[32] When describing the cattle trade near Maldonado, Millau points to the centrality of Montevideo: "the cattle that are slaughtered daily in these possessions and other places are taken from the ranches of Montevideo and sometimes not from those nearby."[33] Moreover, he mentions that cattle and land should be offered to families from the "territory of Buenos Aires, who will happily accept to settle on that area."[34] At this point the author clearly offers a new division for the region. He mentions the port of Maldonado but always in relation to "the countryside of Montevideo."[35]

The centrality of Montevideo to the territory and society of the Banda Norte is emphasized by a whole chapter with the title "News of Montevideo's Port . . . and the state of the city and its countryside."[36] Besides describing the characteristics of the port and its activities in detail and signaling the growing importance of the region to commercial and military vessels, Millau points out that the city is the distribution point for the mail service connecting the region to Spain.[37] To convey the city's recent population growth and increasing significance, the author also describes the urban structure of Montevideo, its religious life, and the origin of the population in detail. Millau reported that although the city has been founded just "a few years ago with some families from the Canaries," its population has increased by "either intermarrying or marrying with a large number of foreigners who have settled there, some working on cultivating the land, some employed in trade and commerce."[38]

Millau's description of Río de la Plata as a place divided into "bandas," or distinct spaces, in which human activities unfolded in particular ways, signals a change in the region's imagined geography. His perception of space derived from his own experience in the region as well as by his informants, and at the same time his descriptions conveyed a representation of the region to inform and influence imperial administrators.

The Portuguese presence in Colônia and extending to the borderlands also received attention from both Millau and Cosme Bueno. The Portuguese presence is described as a distinct feature, one that created disorder. According to Millau, in Montevideo's campaña there were forts and guards to patrol the area against "the continued incursion of Portuguese, some infidels, and vagabonds."[39] Cosme Bueno in his account also described the Banda Norte as the space of interaction between the Spanish and the Portuguese.[40]

Because the authors answered to Spanish administrators and religious authorities, their descriptions of the northern bank of the River Plate emphasized the competing presence of the Portuguese, the illegal connections between the Spanish and Portuguese in that space, and the existence of another important Spanish port in the region besides Buenos Aires. These descriptions suggest that the Banda Norte was a unique territory in which Montevideo occupied a central role as the main Spanish urban settlement for official economic activities and Hispanicized social life and that it was also a space where nonregulated interactions with the Portuguese and indigenous groups took place.

Denouncing the activities of smugglers and unpacified indigenous peoples was also a way of justifying the expansion of Montevideo's jurisdiction. The written accounts circulating in late colonial Río de la Plata and the Atlantic World expressed the influence of Montevideo's elite over the surrounding Banda Oriental. Even though this jurisdiction was contested, it is precisely the existence of border disputes with Portuguese America and with authorities from Buenos Aires that helped consolidate the imagined geography of the region. In that corography, Montevideo's Banda Oriental constituted a distinct and specific region.

AN EVOLVING INTERACTION ZONE

The descriptions produced after 1777 reflect the enlightened and reformist spirit of the Bourbon Spanish empire and the deep administrative, military, and economic changes that were affecting Río de la Plata. The corography between 1777 and 1805 emphasized administrative concerns or measures to improve the economy and society of the region for the benefit of the Spanish metropole. More important, however, the descriptions presented three principal alterations to those of previous periods. First, the North Bank of the River Plate was described as being under the jurisdiction of Montevideo, and the terms *"Banda Norte," "Banda Oriental,"* and *"Província de Montevideo"* were used interchangeably to describe the area. Second, the Portuguese appeared as the inhabitants of the southern provinces of Brazil and were no longer connected to Colônia, although they were still associated with disorder. Third, other inhabitants of the region were depicted as *gauchos,* daily wage laborers or nomadic semioutlaw smugglers. Thus the narratives produced during this period reveal growing regional importance of Montevideo, and reinforced the notion that the North Bank was a distinct and unique zone where illegal contacts and interactions with the Portuguese took place. It was at this very moment when the region began to be described as the Banda Oriental.

One of the first authors to extensively describe the region as the Banda Oriental was the Creole ecclesiastic Manoel Perez Castellano.[41] Perez Castellano was born in Montevideo, received a degree from the University of Córdoba, and resided in Montevideo and its campañas. Between 1778 and 1808, he wrote a series of letters to Benito Riva, an Italian clergyman who was his mentor. In his early letters, Perez Castellano emphasized the differences between Montevideo and Buenos Aires. He stressed prices, reactions to political events, agricultural production, and business practices to distinguish between the Banda Oriental and the Buenos Aires side of the estuary. According to the author, the countryside of Montevideo experienced such an abundance of agricultural production that people from Buenos Aires "already envy [Montevideo] in respect to some merchandise."[42] The representation of Montevideo's hinterland as the Banda Oriental reinforced an oppositional relationship between the two port towns and their countryside.

The distinction between Montevideo and Buenos Aires was also represented in the way Perez Castellano referred to the inhabitants of Montevideo and its hinterland, calling them vecinos, or neighbors, of Montevideo.[43] In one of his first letters, Perez Castellano includes a list of landowners in the countryside, as well as a list of churches and lay brotherhoods established in Montevideo.[44] This information attested to the existence of a community of "notorious" subjects.[45] *Vecinos* was the official term to describe a person who was socially recognized as belonging to a community and eligible to hold public offices as a property owner. Communities in Spanish America were usually organized around the town council. Therefore, in describing the inhabitants of Montevideo as vecinos, the author was also reinforcing the idea that the inhabitants of the Banda Oriental constituted part of a distinct community with a certain degree of political cohesion and autonomy in relation to Buenos Aires.[46]

In the last decades of colonial rule, other authors commonly referred to the area as the Banda Oriental. The appearance of this descriptor in private letters from Creoles (such as Perez Castellano) suggests that it was widespread in the region. From the 1780s to the 1800s, the term would appear in numerous administrative accounts, with the emphasis placed on Montevideo's jurisdiction over the region. "Oriental" originally referred to the land east of the Uruguay River.

During the 1780s and 1790s, Montevideo's perceived distinctiveness gained more widespread attention, which formalized the political and economic links between the city and its countryside at the imperial level. Spanish bureaucrats produced written accounts to inform and recommend imperial policies in the region and represented the Banda Norte, or Banda Oriental, as under the jurisdiction of Montevideo. In addition to the dichotomy between Buenos Aires and Montevideo, the significant presence of Portuguese and indigenous inhabitants and the occurrence of disorder and contraband trade in the Banda Oriental also appeared in these administrative accounts. Whether Creoles like the clergyman Perez Castellano, peninsular Spanish like Intendant Sanz, or foreigners like the English missionary William Gregory, these authors' called for an increase in Montevideo's control over the territory. Moreover, maps produced in the period also show that Spanish cartographers regarded Montevideo as the provincial capital of the Banda Oriental.

In 1785 the intendant of Río de la Plata sent the Council of the Indies a long missive outlining recommendations regarding landownership in the "Banda Norte in the Jurisdiction of Montevideo." The recommendations covered access to land and cattle resources and endowed Montevideo's authorities with jurisdiction to repress contraband in the area. Moreover, the intendant called for expanding the number of regular troops in the garrisons and increasing the authority of the Resguardo, including a "juzgado," or tribunal of justice.[47] These recommendations were based on information made available in reports provided by Cipriano de Melo and Francisco de Ortega, the officers in charge of repressing contraband, as well as on "extended conversations with individuals well informed and experienced in the matters of the country." Nonetheless, according to Intendant Sanz, it was the "comandante de los Resguardos dn. Francisco Ortega . . . [who voiced] more correct ideas and solid knowledge of the problems that caused the landed people to complain [el grito] about the situation in the campaña."[48] The "Arreglo de los Campos"—regulation of the fields—not only shows the influence of local agents in the formulation of imperial politics and the shaping of the legal and imagined geography of the region but also reveals the centrality of Montevideo as the key administrative center of the Banda Norte.

The role of Montevideo as provincial imperial center and source of order in the Banda Norte was reinforced in an anonymously written pamphlet titled, "News from the Río de la Plata," probably penned in the 1790s and early 1800s.[49] This text was produced by a bureaucrat who claimed to have served for eight years in the region and who wanted to inform the Spanish Crown about possible disorders in the fields of Montevideo. The document's author suggested reforms to "maintain and increase the wealth of this kingdom [Banda Oriental]."[50] Portuguese presence and smuggling activities are portrayed as significant aspects of the Banda Norte of the River Plate.[51] As a result, the anonymous writer's account argues for the crucial role of Montevideo as a focus of imperial reforms in order to repress contraband trade. The eastern part of Montevideo's countryside, where the Portuguese were located, was the theater of conflicts, robberies, and illegal transactions between the subjects of the two Iberian empires. On some occasions, gauchos were involved in such activities with the Luso-Brazilians. Thus the author proposed strengthening the authority of Montevideo and its inhabitants over the countryside in order to prevent "disorders."[52]

According to the writer, four categories of people inhabited the country-side of Montevideo: landowners (*hacendados duenos de estancias*), daily wage laborers, or gauchos (*jornaleros, trabajadores, o peones del campo conocidos por gauchos*), Indians in the Jesuit missions, and the Portuguese.[53] It is noteworthy that "Indians" and "Portuguese" were the only categories of people who were localized to specific areas. While the author located the Indians in the Banda Oriental of the Uruguay River, he situated the Portuguese on the "oriental" side of the Yi River. The non-Spanish population of the "countryside of Montevideo" was therefore identified with the "oriental" areas, which were far from Montevideo, on the fringes of colonial rule. Meanwhile, Buenos Aires, the seat of the bishopric and the capital of the viceroyalty, was described as the "Occidental" bank.[54] It is clear that the author perceived the spatial differentiation of the Río de la Plata and recognized Montevideo's centrality to a distinct region, the North Bank, or Banda Oriental.

The spatial subdivision of the viceroyalty of Río de la Plata and the centrality of Montevideo to the Banda Norte also appear clearly in the 1792 account by Francisco Javier de Viana, chronicler and cartographer of the expedition commissioned by the Spanish Crown led by Alejandro Malaspina. Javier de Viana was born in Montevideo and graduated from a Spanish university.[55] He traveled to the River Plate to make trigonometric maps and take precise coordinates to circumnavigate South America via Cape Horn. While Javier de Viana rarely used the term *Banda Oriental,* he did refer to the area as a "pais" (country), and the maps and geographic knowledge his expedition produced were related to Montevideo and its territory.[56] In the beginning of his narrative, the centrality attributed to Montevideo is already evident. The opening chapter of his journal reads, "From the Bay of Cádiz to the Port of Montevideo on the Rio de la Plata."[57] In the next section, the author describes the path to follow from "Trinidad Island to Rio de la Plata," but it leads to Montevideo.[58] In the following pages, he provides detailed instructions on how to enter the port of Montevideo and describes the port of Maldonado, Isla de los Lobos, Isla Gorriti, Punta del Este, and Cabo Santa Maria—all features of the North Bank that aided navigation to Montevideo.[59]

In Javier de Viana's "Diarios de Viaje," the natural features of the North Bank are always described in relation to Montevideo, where Viana and his expedition established their scientific headquarters and observatory. The mapping and observations of fauna and flora departed from Montevideo, and "the naturalists traveled one hundred leagues of the flatlands" from the city. His use of the word *country* to describe the region can be attributed, I believe, to the fact that he was born there and understood the region as a natural whole.

Javier de Viana did not emphasize the use of "Banda Oriental," but his maps and geographic coordinates contributed to the dissemination of a new spatial division of the region. In other words, Javier de Viana's maps and descriptions formalized a reconceptualization of the region already under way by local agents, metropolitan, and foreign actors. Javier de Viana documented Montevideo's jurisdiction over the campaña and represented the North Bank as a space composed of the city and its hinterland. Buenos Aires, the Portuguese, and contraband trade are virtually absent from his narrative. While Javier de Viana mentions Buenos Aires as the capital of a province of the same name, he makes no mention of the viceroyalty or the fact that Buenos Aires was the capital city to which Montevideo was politically subordinated. Only a few members of the expedition went to Buenos Aires to establish coordinates and map the coast, but they quickly "returned to Montevideo."[60] The Portuguese only appear as the first settlers of Colônia do Sacramento, with no further mention of contraband trade.

By the end of the eighteenth century, imperial bureaucrats and administrators joined merchants, travelers, and cartographers in making Montevideo the center of the Banda Oriental, a distinct and separate region in Río de la Plata. In 1799 another anonymous bureaucrat authored an administrative report about contraband and disorder in the countryside of the Banda Norte and presented it to the Council of the Indies.[61] According to the document, the lack of clear royal control and imperial oversight caused border disputes in an area the Portuguese had competed to control for three decades. As a remedy for these problems, the bureaucrat suggested the construction of a "line of fortifications" and an increase in "patrolling troops." In this document, Montevideo is designated as the most suitable base from which to implement such policies.

A Spanish bureaucrat who participated in the demarcation of the borders between Portugal and Spain in the previous decades, Felix de Azara, also reinforced the Montevideo's centrality to a distinct zone in Río de la Plata. In his writings, Azara constantly referred to Montevideo's jurisdiction as the "Fields of the North of the River Plate" and "our countryside of Montevideo."[62] His 1801 "Rural Memoirs of the River Plate" suggested a series of measures to secure Spanish jurisdiction over the borderland, and it made Montevideo the centerpiece of enhanced Spanish control of the North Bank.[63] First, the author represented the vecinos of Montevideo as an organized community that took decisive actions to increase their control over the region, especially to root out illegal trade and robbery.[64], Second, he suggested the creation of parish chapels in the countryside to instruct the population and, thereby, to remedy the problems of disorder.[65] Third, he argued that the Portuguese presence in the areas of Spanish dominion was unavoidable and even desirable, since the Portuguese "washed more often and were more economic, [so] they would be a good example."[66] It is worth noting that Azara's expedition was equipped with personnel and logistical support from the Cuerpo de Blandengues and thus sponsored indirectly by the Montevideo cabildo. Therefore, Azara's expedition was a testimony to the deep ties between Montevideo and the Banda Oriental. By 1804 the centrality of Montevideo to the Banda Oriental is attested in the *Carta geográfica,* a map commissioned by Spanish authorities that labels the region "fertile fields of Montevideo" (map 7).

Foreign merchants and travelers who made Montevideo's deep-water harbor their point of entry into the Río de la Plata also reinforced or formalized the reconceptualization of the Banda Oriental as a distinct interaction zone and as the focal point of its surrounding territory.[67] From 1800 to 1809, two British subjects—one a merchant and the other a missionary—produced accounts describing Montevideo and its surrounding areas from different viewpoints. Both, however, reinforced the specificity of the Banda Oriental and the centrality of Montevideo to the countryside.

After his ship was captured by French privateers while on a voyage to the Pacific Islands and conducted as a prize to the port city, the British missionary William Gregory spent more than a year in Montevideo. Like most travel narratives, his description focused on the city, food, and natural and geographic features. Gregory perceived the countryside of Montevideo as a distinct space: "this district [of Montevideo] differs from other parts of South America."[68] Because of his lack of connections in Montevideo and poor financial situation, the missionary was only able to rent a house on the outskirts of town. He frequently noted the presence of mestizos and Indians in the countryside of Montevideo, which he referred to as the "vicinity of Montevideo." On many occasions, he revealed that he was afraid of interactions with such characters. The vicinity of Montevideo was distinct from the "vicinity of Buenos Ayres," where there was an "abundance of a large quarry of stones, in which a number of the natives are employed."[69] Gregory described the two main cities as physically and societally different.

Under very different circumstances from those of Gregory, British merchant Thomas Kinder arrived in Montevideo in 1809 in search of business opportunities. In his journal, Kinder provided details about the landscape and roads in the countryside, as well as the land routes connecting Montevideo and Rio Grande in Portuguese America along with other information about the geography of the region. Once more, the countryside of the Banda Oriental is portrayed as the hinterland of Montevideo, and the city is a main point of reference and commercial center:

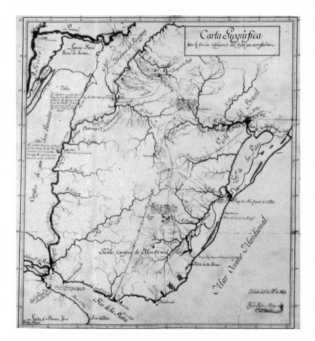

Map 7. Agustin Ibañez, Mapa del territorio ocupado por los Portugueses 1804. Original at the Archivo General de Indias, Ministerio de Educación, Cultura y Deporte.

The country in the neighbourhood of this city is so unvaried that having once rode out and viewed it from two or three different elevations, I found little inducement again to stir beyond its walls. . . . The River Sta. Lucia falls into the "La Plata" about 10 miles to the West of Mtvdeo and from its vicinity all the wood used as fuel in that city is brought in Carts, this as well as every other article requiring human labour to bring it to market is very dear.[70]

Kinder, however, did not venture into the countryside alone. Instead, he relied on local informants he met in Montevideo to help him obtain information about the region.

In this manner, Kinder's experience and account illustrates how local elites influenced the formulation of an imagined geography of sovereignty in the region. Carrying letters provided by another British trader, Kinder stayed as a guest within the walls of the city at the house of a powerful

Montevidean merchant, Francisco Joanicó. Kinder spent much of his time in Montevideo going to cafés, playing backgammon, and chatting with other businessmen. He was explicit about the role of his host in shaping his perception of the region: "During my stay at Montevideo I rode out to visit the countryside with my hospitable friend Francis Juanico, having heard it represented as the best in the country adjacent and well worth seeing."[71] Thus local elites could influence the type and quality of information that shaped the traveler's perspective. As Kinder's account attests, foreign travelers and merchants acquired knowledge and information in interaction zones like Montevideo and the Banda Oriental through local informants and intermediaries. In his particular case, local merchants and elites shaped how he understood and conceived of the region's countryside as a space where roads, resources, and distances were all defined in relation to Montevideo. Buenos Aires, in contrast, appears as another port, maybe a more important center but definitely a different community otherwise unknown without another trip by boat and new letters of introduction. Gregory and Kinder, a missionary and a businessman, had arrived in Montevideo under different circumstances and with different goals, and their varied experiences in Río de la Plata certainly affected the content of their narratives. Nonetheless, they both considered Montevideo a distinct and crucial economic, social, and political center of the Banda Oriental.

REVOLUTIONARY WAVES AND THE ORIENTALES

Napoleon's invasion of the Iberian peninsula and the subsequent crisis of legitimacy that ravaged the Spanish empire served to formalize the spatial divisions of Río de la Plata, and reinforced the Banda Oriental and "*orientales*" as a distinct spatial imaginary and a source of regional identity. Until 1808, the emergence of the Banda Oriental as a distinctive space occurred within the orbit of the Spanish empire, within the viceroyalty of Río de la Plata. The Napoleonic wars marked a political division in Río de la Plata, with different groups claiming sovereignty over territory. The tensions between Montevideo and Buenos Aires reached its climax, and after 1808 Montevideo gained autonomy in relation to Buenos Aires. In

1810 the Banda Oriental was the theater of disputes between Montevidean royalists, Buenos Aires revolutionaries, and the Federalist forces of Artigas in the countryside. The wars of independence cemented the connections between Montevideo and the Banda Oriental. Despite the fragmentation of Spanish rule in the region, all the parties involved acknowledged the North Bank as a distinct region with Montevideo as the main social, economic, and political center. During the revolutionary decade, Montevideo and the Banda Oriental emerged as a sovereign polity—politically and spatially.

In the aftermath of the British invasions (1806–7), the cabildo of Buenos Aires had replaced Viceroy Sobremonte (1804–7) with the military officer Santiago de Liniers, the man who had led the city's militia against the occupying troops. Across Río de la Plata, Montevidean authorities refused to recognize the new viceroy appointed by the capital's cabildo. In 1808, the governor of Montevideo, Francisco Javier de Elio, and Montevideo's cabildo proclaimed a *junta de gobierno* that ruled the province in the name of Ferdinand VII. This moment marked the severing of the administrative links of political dependence between Montevideo and Buenos Aires. In the following years, the Loyalist government of Montevideo would actually support agents plotting against the Buenos Aires government.[72] In 1810 Elío returned from Spain as the Supreme Junta's newly appointed viceroy of Río de la Plata, but the Buenos Aires cabildo did not regonize his authority. As a result, in January 1811 Elio installed Montevideo as the capital of the viceroyalty of Río de la Plata. In his proclamation cutting the political ties between Buenos Aires and Montevideo, Elio addressed the inhabitants of the "Banda Oriental."[73]

The fragmentation of royal authority in the region led many officers and political leaders to appeal to Spanish subjects for support and loyalty. While Elio counted the support of Montevideo's merchants, in the countryside caudillo Jose Artigas (1811–20) launched a revolutionary movement, challenging the authorities of Montevideo. In 1810 and 1811 both loyalist and revolutionary leaders appealed to the "orientales." However, their concepts of "*orientalidad*" were not homogeneous.[74] On the one hand, the governor of Montevideo, Gaspar de Vigodet, claimed loyalty to the king of Spain and asked the orientales to prove their value as good subjects of the monarchy. On the other hand, Artigas, the popular caudillo of the Banda Oriental, called on "good orientales" to defend the revolution. In analyzing the two "proclamations," it is clear that there was neither consensus about who the "orientales" were nor agreement on what their political agenda should be. Nevertheless, both leaders appealed to the people of Banda Oriental—orientales—thereby linking political participation, and shared experiences in the territory to Montevideo and excluding Buenos Aires from the jurisdiction.[75]

Different groups' usage of the term *Banda Oriental* to refer to the city of Montevideo and its countryside was reiterated during the turbulent years of the wars of independence. The works of Damaso Larrañaga (1771–1848), a Creole intellectual who was born in Montevideo and founded the city's first public library (later the National Library of Uruguay), reinforced the perception of the Banda Oriental (and its capital Montevideo) as an autonomous region, regardless of the political projects at stake. Larrañaga was an active political actor and was involved in several competing political projects in the area. He was involved in Montevideo's Junta Gubernativa against Buenos Aires (1808–14), Artigas's administration (1815–16), and subsequently became an active participant in the Cisplatine administration (1816–22). By portraying Montevideo and the countryside as a cohesive unit, he reinforced a perception of the region as a distinct and separate space from Buenos Aires.[76] Larrañaga refers to the Banda Oriental as "patria" or "pais" (country).[77] Like Javier de Viana before him, he also emphasized the centrality of Montevideo and used words that suggested the existence of a shared regional identity. Furthermore, on several occasions he used the possessive pronoun *ours* in reference to the landscape and customs of the region.[78] This is significant considering that both authors were from the region and that the word *patria* was associated with place of origin in the eighteenth century. This suggests that native authors' descriptions of the territory were shaped by their sense of belonging to its community.

The struggles for independence cemented the ties between Montevideo and the Banda Oriental. Whether royalist, revolutionary, Montevidean, Artiguista, or porteños, each party recognized the North Bank as a distinct region in which Montevideo occupied a central social, economic, and political role. Artigas's proclamation of autonomy from Spain in 1815 effectively made the Banda Oriental a sovereign state, and was followed by Portuguese occupation of the region. In 1817 Luso-Brazilian troops occupied Montevideo and its countryside. Three years later Artigas's army was defeated and the Banda Oriental was annexed to Brazil as the Cisplatine Province, or the Estado Oriental.[79] Under Luso-Brazilian rule, the region opened to foreign agents, especially British and French subjects.[80] During this period, the number of European travelers increased substantially due to the political turmoil and the potential commercial opportunities in the Banda Oriental.[81]

CONCLUSION

During the eighteenth century there were important economic, social, and political changes in Río de la Plata, changes that were reflected in the way inhabitants, travelers, and imperial agents perceived, experienced, and portrayed space there. The analysis of the written accounts produced in the Río de la Plata interaction zone reveals transformations in the imagined geography of the region. The toponymy used to describe the region across the Río de la Plata from Buenos Aires changed from Otra Banda to Banda Norte to Banda Oriental, revealing the emergence of the North Bank as a distinct space. These changes indicate how different social groups perceived and represented spatial changes that were connected to the emergence of Montevideo as a hub of transimperial commerce and a regional center of the Banda Oriental.

Accounts about Río de la Plata evolved toward a more complex spatial division within the region, with the emergence of the area called Banda Norte, or Banda Oriental, for which Montevideo functioned as the main economic, political, and social center. The accounts produced by British and Portuguese authors in the first half of the eighteenth century do not describe the North Bank of the River Plate as a distinct space within the Spanish dominions, and Montevideo appears as a town within the jurisdiction of Buenos Aires. By the last quarter of the eighteenth century, written accounts produced by Spanish subjects portrayed the area adjacent to Montevideo as the Banda Oriental or Banda Norte—a space with different characteristics from other areas under Buenos Aires's jurisdiction. This change in spatial representation was gradual and nonlinear, and it was intimately tied to the opportunities opened by the imperial reforms that increased the administrative and economic status of Montevideo, as well as the expulsion of the Portuguese from Colônia. Moreover, the subsequent relocation of transimperial networks to Montevideo and the countryside of the Banda Norte contributed to the region's specificity as a borderland with the Portuguese and an area plagued by contraband trade. The presence of equestrian nomadic indigenous groups in the region justified Montevideo's significance and increasing authority in directing Spanish control over the region. As a result, Montevideo became a crucial administrative and commercial center and a hub for transimperial agents in the Río de la Plata interaction zone.

The central role of Montevideo in the imagined geography of the Banda Oriental was reinforced and consolidated during the wars of independence. Royalists, revolutionaries from Buenos Aires, Artigas and his armies, and Luso-Brazilians represented the space of Banda Oriental as a unit in which Montevideo was the main urban center. The spatial representation of the Banda Oriental deployed by royalists, monarchists, Artiguistas, Luso-Brazilians, and foreign travelers included areas that were previously under the control of Buenos Aires. Nevertheless, these contested areas became part of the Banda Oriental and the jurisdiction of Montevideo during the revolution. The evolution of the toponymy reveals the wider social, political, and economic changes in the region and highlights the dynamic nature of spatial formation, the agency of local inhabitants, and the significance of transatlantic interactions in shaping spatial representations of the region.

6 Traversing Empires

THE ATLANTIC LIFE OF DON MANUEL
CIPRIANO DE MELO

In the eighteenth century, powerful social, political, and economic networks crossed political boundaries, connecting societies on both sides of the Atlantic Ocean. These networks were avenues through which individuals circulated, establishing connections in different regions in order to mobilize resources both locally and remotely. Born in Lisbon around the year 1742, Manuel Cipriano de Melo grew up in Buenos Aires and later established businesses in West Africa, Salvador de Bahia, Colônia do Sacramento, Rio de Janeiro, and London, before finally settling in Montevideo. Throughout his life, Cipriano de Melo switched imperial allegiances and relocated many times; nevertheless, he maintained enduring commercial, familial, and religious networks. This dynamic and sometimes convoluted career did not prevent him from attaining high office in the Spanish bureaucracy of Montevideo, nor did it keep him from becoming one of the most prominent members of Montevideo's community.

Cipriano de Melo's life is representative of the fluid transimperial networks evident in the eighteenth-century Atlantic World and offers an opportunity to analyze the relationship between an individual and these networks. Transimperial networks acted as a conduits through which individuals could obtain social, economic, and political support, locally or remotely. Furthermore, the control of such networks enabled local groups to develop a sense of community within the realms of the Spanish and Portuguese empires, providing peripheral communities with social, political, and economic opportunities that served as alternatives to the ones offered by the local centers of power.

Focusing on how individuals manipulated and inserted themselves in transimperial networks reveals important connections between different empires in the Atlantic world. Research on this topic has been revitalized in recent decades by a series of works that emphasize the interconnection of social and economic processes that unfolded on the three continents of the Atlantic basin.[1] However, these groundbreaking works are limited in scope: first, by geography—the North Atlantic—and, second, by the political boundaries of empires, for example, the British Atlantic or the Spanish Atlantic. Consequently, these studies emphasize processes that unfolded within political units that resemble contemporary national or imperial political boundaries. In this manner, the study of interaction between empires has positioned the state at the center of analysis, thus favoring research on diplomatic and military aspects of transimperial interaction.

In different areas of the Atlantic, human interactions moved beyond the boundaries designated by the political metropoles.[2] As a locus of transimperial interaction, the Río de la Plata region is one of the prime examples of such dynamics. In the eighteenth century, Río de la Plata emerged as a stage for colonial disputes between Spain and Portugal and as a locale of interest for Great Britain and France. In this context, social networks were crucial for transimperial commercial and political dynamics.

In Río de la Plata, specifically, in Montevideo, the control of transimperial networks, combined with a specific interpretation of imperial law, fostered the emergence of distinctive communities within imperial realms: one with interests centered in Montevideo and the adjacent territory of Banda Oriental and one centered in Buenos Aires. This process of colonial regional identity formation unfolded in a context that predated the emergence of modern nations.[3]

As a Portuguese merchant who served both Iberian empires in distinct moments of his life, Cipriano de Melo extended networks beyond imperial limits allowed him to better manipulate resources and improve his position within the empire he was serving at the moment. His life story illustrates the wider impact of his connections. Cipriano de Melo's experiences were representative of those of many of his contemporaries; however, he was able to capitalize on many of these and turned the events of his life into opportunities to create a hub for multiple networks. More than just the biography of an individual, his actions serve as a backdrop for analyzing the significance of networks in imperial borderlands during the late colonial period.[4]

The eighteenth century was marked by a series of treaties between Atlantic empires that reflected significant changes in the balance of power in Europe and in American territories. Portugal and Spain, since the War of Spanish Succession (1705–13), were increasingly economically and politically dependent on England and France, respectively. As the Iberian powers perceived their position as second-tier powers among Atlantic empires, their rivalry escalated, as one country tried to improve its position at the expense of the other.[5] After the Seven Years' War, a wave of reform swept the Atlantic, triggering a comprehensive imperial reorganization in Atlantic colonial empires. While Britain and France eventually had to deal with revolutionary movements in the Americas and in Europe, the Iberian monarchies implemented policies in their American colonies aimed at restructuring colonial administrations, known in the historiography as the Bourbon and Pombaline reforms. The 1760s and 1770s, according to the historian Dauril Alden, marked the climax of Luso-Spanish rivalry in the Americas. The Río de la Plata region was a crucial area of dispute.[6]

The Río de la Plata region had been a subject of tension between Spain and Portugal since the seventeenth century. Although peripheral in the Spanish mercantile system, the region attracted foreign traders interested in the interior markets in hides and especially the silver that came into the local economy from Potosí. The founding of Colônia do Sacramento, across from Buenos Aires in 1680, was a key Portuguese move to secure territorial expansion and navigation in the La Plata estuary, as well as the creation of a commercial hub for tapping silver from the Spanish empire. Colônia do Sacramento, for almost a century, was a major contraband entrepôt that supplied the region with sugar, textiles, rum, slaves, and other Atlantic products. It epitomized the creation and maintenance of enduring social and commercial networks that linked Portuguese and

Spanish America.[7] The Portuguese presence in the Río de la Plata basin, however, was never fully accepted by the Spanish Crown. On several occasions, Spanish forces conquered Colônia (1680, 1705, 1762), but Portugal was able to regain the city by diplomatic means and with strong British support. In 1777, however, diplomacy and British support were not enough to prevent a new and long-standing Spanish conquest of the town.

Beginning in the mid-1770s, reforms radically changed the geography of power in the Río de la Plata region. Of these reforms, the most important ones were the creation of the viceroyalty of Río de la Plata with its capital in Buenos Aires, the expulsion of the Portuguese from Colônia, and the establishment of Montevideo as the main Spanish port in the region. After the conquest of Colônia do Sacramento by Spanish forces in 1777, many Portuguese subjects relocated to Montevideo and the countryside of the Banda Oriental. Using previously established networks, the newly arrived inhabitants acquainted themselves with mercantile groups centered in Montevideo in order to renew smuggling connections with Portuguese and British traders. Furthermore, the Bourbon reforms established Montevideo as a mandatory port of call and as the only port authorized to disembark slaves in Río de la Plata. Montevideo also became the base of the Spanish South Atlantic fleet and the seat of the authorities in charge of policing contraband both at sea and on land.[8] The first officer appointed by Viceroy Cevallos for the position of repressing contraband trade in Montevideo was don Manuel Cipriano de Melo.

Born into a wealthy family in Lisbon in 1740, Cipriano de Melo was orphaned before he turned ten years old. Thanks to family connections, he was sent to Brazil and placed under the care of the governor of Rio de Janeiro, Gomes Freire de Andrade. In 1749 the governor sent him to Río de la Plata and entrusted his care to the governor of Colônia, don Garcia de Bivar. However, once in Río de la Plata, Cipriano de Melo soon ran away from Colônia to Buenos Aires, where he ended up under the patronage of the Spanish governor, Joseph de Andonaegui.[9]

Between 1754 and 1756, the Guaraní Indians from the Siete Pueblos Missions of Paraguay rebelled against the provision in the Treaty of Madrid (1750) that stipulated the exchange of Colônia do Sacramento for the interior territory of the Jesuit missions. In 1754 Cipriano de Melo participated with the Spanish forces during the resulting Guaraní War (1754–56). On one occasion, Cipriano de Melo traveled to the theater of war in a canoe. As a protégé of the governor of Buenos Aires, Cipriano de Melo most likely had the opportunity to interact with other regional authorities, such as the governor of Colônia do Sacramento and, most important, the governor of Montevideo, José Joaquín de Viana. While still a teenager, Cipriano de Melo was able to familiarize himself with the region and with the authorities with whom he shared experiences in the theater of war.

Once the joint Iberian campaign against the rebellious Guaranís had ended, Cipriano de Melo went to Cádiz, where he studied nautical sciences and was introduced to its theater culture and playhouses. After concluding his studies, Cipriano do Melo returned to Lisbon and collected his inheritance. Afterward, he returned to Río de la Plata, arriving in Colônia do Sacramento with his heavy luggage and four slaves.[10]

In Colônia do Sacramento, Cipriano do Melo established himself as a ship pilot in the Río de la Plata estuary.[11] During the 1762 military campaign against Colônia do Sacramento led by the new governor of Buenos Aires, don Pedro de Cevallos, Cipriano de Melo switched imperial allegiance and was named pilot for the Spanish fleet that attacked Colônia. He actively fought the Portuguese and British during the naval blockade of Colônia and took 260 British prisoners. Nevertheless, Cipriano de Melo again was working under the Portuguese flag in 1763, when Colônia was returned to Portuguese control as part of a diplomatic agreement.[12]

In the following decades, Cipriano de Melo crisscrossed the Atlantic Ocean conducting business in Colônia do Sacramento, Salvador de Bahia, Rio de Janeiro, Lisbon, West Africa, and London. During this period Cipriano was involved in a couple of slave trade expeditions to Africa, as well as in shipping textiles, sugar, and tobacco to the southern Luso-Brazilian ports. In 1765 Cipriano de Melo was once again in Río de la Plata. In Colônia do Sacramento, Cipriano de Melo married Ana Joaquina da Silva, the daughter of an important local merchant, and received a dowry of 30,000 pesos.[13] In addition, Cipriano de Melo established himself as a trader and pilot due to his closeness with the authorities, such as the governor and prominent businessmen of the Portuguese colony.[14] In doing so, he crossed imperial boundaries, trading sugar, tobacco, textiles, woods, furniture, paper, and slaves.

Among his business partners were some of the wealthiest merchants of Colônia do Sacramento and Rio de Janeiro, as well as government authorities. Cipriano de Melo conducted extensive business with the powerful Colônia do Sacramento–based merchant Coronel João de Azevedo Souza, who often advanced money to the local government, and associated with the powerful merchant of Rio de Janeiro, don Brás Carneiro Leão.[15] Among his other business partners in Colônia were the merchants Mamede João and Joseph da Costa Ferreira and the famous smuggler João da Cunha. In addition, Cipriano de Melo was included by the governor as one of the honorable people of Colônia do Sacramento who were asked to give a statement to the Concelho Ultramarino regarding the state of the colony.[16] Through his business partners in Colônia, Cipriano de Melo gained access to networks in Rio de Janeiro, which directly connected him to some of the wealthiest merchants of that city, who conducted extensive business in the South Atlantic slave trade.[17]

In 1777 a Spanish fleet transporting more than ten thousand troops, led by the newly appointed Spanish viceroy, don Antonio Pedro de Cevallos, arrived in Río de la Plata. Cevallos had orders to establish the viceroyalty in Buenos Aires and to expel the Portuguese from Colônia do Sacramento. Once again, Cevallos commissioned Cipriano de Melo as a pilot for a squadron of ships dispatched to conquer Colônia do Sacramento. In June of that same year, Colônia fell into Spanish hands and was leveled. Subsequently, Cipriano de Melo and hundreds of Portuguese citizens swore an oath of loyalty to the king of Spain. Thereafter, Cipriano de Melo relocated to Montevideo, where, as a reward for his service to the Spanish Crown, he was appointed to the new office charged with the repression of contraband trade, the Comandancia del Resguardo.[18]

Once relocated to Montevideo, Cipriano de Melo was in a strategic position, not only because of his place in the Spanish bureaucracy, but also due to his connections and capital. As the *segundo comandante* of the Resguardo, Cipriano de Melo was charged with controlling ports and regulating navigation in lakes and lagoons, with thirty-two men under his authority. More important, he was both the person responsible for determining the legality of ship arrivals in the port and the person in charge of inspecting their cargo. Furthermore, Cipriano de Melo successfully collected compensation from the Spanish Crown for the estates he had lost in

Colônia do Sacramento due to expulsion of the Portuguese. He was granted a license to import 32,000 pesos worth of slaves or merchandise from Brazil—tobacco, sugar, cachaça, and other goods.[19] Taken together, these factors ensured his privileged insertion into Montevideo's society.

Reestablished in Montevideo, Cipriano de Melo had all of the necessary resources, means, and knowledge needed to reconnect the commercial routes between Rio de Janeiro and Río de la Plata, the hub of which was formerly located in Colônia do Sacramento. Cipriano de Melo not only secured the legal ability to ensure the safety of the operations due to his office but also attained enough capital to finance his own business ventures. If knowledge about Luso-Brazilian markets and products was important, then insertion into the local community was also crucial: an important group of merchants, who were eager to profit from Montevideo's newly acquired status within the Spanish empire welcomed Cipriano de Melo into their fold. These kinds of local arrangements were fundamental to the growth of the local mercantile and political community.

In 1780 a close associate of Cipriano de Melo, the Montevidean merchant Francisco Maciel, departed on a business trip to Rio de Janeiro. According to the Luso-Brazilian viceroy don Luis de Vasconcelos, Maciel acted as a delegate representing the interests of Montevidean merchants. He met with merchants and authorities in Rio de Janeiro in order to acquire ninety slaves and to purchase tobacco, sugar, and textiles. However, the most important part of his visit was to reestablish the trade route between Rio de Janeiro and Río de la Plata. Under the pretext of needing repairs, Maciel ensured that Portuguese ships would be welcome in Montevideo by Segundo Comandante Cipriano de Melo.[20] Although suspicious of the proffered strategy, the viceroy was reassured by Carneiro Leão, a merchant of "good reputation and large credit" in Rio de Janeiro, who vouched for the trustworthiness of the authorities and merchants of Montevideo and assured the safety of the ships.[21]

Between 1781 and 1786, seventy-four Portuguese ships arrived in Montevideo, forty-three of which had declared at departure their destination as other Portuguese ports, usually Rio Grande or Santa Catarina. Among the captains who frequently traveled this route were Portuguese pilots navigating Spanish and Portuguese vessels. Moreover, some of these Portuguese captains were Cipriano de Melo's business partners and friends who traveled the route between Montevideo and Rio de Janeiro. In Montevideo, some of them were hosted at Cipriano de Melo's house or were guests at his dinner table.[22]

Cipriano de Melo also participated actively as a merchant in the Río de la Plata–Luso-America route. In 1779 Cipriano de Melo petitioned the Spanish Crown for permission to collect the money owed to him by Luso-Brazilian merchants, approximately 32,000 pesos. To support his claim, he collected the statements of many businessmen located in Colônia do Sacramento, Buenos Aires, and Montevideo, who confirmed the well-known fact that Cipriano de Melo had credits in the cities of Rio de Janeiro and Salvador de Bahia, as well as on the island of Santa Catarina. Moreover, Cipriano de Melo also had several statements from a Spanish officer, who had fought alongside him in 1777, that attested to the good service performed by Cipriano de Melo for the Spanish Crown. The Crown granted Cipriano de Melo's petition and further authorized Viceroy Cevallos to compensate him for his lost property in Colônia do Sacramento, which included the property of his father-in-law, don Manuel Pereira Gonzales, who had fled to Rio de Janeiro in 1777.[23]

Cipriano de Melo found important allies among the merchants and authorities of Montevideo (figure 3). The Viana family and their allies were most responsible for Cipriano de Melo's integration into Montevideo's society. They also stood to profit both from the new status of Montevideo as an Atlantic port and from their dealings in the port of Buenos Aires. The group included the former governor of Montevideo, José Joaquín de Viana; his cousin, Melchor de Viana; the merchant don Francisco Maciel; and, later, Cipriano de Melo himself. The Viana familial networks connected them to the first settlers of the Banda Oriental and guaranteed that their families received favors from the Crown in compensation for their efforts to build the city.[24]

The first governor of Montevideo, don José Joaquín de Viana, married doña Francisca de Alzaybar, the sister of don Francisco de Alzaybar, who was the first settler and a *latifundia* owner in the Banda Oriental. In two separate terms in office, Viana governed Montevideo for fifteen years (1751–64; 1771–73). During these periods, the governor was able to build strong networks in the city. The connection with the Alzaybar family not only assured access to ample economic and social resources in the area but

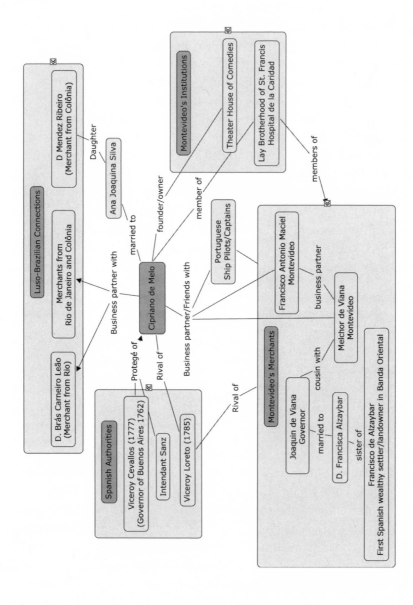

Figure 3. Networks of Don Manuel Cipriano de Melo.

also ensured *mercedes* (rewards) from the Crown for the Alzaybar family, who assisted settlers and patrolled Río de la Plata.[25] Moreover, Viana had led Spanish troops during the Guaraní War, which entitled him to royal favors. In the following decades, Joaquín de Viana was responsible for distributing land, choosing the two subsequent governors of Montevideo (Agustín de la Rosa and Joaquín del Pino, respectively), and in the process secured a prominent estate for his family and himself in the region.[26]

Joaquín de Viana built an extensive network of relatives, fictive kin, and business associates who were prominent in the later decades of the eighteenth century in Montevideo. For example, Joaquín de Viana was a cousin of Melchor de Viana, who traded slaves and all type of goods from Europe and the Americas, which made him one of the most important merchants in Montevideo. Furthermore, Joaquín de Viana named the sister of another powerful Montevidean merchant, Francisco Maciel, the executor of his estate. Maciel was one of the most active slave traders in Montevideo. Another important character in the Viana faction was don Francisco de Medina, a wealthy trader who was responsible for the creation of the first *saladero* (estate for production of jerky beef) in the Banda Oriental.[27]

Viana's connections, however, extended beyond the merchant community of Montevideo. The Montevidean governor was a political protégé of Viceroy Juan José Vértiz, who ruled in Buenos Aires as governor from 1770 to 1776 and as viceroy from 1778 to 1784. Among the merchants of Buenos Aires, Martín de Altolaguirre, Manuel Belgrano Perez, and Tomás Antonio Romero were very active in operating with this group in Montevideo in the early 1780s.[28]

After the fall of Colônia do Sacramento, this network of local elites welcomed Cipriano de Melo in Montevideo and incorporated him as a business associate and friend. Cipriano de Melo, Melchor de Viana, and Francisco Maciel hired the same vessels and the same pilots and, most important, shared the same networks in Rio de Janeiro and Salvador da Bahia.[29] These merchants utilized the same agents and submitted orders for goods as a group, relying on Cipriano de Melo's contacts to acquire general and specific products, such as chairs made of the fine Brazilian wood jacaranda, and even slave cooks from Bahia.[30] These types of operations relied directly on trust. Because of the nature of trans-imperial trade, the level of informality was much higher than in traditional intra-imperial trade networks. The latter system relied on legal regulation much more than it did interpersonal relationships. The transimperial connections of Cipriano de Melo benefited groups centered in Montevideo as well as merchants in Buenos Aires who were active in the slave trade and trade with foreign colonies. Montevideo became the preferred Atlantic port of the region, not only due to the Bourbon reforms, but also because of its Luso-Platine networks. As a result, Montevideo became the preeminent port for both legal and illegal trade.

Because he profited from the new offices and regulations created by the Bourbon reforms, Cipriano de Melo had a relatively easy task reestablishing himself in Montevideo. He also mobilized his connections in Portuguese America. During periods of war between Spain and Great Britain, increasingly lax regulation of neutral trade allowed transimperial networks to function even more actively and with a higher level of legality. The intense traffic in the port of Montevideo in the years after the downfall of Colônia had initially been welcomed by traders in Buenos Aires. However, the growing control of transimperial trade by Montevideo's merchant community and officials began to trouble important factions in Buenos Aires.

By the mid-1780s, some of the merchants and authorities in Buenos Aires were dissatisfied by the fact that Montevideo was the only port authorized to dock transatlantic arrivals. As a result of this arrangement, the merchants of Buenos Aires depended on their agents and business associates in Montevideo, which allowed the merchant community of Montevideo to increase their own business by profiting from the condition of being the port of Buenos Aires. As a result, Montevideo benefited directly from Buenos Aires's economic growth and commercial prosperity. During the 1780s, an emergent group of Buenos Aires merchants who were active in enterprises such as the slave trade, trade with foreign colonies, and free trade with other ports in the Spanish empire had important interests in Montevideo's port. The most visible members among this group were Tomás Antonio Romero; his son, don José de Maria; and don Manuel de Aguirre.[31]

The nomination of a new viceroy for Buenos Aires in 1784, however, triggered conflict among some factions of the mercantile communities in both port cities. Important segments of the mercantile community of Buenos Aires welcomed the arrival of the viceroy, Cristóbal del Campo, marquis de Loreto (r. 1784–89), to Buenos Aires. Determined to put an end to the intense transimperial traffic channeled through Montevideo, the viceroy enacted measures designed to constrain the "excesses" of autonomy and the contraband activities of Montevideo's authorities.[32]

Beyond the contraband issue, the conflict involved a dispute between Viceroy Loreto and the intendant of Río de la Plata, don Francisco de Paula Sanz. In Río de la Plata, the viceroy and the intendant often had overlapping or loosely defined jurisdiction.[33] In addition, the arrival of the marquis de Loreto generated divergent opinions about policies regarding trade with neutrals and how best to stimulate local industries. On the one hand, Intendant Sanz sought to protect trade and local shipyards and factories; on the other, Viceroy Loreto aimed to protect monopolistic policies. The conflict could be understood as competing visions of imperial policy or as the conflict between the old and the new structure of power created by the Bourbon reforms. Nevertheless, personal grievances between the two men, combined with their loyalties to the various factions which they served, should be acknowledged.

One of the most visible targets of the porteño reaction was Cipriano de Melo. The viceroy and other authorities accused him of supporting contraband trade by allowing Portuguese ships to harbor in Montevideo, thus facilitating the illegal introduction of goods and subjects into Spanish dominions.[34] The events that culminated in a series of lawsuits against Cipriano de Melo began when one of his Portuguese business partners, the pilot and well-known smuggler don Antonio Juan de Acuña, was arrested after illegally entering Montevideo, where he stayed for two days at the house of Cipriano de Melo. Acuña had arrived in the city onboard a Portuguese brigantine two days earlier. According to his statement, he went to Cipriano de Melo's house because of his connections to Melchor de Viana. Acuña justified his presence in the city by claiming that he needed to collect a debt from this important merchant.

The episode gave birth to a long lawsuit in which the authorities in Buenos Aires made a case against Cipriano de Melo while also questioning the ability of Montevidean authorities to control transatlantic trade. The dispute centered on who had jurisdiction to inspect the ships and authorize the disembarkment of goods. The case was further complicated in two ways: first, Acuña's alleged infractions fell under the jurisdiction of customs officials, who at that time were under the direct influence of the new viceroy and porteño authorties; and second, letters, receipts, and account books of operations involving Cipriano de Melo; his wife, Ana Joaquina; Melchor de Viana; Francisco Maciel; and other important Montevideo merchants had been found among Acuña's confiscated belongings. This legal case foreshadowed the conflicts between Buenos Aires and Montevideo merchants that surfaced in the 1790s, in the aftermath of the creation of the porteño Consulado de Comércio.

In the 1784 lawsuit, prosecutors exposed an intricate network of cooperation among the Montevidean merchants. According to evidence cited in the case, Cipriano de Melo and his wife operated a business that sent illegally imported slaves to Alto Peru. Using one of their own slaves to manage the deliveries, the couple had allegedly exported anywhere from twenty-seven to three hundred slaves.[35] The viceroy also questioned the legitimacy of Cipriano de Melo's license to introduce 32,000 pesos from Luso-America. According to Viceroy Loreto, Cipriano de Melo had stated that he transported less than 5,000 pesos to date. However, the viceroy argued that Cipriano de Melo had five ships under his command in Brazil; thus, the viceroy calculated that the amount carried by each ship would be roughly 1,000 pesos, which was not enough to cover the cost of the ship and its crew.

The evidence also exposed even larger underground networks of contraband trade that involved the Portuguese pilot, Juan de Acuña, and the Montevidean merchants Leonardo Pereyra, Melchor de Viana, Francisco Maciel, and Francisco de Medina. Acuña's papers revealed that, for more than four years, these merchants had been smuggling slaves, sugar, tobacco, and other goods and had been illegally exporting hides to Rio de Janeiro and Salvador de Bahia. These operations amounted to more than 51,400 pesos fuertes.[36] Among his partners in Rio de Janeiro, Cipriano de Melo counted Antonio João da Costa, João da Costa Pinheiro, João Diniz Vieira, and Brás Carneiro Leão. The representative of the group in Salvador de Bahia was don Francisco José de Lucena. It is revealing that the group had more connections to Rio de Janeiro than to Salvador de Bahia. In addition to the larger number of associates in the Fluminense port, Maciel complained about a former partner from Bahia, Manoel José Froes, who had not paid for the 5,697 hides sent to him on account. The Montevidean merchants spread this information, not only to their associate in Salvador de Bahia in charge of collecting the debt, but also among their business associates in Rio de Janeiro. Such behavior was characteristic of business organizations in Old Regime societies: network structures ensured trust and the safety of operations.[37]

Among the confiscated papers were lists of goods ordered by Cipriano de Melo—for his family, the governor of Montevideo, and Primer Comandante del Resguardo don Antonio Pereira—that included furniture made from jacaranda wood, shirts, velvet dresses, and *salterio* scores and even a slave musician and slave cooks. All of these items and slaves were intended for personal or household use by their families. In addition, authorities found lists that specified items for sale.[38]

The viceroy used the evidence found among Acuña's belongings to argue against the primacy of Montevideo as a mandatory port of call for the region. He bolstered his argument by highlighting the corruption of the Montevidean authorities, whom he accused of protecting smuggling with the Portuguese. Moreover, the viceroy advocated against the liberal policies of neutral trade and saw the need to "close the door to Portuguese traders," as well as to the British, "even if it meant allowing their ships to sink in front of the harbor." The marquis de Loreto also leveled direct charges against Cipriano de Melo, whom the viceroy defined as a "corrupt official, who was receptive to bribes," "a foreigner," and "a Portuguese, whose conduct and performance were so damaging to the Royal Treasury."[39]

In his defense, Cipriano de Melo presented a list of all the services he had performed for the Spanish Crown: participation in military actions during the war of 1777, the conquest of Colônia do Sacramento, and expeditions to ensure the control of Patagonia and the Malvinas (Falkland Islands). Furthermore, he provided a list of all his contraband confiscations since he took office as Segundo Comandante del Resguardo. He also cited canons of natural law justifying the licenses for foreign ships to enter Montevideo's harbor for repairs and reviewed the royal ordinances regarding trade with neutrals.[40]

Most important, Cipriano de Melo adamantly affirmed his loyalty to the Spanish Crown, stating, "It is a public and well known fact that I was a resident [*vecino*] of Colônia do Sacramento; thus, I shall not be considered a foreigner, and rather I should be reputed as a Spaniard, with all the rights and privileges that Spanish subjects enjoy." He argued that, according to the laws of conquest, residents who wanted to swear loyalty would enjoy full rights as vassals of the Spanish Crown.[41]

Cipriano de Melo also stated that the arrival of the Portuguese traders ensured the continued flow of slaves during the years of war with Great Britain. Furthermore, he used this argument to justify his involvement with Antonio Juan de Acuña, who, according to Cipriano de Melo, was one of the agents involved in the slave trade. The Bourbon reforms had intended to stimulate the introduction of slaves into the Americas in order to increase agricultural production. However, policies intended to foster the acquisition of slaves in the empire ultimately reinforced the traditional commercial route between Río de la Plata and Rio de Janeiro. After the wars of 1777, the king had authorized certain subjects to import their capital from Portuguese America into Spanish America. The intendant of Río de la Plata, Francisco de Paula Sanz, stated that the trade with the Portuguese benefited the empire, mainly owing to the introduction of slaves. Moreover, Intendant Sanz argued that such flows of capital favored the Spanish empire and therefore should not be considered contraband.[42]

What had started as a local conflict soon reached the Council of the Indies in Seville as a confrontation between the intendant, under whose jurisdiction the Comandancia del Resguardo functioned, and the viceroy, who controlled the customs officials. In short, the local conflict turned into an imperial conflict between the supporters of the newly instituted reforms and the old power structure. Such a dispute clearly exemplifies how local elites and authorities interpreted and manipulated colonial regulations according to their own interests. In 1788 Sanz was sent to Potosí as the new intendant of Alto Peru and the viceroy was replaced in Buenos Aires. Montevideo's officials retained jurisdiction over all transatlantic arrivals in Río de la Plata. In spite of the fact that the port activity of both cities complemented one another, such an outcome did not mean an end to the conflict between the factions of the mercantile communities of Montevideo and Buenos Aires.

In 1791 Buenos Aires merchants opposed to transimperial trade renewed the attacks on Cipriano de Melo by presenting more charges to the Council of the Indies, accusing him and his business associate don Manuel Diago of contributing to fraud, which had led to the bankruptcy of the Customs House of Buenos Aires and of smuggling goods to Brazil and La Habana.[43] In his defense, he emphasized the lack of evidence connecting him to the corruption in the Customs House and instead blamed the influence of Viceroy Loreto over the *fiscal* of the Council of the Indies. Cipriano de Melo denounced the viceroy for the false accusations against him and the fiscal for his failure to process the documents he had sent to the council. Moreover, Cipriano de Melo accused them both of persecuting him, "since he had sworn vassalage to the King of Spain, thus having denied his status as a Portuguese subject."[44]

As for the smuggling charges, Cipriano de Melo presented in his defense that all the trade with La Habana had been conducted by his wife, Ana Joaquina da Silva, and thus was not his business. After a long, drawn-out lawsuit, it was decided that his wife had obtained his consent to engage in commerce; Cipriano de Melo was found guilty of smuggling slaves and other goods. He was jailed in Buenos Aires for a brief period in 1788. However, the king reaffirmed Cipriano de Melo's status as a naturalized Spaniard and allowed him to retain his office but forbade him to trade in slaves and other goods. The ban did not prevent his wife from conducting a series of commercial transactions that involved slaves, sugar, and tobacco, as well as a series of deals with Potosí, Chile, La Habana, Brazil, and Europe.[45] Diago, furthermore, retained his right to engage in trading activities. The commercial partnership between Diago and Cipriano de Melo lasted until the death of the latter in 1813.

Even after the incidents of 1788, Cipriano de Melo continued to be an active member of Montevideo's elite. He founded the city's first theater, known as the House of Comedies, and served as manager of Hospital of Charity, an institution owned and operated by the lay brotherhood of Saint Francis. During the 1790s, he actively involved himself with the Luso-Brazilian community residing in Montevideo, sponsoring and assisting newly arrived immigrants from Brazil, especially artisans. He also maintained active networks with Portuguese authorities, including granting clearance to Portuguese vessels that arrived in Montevideo transporting Franciscan missionaries.[46] These facts point to the successful integration of Cipriano de Melo into the city's institutional and social life and highlight the transimperial nature of local society and community institutions.

The 1790s marked the beginning of a phase in which Cipriano de Melo was no longer allowed to engage directly in the Atlantic trade. Nevertheless, he continued as the authority in charge of suppressing contraband trade in the port of Montevideo, often ensuring that his business associates could trade freely. In Montevideo, Cipriano de Melo personally inspected many of the vessels arriving from foreign colonies.[47] Often these ships carried old acquaintances or business partners and their agents as passengers. Due to his office, Cipriano de Melo could delay or expedite the clearance of arriving vessels and determine the legality of the cargo. In addition, Cipriano de Melo's friends and business associates increased their participation in regional and transatlantic commerce. Manuel Diago, Francisco Maciel, and Matteo Magariños, who served as Cipriano's attorney, were all founding members of Montevideo's Junta de Comércio (1794), and Maciel and Magariños served as the Junta's delegate to the Consulado in Buenos Aires.[48] In addition to their privileged position in the merchant community, both Maciel and Magariños dispatched many merchant ships to Brazil, and they also represented the interests of powerful Buenos Aires merchants such as Francisco Belaustegui and Juan Viola (Magariños) and Manuel de Aguirre, Pinedo y Arroyo, and Santiago Barros (Maciel).[49] As a result, although Cipriano de Melo was officially forbidden from engaging in transatlantic, he could use his office strategically to give advantages to his business associates, who maintained networks with both Portuguese America and Buenos Aires.

Cipriano de Melo also increased his activities in the Merin Lagoon and in the borderlands between Brazil and the Banda Oriental in the 1790s and 1800s. During this period, he conducted several raids, established guards, and deployed canoes to repress contraband in the waters of the Merin Lagoon.[50] In these antismuggling operations, Cipriano de Melo counted on the help of Rafael Pinto Bandeira, a Portuguese merchant and official. Bandeira had been accused of monopolizing contraband trade in the area, but these accusations never resulted in a conviction.[51]

The last decade of the eighteenth century witnessed warfare involving Spain and other Atlantic empires. The new conflicts encouraged Spanish officials to enact laws authorizing trade with neutrals. Between 1795 and

1797 Montevideo's harbor was open officially to vessels originating from Portugal and other friendly nations. As had occurred in the previous decade, Río de la Plata merchants from Montevideo along with some factions from Buenos Aires found these years full of opportunities for transimperial trade. The 1790s, however, marked yet another dispute between groups centered in Buenos Aires and groups in Montevideo. This time, commercial interests opposed old allies: Montevideo's authorities and merchants versus the group of Buenos Aires merchants involved in trade with foreigners.[52]

During the mid-1790s, obvious signs of the rupture of the alliance between Montevidean traders and the nonmonopolistic merchants of Buenos Aires and of their struggle for primacy in transimperial trade surfaced. As the head of the agency in charge of repressing contraband, Cipriano de Melo undertook a series of confiscations that targeted the vessels and crews of the porteño merchants involved in transimperial trade. The lawsuits, combined with the contraband confiscations generated in the 1790s, testify to the split between the Montevidean faction comprised of Maciel, Cipriano de Melo, and Melchor de Viana from Montevideo and the faction comprised of Tomás Antonio Romero, Pedro Duval, and José de Maria, among others, from Buenos Aires.[53]

The monopoly enjoyed by Montevideo's harbor authorities on transatlantic arrivals lay at the root of the conflict between these mercantile factions. In the 1790s the mercantile community of Buenos Aires already was internally divided, between the merchants who opposed trade with neutrals and those in favor of such practices.[54] As a result, mercantile factions in Buenos Aires initiated a lawsuit in which merchants, with the support of the Consulado de Comercio, argued against the position of Montevideo as the privileged port city in Río de la Plata.[55] This time, however, the most visible targets from among the Montevidean authorities were Cipriano de Melo and the new viceroy of Río de la Plata, Olaguer Feliú, himself a former governor of Montevideo.

The main incident that exposed the political opposition of these once allied merchants from Buenos Aires and Montevideo involved the primacy of Montevideo as a mandatory port of call in the region. The porteño traders decried the excesses of the viceroy and of Comandante del Resguardo Cipriano de Melo, who, they argued, "threatened the primacy of the Capital

Buenos Aires" and imposed "miserable losses" in free trade.[56] The group of merchants from Buenos Aires, represented by Manuel de Aguirre, José de Maria, and Pedro Duval, complained about the enforcement of the policy that stipulated that all ships from foreign colonies must harbor first in Montevideo.

The pivotal episode in this conflict was the refusal of entry into the port of Buenos Aires for two ships coming from the Islas Mauricio and from Pernambuco in Portuguese America in late 1798. Duval and Aguirre, two powerful merchants in Buenos Aires and members of the Consulado de Commerce, owned the ships at the center of the dispute. The merchants complained that their ships, loaded with perishable cargo and slaves, had been denied safe harbor in Buenos Aires due to the decree by Viceroy Olaguer Feliú that required all transatlantic trade to be conducted through the port of Montevideo. Moreover, the merchants petitioned the viceroy to designate an officer to inspect the ships, without them having first to sail back to Montevideo. Viceroy Olaguer Feliú chose Cipriano de Melo to perform the task. Cipriano de Melo, however, was not in Buenos Aires and, consequently, the ships were forced to sail out of that city.[57]

In an attempt to circumvent a return to Montevideo, Duval and Aguirre directed their ships to sail to Colônia do Sacramento, which was under the jurisdiction of the porteños, and then to return to the harbor of Buenos Aires under the guise of ships arriving from another Spanish port. This maneuver did not produce the expected result, however, and the ships eventually departed for Montevideo. The merchants complained that such rules not only impeded the shipment of their cargo but also caused damage and the death of a number of slaves when the ships were caught by a storm en route to Montevideo.[58] The merchants also argued that Buenos Aires should be allowed to receive slave ships, not only because the city provided the capital to finance such expeditions, but also because the port had better logistics for the disembarkation of slaves.

Duval and Maria called the Comandancia de Resguardo officers "bad and unfaithful bureaucrats" and declared that the authorities in Montevideo, including the viceroy, wanted to maintain the monopoly on both transimperial and contraband trade.[59] Implicit in the accusation was that illicit trade did not occur in Buenos Aires. Moreover, the porteño merchants and their allies argued that the extension of the authority of a Montevidean official, in this case Cipriano de Melo, to Buenos Aires constituted a serious offense to the bureaucrats of the viceregal capital. In their estimation, the change would "represent the influence of Montevideo over Buenos Aires." They also claimed that Viceroy Olaguer Feliú spent more time in Montevideo, where he kept his home, than in Buenos Aires.[60]

Moreover, Maria also alleged that Olaguer Feliú had failed to honor the licenses for transimperial trade granted by the former viceroy and that such measures unfairly targeted Buenos Aires merchants.[61] In addition, Maria stated that the viceroy associated closely with a certain "Melo" to whom he gave more authority than was legal.[62] Maria and Duval stated that they did not want to "mention the details of Feliú's presence in Montevideo in order to refrain from reproducing rumors and from demonstrating a lack of 'decorum'" and to avoid the provocation of further unrest in the streets of Buenos Aires.[63] Such statements made clear the division between the communities of the two port cities: even though the conflict started as a political and economic question, the merchants were able to use their vertical and horizontal networks to mobilize people beyond the strict confines of the mercantile community.[64]

The dispute culminated with the attempt of Montevideo merchants congregated in the Junta de Comércio to create their own Consulado de Comercio and practically gain legal commercial autonomy in relation to Buenos Aires. Although Cipriano de Melo had not been allowed to engage in Atlantic trade since the late 1790s, his business partner, Manuel Diago, was an active member of Montevideo's merchant community and in the Junta de Comércio. Montevideo's Junta de Comércio (a regional merchant guild dependent on the Buenos Aires Consulado) sought to enhance the role of Montevideo's port in the region. Because Buenos Aires merchants depended on Montevideo's port authorities, merchants, and connections to transimperial trade, Montevideo's community tried to profit the most from such a strategic position.

Conversely, the merchants of Buenos Aires made an effort to authorize the port of Ensenada de Barragán, a bay south of Buenos Aires, as a transatlantic port. The initiative of the merchants of Buenos Aires proved temporarily successful. From 1801 to 1802, the port of Ensenada de Barragán was declared a physical extension of the port of Buenos Aires, and it opened to Spanish vessels navigating transatlantic routes. However, foreign vessels were excluded. Despite the Council of the Indies' refusal to create a new Consulado de Comercio in Montevideo, it was receptive to the arguments in favor of the return to primacy of the port of Montevideo.[65] After 1802 Montevideo once again became the primary port of call for transatlantic voyages in the Río de la Plata estuary. Thus, by the beginning of the nineteenth century, a new balance of power had been created in Río de la Plata. Although they continued to conduct business together, the communities of merchants from Montevideo and Buenos Aires clearly had different interests.

Cipriano de Melo had been a protagonist in many of the conflicts generated by the emergence of Montevideo as a regional center of power. In the first decade of the nineteenth century, however, his actions did not have the same results as in the previous decades. Nonetheless, he kept alive his networks and influence in the region. In 1809 the governor of Rio Grande do Sul, the southernmost captaincy of Brazil, sent Cipriano de Melo boxes of sweets in reciprocation for Portuguese newspapers that he had received earlier. The governor thanked Cipriano de Melo, saying that he had not been able to get hold of a Portuguese newspaper in months. Although minor, this episode demonstrates that Cipriano de Melo continued to nourish his important transimperial connections.[66]

When the movement for independence began, Cipriano de Melo supported the Junta de Montevideo created in 1808 and the Portuguese invasion of the city in 1811. He also maintained strategic connections and a privileged position to influence the political events. His business partners, Manuel Diago and Francisco Joanico, and his attorney, Matteo Magariños, were among the twenty-two representatives elected to participate in the Cabildo Abierto that created the Junta of 1808, which officially severed the political ties of subordination to Buenos Aires. In 1813 Cipriano de Melo died in the comfort of his home while Montevideo was under military siege by troops sent from Buenos Aires.[67] By the time of his death, there remained to be collected more than 37,000 pesos from his business associates in Montevideo and Rio de Janeiro. Of this total, 36,000 pesos related to trade activities, and 1,000 pesos pertained to a loan extended to a Portuguese artisan whom Cipriano de Melo had helped to establish in Montevideo. The total capital amassed by Cipriano de Melo in his lifetime amounted to more than 186,000 pesos.

The life story of don Cipriano de Melo and his connections beyond imperial limits—ranging from Alto Peru to Rio de Janeiro to Africa and Europe—expose the fluidity of political boundaries during the late eighteenth century. Moreover, Cipriano de Melo's case illuminates the significance of transimperial networks for borderland regions and demonstrates how the manipulation of transimperial resources, together with imperial law, enabled local groups to improve their status within the imperial system. Improved status, in turn, was used to gain autonomy in relation to the regional centers of power.

The political and economic conflicts in which Cipriano de Melo participated were in large part disputes between the opposing political and commercial interests of the viceregal capital of Buenos Aires and the growing provincial capital of Montevideo. Indeed, the Bourbon reforms and the transimperial networks connected to Portuguese and Anglo-America constituted the roots of Montevideo's emergence as a regional center. Montevideo's society developed a greater sense of its own economic and political influence within the realms of the Spanish empire by manipulating the imperial discourse and new regulations to their advantage and further benefited from the social and economic capital that they transferred from Colônia do Sacramento. The life story of Cipriano de Melo, whose experiences were shared by many of his contemporaries, adds a new layer of understanding of the changes occurring in the late colonial period in the Atlantic. The social networks that transcended the political limits of Atlantic empires were crucial in shaping political, economic, and social processes unfolding in imperial spaces.

7 Postponing the Revolution

TRANSIMPERIAL COMMERCE AND
MONARCHISM IN THE BANDA ORIENTAL

In response to the crisis of legitimacy triggered by Napoleon's invasion of the Iberian Peninsula in 1808, different reactions and political projects emerged in the Spanish American colonies. Historians of Latin America have emphasized different factors that shaped revolutionary and royalist projects: grievances regarding imperial reforms, elite factionalism and regional economic interests, Peninsular versus Creole rivalry, and, often, the willingness of local elites to establish free trade.[1] The maintenance and control of transimperial networks of trade was a central preoccupation of commercial and political elites during the independence era. A close analysis of the Río de la Plata commercial and political processes between 1810 and 1822 illuminates the relationship between transimperial trade and the emergence of different political projects during the revolutionary decade of the 1810s. Moreover, it contributes to the understanding of the plural meanings of sovereignty and monarchism during the age of revolution in Iberian America.[2] In Montevideo, monarchist political projects were connected to transimperial commerce and the maintenance of Old Regime institutions.

While Buenos Aires was one of the first Spanish colonial centers to break free from Spanish rule and to declare free trade, Montevideo became the bastion of Spanish loyalism and, later, monarchism in the South Atlantic. Between 1810 and 1814, loyalist Montevideo not only maintained control over previously existing transimperial networks of trade but also increased its volume of trade with foreigners, including commerce with U.S. merchants. Royalist Spanish rule did not last, however. Revolutionary forces, first from Buenos Aires, in 1814, and later, in 1815, José Gervasio Artigas's forces took control of the city. Portuguese troops invaded Montevideo in 1816 and returned the city and its hinterland to the monarchical rule but this time as part of the Luso-Brazilian empire until 1822. Under Portuguese monarchical rule, political institutions centered in Montevideo exerted control over the whole territory of the Banda Oriental for the first time. The creation of a provincial assembly, composed of the representatives of each cabildo, symbolized the provincial scope of the political institutions and reinforced Montevideo's central role in the Banda Oriental. For Montevideo's commercial elites, royalism and monarchy were the preferential option to increase transimperial trade, to maintain Old Regime institutions and the colonial status quo, and to boost Montevideo's autonomy in relation to Buenos Aires.

During the last decades of Spanish colonial rule, political and commercial disputes emerged between elites from Buenos Aires and Montevideo and influenced the different responses to the political crisis in 1808, namely, the creation of a revolutionary junta in Buenos Aires and the emergence of Montevideo as a bastion of loyalism. Under monarchical rule (1810–22), there was an increase in the number of Portuguese, British, and American vessels entering Montevideo's harbor. During the age of revolution, Montevideo's merchant elites repudiated rebellion and upheaval and deepened their commitment to monarchism and to the Old Regime political projects of the Spanish or Portuguese Crown. Monarchism was used by Montevideo's elites to assure political autonomy from revolutionary Buenos Aires and to profit from trade with foreign merchants, especially Portuguese, English, and Anglo-Americans. During this period Montevideo lost its status as the official port of Buenos Aires. For the commercial elites of Montevideo, the maintenance of well-known commercial routes and transimperial commercial links was a primary preoccupation during the revolutionary period.

PLATINE RIVALS: THE CRISIS OF THE SPANISH
MONARCHY IN MONTEVIDEO AND BUENOS AIRES

The process of independence in Río de la Plata was complex, involving many different regional factions and international political agents. While Buenos Aires broke away from Spanish rule early in the 1810s, Montevideo remained a bastion of royalism in Río de la Plata until 1814. During this period, Montevideo's elites maintained the centrality of the pueblos as the source of sovereignty in the area and Montevideo's role as the political center of the province. At the same time that they claimed local sovereignty, they implemented trade regulations to increase commercial intercourse with foreign powers, specifically, with the commercial community of Rio de Janeiro. The different ways the political and economic elites of Buenos Aires and Montevideo reacted to the monarchical crisis in Spain was indicative of rivalries that had been unfolding during the last decades of the colonial period.

By 1808 Buenos Aires and Montevideo elites were at odds with each other over legal and commercial matters. The powerful merchants of Buenos Aires—the wealthiest and most dynamic commercial community in the Río de la Plata port complex—resented Montevideo's commercial autonomy, the need to maintain agents in the city, and the required payment of taxes and fees to local authorities there. The still interlocked but increasingly divergent commercial communities began to unravel in the aftermath of the British invasions of 1806 and 1807. In 1806 a small British fleet sailing from Cape Town invaded and occupied Buenos Aires. Viceroy Sobremonte (r. 1804–7) fled the city, and the French-born Spanish officer Santiago de Liniers led the popular resistance. To expel the British in 1806, Montevideo's troops supported the urban militias of Buenos Aires. However, a new invasion occurred in 1807, this time in Montevideo and Buenos Aires. For the second time, in July 1807, the inhabitants of Buenos Aires resisted the British invasion, and British forces were expelled by August. British merchants were allowed to remain in Montevideo for seven months before returning to Europe.

Montevideo's merchants profited greatly from acquiring European goods from British traders at bargain prices during the British occupation of their city. According to the historian Arturo Bentancur, in 1807 more than a million pounds worth of British goods were introduced in Río de la Plata, the majority at Montevideo.[3] Furthermore, under British occupation, the port of Montevideo was open to trade with neutral nations, namely, the United States and Portugal, allowing the city's traders to export hides and other agricultural goods and to import slaves.[4] These maneuvers caused revolt among merchant circles of Buenos Aires.[5] In the aftermath of the British invasions, Santiago de Liniers emerged as interim viceroy of La Plata, supported by the Buenos Aires Creoles. Subsequently, Liniers attempted to strip Montevideo of her status as the base for the South Atlantic fleet and to terminate the city's jurisdiction over the Malvinas Islands and the Patagonian settlements.[6] Specifically, Liniers wanted to end Montevideo's primacy in trade with foreign ships and the city's status as the only port authorized for the disembarkation of slaves.

Liniers's rise to leadership sundered the Spanish territories of Río de la Plata by provoking strong opposition from merchants and authorities in Montevideo. Montevideo's governor, Francisco Elío, and the city's merchant community rejected Buenos Aires's measures by deploying the tactic "obedezco pero no cumplo," effectively not enforcing the interim viceroy's orders. Montevideo merchants also stopped transferring the revenues derived from the *averia* to the Consulado de Buenos Aires. Furthermore, Montevideo's authorities sent two delegates (Nicolas de Herrera and Juan Perez Balbas) to Spain in order to obtain a consulado and to enhance the city's political and economic rights within the empire.

To aid their petition for an autonomous consulado de comercio, Montevideo's merchants and authorities cited the crucial role of the troops, supplies, and capital the city's residents had given to Buenos Aires during the British invasions. Montevideo merchants had raised approximately 100,000 pesos to support Spanish resistance in the region, and they provided material and human resources to the defense of Río de la Plata.[7] For example, Francisco Maciel offered warehouses and seventy slaves, while Matteo Magariños organized and funded a militia unit of 350 men and provided more than seven hundred horses to the Spanish forces.[8] Many other merchants contributed with smaller amounts, varying from 300 to 1,000 pesos, and offered donations in kind, such as bread, horses, mules, rice, and the service of slaves. The city's defense against the British helped gain it the title of "very loyal and reconqueror city" (*muy leal y reconquistadora ciudad*), which granted Montevideo official recognition, allowed the guard of the cabildo to carry heavier weaponry (maces), and entitled its residents to small commercial privileges.

In the following months, the political crisis triggered by Napoleon's invasion of the Iberian Peninsula led to the escalation of the political and commercial divergences between Buenos Aires and Montevideo elites. When Napoleon's emissary to Río de la Plata, the marquis of Sassenay, arrived in Buenos Aires he requested the viceregal authorities to swear loyalty to Joseph Bonaparte. The failure of the French-born interim viceroy, Liniers, to immediately reject Bonaparte's regime triggered even more bitter confrontations. In Montevideo, Governor Elío and the cabildo raised serious suspicions about Liniers's loyalty. Beyond that, they questioned the legitimacy of his tenure as viceroy, since metropolitan authorities had neither made nor confirmed his interim appointment.

Eventually, Santiago de Liniers swore loyalty to Spain's Supreme Junta, joining the Audiencia and the Buenos Aires cabildo and sought to strengthen his political grip on Montevideo. In September 1808, Liniers sent ship captain Juan Angel de Michelena to replace Elío as Montevideo's governor. When this news broke in Montevideo, people gathered on the streets, and strong popular support for Elío emerged in the city. On September 21 a cabildo abierto was called in Montevideo to deliberate the proper response to Michelena's arrival as an agent of Buenos Aires. The people elected twenty-two representatives to the cabildo abierto, fourteen of whom were merchants and active members of the Junta de Comércio de Montevideo.[9] The cabildo abierto decided to form a *junta gubernativa* (governing committee), with Montevideo's governor, Francisco Elío, as the president. Montevideo's junta swore loyalty to Ferdinand VII and the junta of Seville, prevented Michelena from replacing Elío, and rejected the authority of Buenos Aires's interim viceroy, Liniers. In practice, these events meant severance of the political ties between Buenos Aires and Montevideo.

Montevideo's cabildo abierto and junta gubernativa included most of the prominent merchants that had been involved with the Junta de Comércio in the previous decades. The election of the Junta members reinforced the primacy of commercial interests in shaping the historical process in Montevideo. Well known and affluent merchants such as Matteo Magariños, Francisco

Vilardebó, Joaquin de Chopitea, Manuel Diago, Jaime Ylla, Antonio de San Vicente, Pasqual Parodi, Francisco Berro, and Pedro Irrazquin were members of the junta of 1808. Most of these merchants were deeply involved in transimperial trade networks, and several of them were partners with Buenos Aires commercial houses. As a result, while the junta of 1808 marked the political divergence between Montevideo and Buenos Aires, trade networks still connected individual merchants of the two cities.

Montevideo's early political autonomy lasted until the arrival of Viceroy Baltasar Hidalgo de Cisneros (r. 1809–10), appointed by the Seville junta. For a brief time, Cisneros was able to fulfill his duties as viceroy of La Plata, but on May 25, 1810, the cabildo of Buenos Aires ousted him.[10] The coup marked the political independence of Buenos Aires from Spain. The response of Montevideo to the events in Buenos Aires was to call for its own cabildo abierto once again in order to decide how to confront the crisis of authority in the metropole and Buenos Aires.

Montevideo's 1810 cabildo abierto decided to establish its own autonomous junta, which swore loyalty to Seville's Supreme Junta and repudiated the leadership of Buenos Aires. From that moment on, Montevideo became the center of Spanish loyalism in Río de la Plata. In 1811 the Cádiz junta named Elío the new viceroy of Río de la Plata. The Buenos Aires Junta, however, did not recognize Elío's authority and did not allow him to disembark at the port. Elío returned to Montevideo, where the local population and the local junta proclaimed the former governor the new viceroy of La Plata and Montevideo the new capital of the viceroyalty. Central to the interest of Montevidean elites was the maintenance of colonial institutions and transatlantic trade.

One of the first actions of Montevideo's new junta was to enact new regulations allowing and ensuring the arrival of foreign merchant vessels in the city's port. In addition to reinforcing procedures already in place, the Regulation of Foreign Vessels of 1811 made it mandatory that all arriving consignments had to be handled by a local merchant registered with the local junta de comercio.[11] As a result, despite Montevideo's efforts to increase its commercial autonomy, which dated to the 1790s, it was the political crisis caused by the British invasions and the Napoleonic wars that allowed the city's elites to effectively pursue autonomy in relation to Buenos Aires, and monarchism was the preferred political option.

Support for the monarchical project, however, was not unanimous in the Banda Oriental, and competing political projects emerged that co-opted a number of pueblos and cabildos in Montevideo's countryside. In addition to confronting the Buenos Aires revolutionary forces in the interior of the Banda Oriental, the royalists of Montevideo faced a third political challenge based on federalist ideas that emerged under the leadership of Artigas. Between 1810 and 1814 the city and port of Montevideo, however, successfully remained loyal to the Spanish monarchy and kept active trade networks with Portuguese America, the United States, and Britain. For Montevideo's merchant class, defense of the monarchy meant defense of transimperial trade.[12]

LOYALISM AND TRANSIMPERIAL TRADE

Between 1810 and 1814 Montevideo's port became progressively more dependent on trade with foreign merchants. Specifically, the number of Portuguese and English vessels entering the city's port grew in importance. During this period a total of 862 ships entered the port of Montevideo (table 3). Of this total, Spanish ships constituted 53.4 percent (461); Portuguese ships, 20.4 percent (176); British vessels, 15.1 percent (131), and U.S. ships, 10.7 percent (92). It is noteworthy, however, that of the 461 Spanish vessels that entered Montevideo's port, at least 31 stopped on the coast of Brazil on the way from Iberia to Río de la Plata. As a result, more than half of all the vessels that entered Montevideo sailed directly from a foreign port, with Portuguese America being the immediate port of origin for 24 percent of all ships that entered the city's harbor in the period.

The significance of commercial intercourse between Montevideo and foreign merchants during the period 1810–14 reached levels never recorded in previous decades. Even though Montevideo had increasingly concentrated networks of both legal and illegal transimperial trade since the 1780s, for the first time more than half of the vessels entering Montevideo came from foreign ports. Rio de Janeiro was the main foreign port of origin for the ships entering Montevideo, with a total of at least ninety-eight vessels.[13] Other Luso-Brazilian ports of origin included Bahia (twenty ships), and the generic term *Costa do Brasil* appeared as the ori-

Table 3 Ships Entering the Port of Montevideo, 1810–1814

Year	Flag					
	Spanish	Portuguese	English	U.S.	Other	Total
1808	58	11	10	4	1	84
1809	83	23	29	5	1	141
1810	118	30	56	24	1	229
1811	91	25	23	50	2	191
1812	60	26	10	9	0	105
1813	37	40	0	0	0	77
1814	14	21	3	0	0	38

SOURCE: AGNU, Ex AGA Libro 95, Aduana, Libro de Entrada de Embarcaciones.

gin of nine ships. Ports located geographically closer, such as Rio Grande (3) and Santa Catarina (1), were inconsequential to Montevideo's trade during the period. These data suggest that geography was not a determining variable for transimperial interaction. Instead, commercial networks and long-standing trade partnerships, which had developed during the late colonial period, were the main factor in trade patterns with Luso-Brazilians. Moreover, after 1812, Rio de Janeiro became the seat of a Spanish minister in charge of representing the Spanish junta at the Portuguese court. As a result, Rio de Janeiro appeared not only as a commercial hub but also as a monarchist political center for Río de la Plata.

British ports served as the second most important commercial connection to Montevideo between 1810 and 1814. London was the origin of sixty-two ships, while Liverpool and Belfast contributed half a dozen ships each. It is noteworthy that British vessels sailed from Hamburg (present-day Germany), the South Sea, and Rio de Janeiro. After the transfer of the Portuguese court to Rio de Janeiro in 1808, the Brazilian capital had become the home of several British diplomats in charge of dealing with Portugal, Spain, and the Spanish colonies. Most notably, the first printing press of Montevideo, sent by the Portuguese court in 1809, arrived in Río de la Plata on board a British vessel.[14]

Of the U.S. ships that entered Montevideo, the principal ports of origin were Philadelphia (6), Charleston (5), Baltimore (4), and Hamburg (6). One vessel each originated in Newport, Rhode Island, and Norfolk, Virginia. Unfortunately, in most of the recorded arrivals of American vessels the port of origin was simply recorded as "United States" or "Foreign Colonies." The steep increase in the number of American vessels in 1810 and 1811 must be understood in the broad Atlantic context. Since late 1810 some specially licensed U.S. merchant ships enjoyed de facto neutral status in Atlantic waters, due to British interest in securing foodstuffs to supply the troops fighting Napoleon in the Peninsular War.[15] The later virtual disappearance of U.S. vessels coincided with the outbreak of the War of 1812.

Between 1810 and 1814, while Montevideo remained the loyalist bastion in the South Atlantic, there was a marked increase in trade with foreign powers. Making use of previously established networks, Montevideo's mercantile community was able to successfully keep trade operations flowing. Furthermore, while Montevideo's elites intensified their connections with Portuguese and Anglo traders, they simultaneously attempted to prevent Buenos Aires's direct transatlantic commerce by issuing letters of marque to Montevidean ships against porteño vessels.[16] For Montevideo's elites, the defense of the Spanish monarchy meant not only official sanction to trade with foreign powers but also a violent political rupture with Buenos Aires.

The loyalist project in Montevideo received strong support from the city's mercantile groups connected to transimperial trade. Merchants such as Matteo Magariños, Francisco Joanico, Manuel Diago, Carlos Camuso, Manuel Vidal, and Juan Duran lent money to the local administration and participated in trade with foreign merchants, especially from Brazil. Magariños distinguished himself by having strong connections with merchants previously involved in trade with Luso-America and other foreign markets. He was one of the most active merchants shipping to and from Brazil, and had imported slaves since the early 1800s. During the British invasions, Magariños made patriotic donations to the Crown and lent money to the city's defenders. Between 1805 and 1808, Magariños sent at least three ships to Brazil.[17] His connections in Rio de Janeiro were built from networks formed by a previous generation of merchants active in Montevideo.

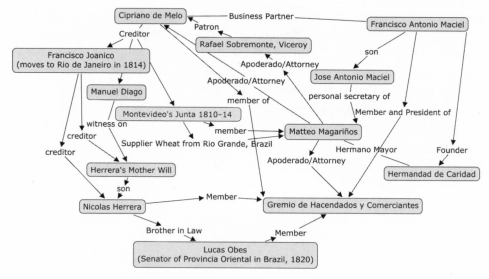

Figure 4. Networks of Matteo Magariños.

Magariños established strong networks with Montevideo's merchants who were involved in trade with Luso-America and the British in the last decades of the colonial period. Magariños served as the attorney (*apoderado*) for merchants like Maciel and Cipriano de Melo—both of whom played an essential role in the maintenance of transimperial trade networks between Brazil and Río de la Plata in the 1780s and 1790s, especially with Rio de Janeiro and Bahia. Magariños was also an important member and attorney for the Landowners and Merchants Guild of Montevideo. He was an active member in local institutions, becoming the head (*hermano mayor*) of a lay brotherhood, Hermandad de Caridad, and a respected member of the city's governing bodies. Between 1810 and 1814, Magariños used his networks in Brazil to purchase and supply wheat to the city during the siege imposed by Buenos Aires's forces. With his commercial networks, he also connected two generations of merchants who conducted business from the 1780s through the 1820s (figure 4). Moreover, his active participation in municipal and local politics, such as his support for the juntas, the merchant guild, and the religious institutions that promoted philanthropy in Montevideo, provided a higher level of institutionalization and continuity for transimperial commerce. These institutions would be crucial in supporting not only the monarchist project against Buenos Aires but also the Cisplatine project in the second half of the 1810s.

Between 1810 and 1814, the political situation allowed Montevideo merchants to use their economic strength and to mobilize resources through their social networks in support of monarchist interpretations of sovereignty and the maintenance of the Old Regime commercial order. The merchants involved in trans-imperial trade became the most active commercial faction operating in Montevideo. Such a development is evident from the analysis of Montevideo's port activity (see table 3) and of the accounts of foreign traders who passed through the city to conduct business. The English merchant Thomas Kinder reported staying at Francisco Joanico's house and having interacted with other merchants who were experienced in the trade between Brazil and Río de la Plata.[18] The crisis of legitimacy in Spain permitted the mercantile elites of Montevideo to simultaneously expand their activity in Atlantic trade and mobilize resources to maintain late colonial commercial and political institutions.

In 1814, however, after a prolonged military siege, Buenos Aires troops succeeded in invading and conquering Montevideo, putting an effective end to Spanish rule in Río de la Plata. Buenos Aires's political project was designed in part to channel maritime trade to ports controlled by porteño elites, such as Buenos Aires or Ensenada. Moreover, old rivalries and political factionalism were important variables in the new arrangement of power in Montevideo. After the fall of monarchist Montevideo, a number of Spanish, Creole, and foreign merchants, including Matteo Magariños and Francisco Joanico, fled the city to seek asylum in Europe and Brazil. The Luso-Brazilian court of Rio de Janeiro became a center for European diplomacy in the South Atlantic and a center for exiled merchants and political leaders from Montevideo.

The success of the porteño forces in Montevideo was short lived, however. In the countryside of the Banda Oriental, another revolutionary project gained traction and opposed the supremacy of Buenos Aires as the main port city of the Banda Oriental. In 1815 Artigas's federalist forces invaded and occupied Montevideo, establishing control over the whole territory of the Banda Oriental (including areas previously disputed with Buenos Aires). Artigas declared the Estado Oriental an autonomous sovereign state and made it a participant in the Liga Federal de Pueblos Libres.[19] Artigas's control of Montevideo did not last long, however.

The ascension of the Artiguista project in the Banda Oriental faced strong opposition from the Creole and Spanish elites of the region. Although the anti-Artigas and antirevolutionary groups had heterogeneous interests, by 1817 landed and mercantile elites had in common support for monarchical projects. Specifically, Spanish royalists involved in export and transimperial trade and with strong links to Luso-Brazilian ports did not find their interests supported by the leader of the orientales. Artigas's support for land redistribution inspired fear among the landed elites that exported agricultural goods. Furthermore, Artiguista officials confiscated goods and physically abused merchants in Montevideo.

In 1816 the Luso-Brazilian intervention initiated a campaign to cease "the terrors of anarchy" and maintain "order" with the aid of Montevidean elites and the acquiescence of the authorities from Buenos Aires.[20] Support for a Luso-Brazilian intervention and, later, for a monarchical project brought different elite groups together, including merchants connected to Brazil, Spain, and other Atlantic locations. Although they regarded the Luso-Brazilian intervention as an antidote to the revolutionary project of Artigas, Spanish royalists still hoped for a Spanish reconquest of Río de la Plata until 1821.[21].

THE LUSO-BRAZILIAN OCCUPATION, THE CISPLATINE PROVINCE, AND THE MAINTENANCE OF THE OLD ORDER, 1817–1822

Monarchism was intimately associated with the maintenance of transimperial trade networks and the preservation of forms of political participation and institutions from the colonial period. Monarchism represented the continuity of Old Regime principles of representation in which corporations were at the core of political life and provided safety and stability for the elites involved in transimperial trade. Furthermore, the maintenance of corporate structures of political participation at the core of the cabildos prevented popular participation based on individual citizenship that characterized revolutionary projects in other parts of Spanish

America, specifically, Buenos Aires. The monarchical form of government, however, faced challenges from various political interest groups in the Banda Oriental, changing patterns of trade in Río de la Plata, and the processes unfolding in other regions of Atlantic World, especially Europe. Montevideo's monarchists envisioned the maintenance of Old Regime political institutions as the base on which transimperial trade could flourish.

To those who favored the monarchical project and the commercial benefits it provided, the principal challenge emanated from Artigas's Liga Federal, or Federal League, also known as the Liga de los Pueblos Libres, or League of the Free Peoples. Artigas's federation included the Banda Oriental and the provinces of Corrientes, Entre-Rios, Misiones, Santa Fe, and Córdoba. It emphasized the autonomy and sovereignty of provinces and towns, wherein cabildos were the bastions of local power.[22] Specifically, the Artiguista government in the Banda Oriental maintained the autonomy of provinces based on *soberanía particular de los pueblos* (particular sovereignty of the towns), a principle derived from Spanish legal tradition according to which sovereignty emanated from local communities, which in association recognized a common authority.[23] This definition of sovereignty derived from law canons that were prevalent in Iberian legal traditions. The novel element of Artigas's federalist state, however, resided in the new form of popular representation and the radical program of land redistribution, benefiting the "most unfortunate orientales" at the expense of the property of "bad Europeans and even worse Americans." These elements marked a departure from colonial legal traditions by locating the political process in the individual citizen rather than corporate bodies.[24]

Artigas's rule triggered strong opposition from landed elites and merchants in Montevideo, who described the state of the Banda Oriental under Artigas as "anarchic" and "violent." According to the merchant and lawyer Lucas Obes, Artigas's radicalism was only comparable to the *sansculotes* of revolutionary France.[25] In early 1816 the merchant and landowning elites of Montevideo requested the intervention of the Luso-Brazilian empire against Artigas. In May 1816 more than ten thousand Luso-Brazilian troops entered Montevideo and the Banda Oriental to end the "anarchy and violence." In January 1817, the cabildo of Montevideo sent two delegates to the Portuguese court in Rio de Janeiro with powers to negotiate the incorporation of the Banda Oriental into the Luso-Brazilian empire. Their main goals were to pacify the country and promote trade.

The representatives of Montevideo's cabildo carried an instruction list with twelve articles to negotiate the incorporation of the Banda Oriental into the Luso-Brazilian empire. Six articles referred to matters pertaining to the legitimacy of the envoys as representatives of Montevideo and the question of sovereignty of the Banda Oriental. Two articles referred to free trade and maritime commerce, one article concerned religion, and other three regulated the appointment of benemerit men (*hombres benemeritos*) to oversee local administration and promote the general happiness of the province.[26]

Another element that speaks to the central role of trade in the Cisplatine project is the exchange of territory for improvements in the lighthouse on the island of Flores. The cabildo of Montevideo proposed the exchange of a tract of territory a mile north of Santa Tereza, following northwest to the fort of San Miguel, along the coast of the Merin Lagoon to the headwaters of the Yaguaron River.[27] This territory would be given to the Luso-Brazilian empire in exchange for the speedy construction of new structures to ensure the safety of navigation and commerce in Río de la Plata. The immediate justification for such a treaty was the shipwreck of a smack from Maldonado in the previous months that caused the loss of cargo and resulted in the death of fifty persons. According to the treaty, property and political rights of "vecinos" established in the territory should be respected and both the forts of Santa Tereza and San Miguel should remain under the control of the authorities in Montevideo. For the Cisplatine authorities, maintenance of commercial shipping lanes was the central axis of the monarchist political project.

Further examination of the legal principles of this political project in the Banda Oriental reveals the challenges faced by the Luso-Brazilian administration. First of all, although Montevideo's cabildo had asked for Luso-Brazilian intervention against Artigas, it recognized the same territorial limits for the province claimed by the *jefe de los orientales*. Furthermore, the instructions for annexation were given to the representatives by Montevideo's cabildo "in the name of all the Pueblos of the Banda Oriental through the representatives elected by the Pueblos."[28] As the historian Ana Frega has pointed out, this was not an accurate representation of the political situation of the Banda Oriental, since most of the pueblos and cabildos in the interior were members of the Liga Federal.[29]

By keeping the pueblos at the center of political life and the source of sovereignty, the elites of Montevideo not only aimed to maintain colonial legal traditions but also attempted to capitalize on the principles of sovereignty stipulated by their rivals' political project. As a result, the maintenance of the principle of soberanía particular de los pueblos, represented an avenue connecting the Luso-Brazilian annexation to the Artiguista project, thus facilitating the co-optation of leaders and rural communities.

The question, then, is how the incorporation would represent the end of anarchy. Why did monarchist elites (merchants and landowners) espouse their support for the same institutions and principles that the "radical" Artigas elaborated? And how did the discourse and political principles of the cabildo of Montevideo differ from those of the revolutionary and federalist Artigas?

Although both projects recognized that sovereignty emanated from the communities, the pueblos, and their cabildos, the crucial difference between the two resided in the form of political participation they advocated. An important clue appears in the first sentence of the cabildo's commission to the delegates to Rio de Janeiro: it gave powers to the representatives in the name of "all the Pueblos of the Banda Oriental," a mandate determined "by election" of their representatives. The principle that sovereignty emanated from the pueblos with "equal but different rights" and represented corporations was reinforced by the cabildo's request to join the Luso-Brazilian empire. In emphasizing the election of representatives and the rights of corporations, the monarchist project abandoned the principle of proportional representation based on population to determine the number of representatives.[30] The return to corporate forms of representation implied the demobilization of rural plebeians. Conversely, the maintenance of Old Regime political institutions attracted the support of merchants and traditional elites, such as two of the most visible political leaders of Montevideo in the early nineteenth century, Lucas Obes and Nicolas de Herrera, who had been critics of the Portuguese a few years earlier.[31]

In 1816 a heated debate played out in the political press in Río de la Plata. The dispute was not about where sovereignty resided but rather how sovereign bodies, the cabildos, should vote and conduct elections. The disagreement centered on a matter of political participation within the sovereign body. In the pages of the *Gazeta de Buenos Aires,* the debate involved political leaders of the cities on both banks of the Rio de la Plata. The polemic encapsulated the discussion distinguishing between *cabildos abiertos* and *representatives.* The former allowed active participation of plebeian groups, while the latter enjoyed more exclusive participation.

The cabildos abiertos were extraordinary open town hall meetings normally called in moments of crisis during the colonial period. They became popular in the region during the English invasions of 1806 and 1807 and reappeared with strength during the crisis of legitimacy triggered by Napoleon's invasion of Spain.[32] The popularization of cabildos abiertos was a product of intense popular mobilization and political participation that characterized the initial stages of the revolution in Río de la Plata, represented best by the Buenos Aires May 25th Movement.[33] The cabildos abiertos allowed a much larger number of people to elect leadership and pass resolutions, and, most important, the number of representatives was based on the number of individuals with voting rights in the cabildos. The cabildo abierto system marked a departure from the regular form of cabildo from the colonial period. In regular cabildos, only a few elected officials participated in decision making, the number of representatives was based on corporations rather than individuals, and access to these offices reflected a level of wealth and social status within the community.[34]

During the revolutionary decades in Río de la Plata, the centralist government of the United Provinces in Buenos Aires as well as the monarchists of Montevideo espoused their support for the representative system. The monarchists advocated one model that preserved the political leadership of the established elites, the *familias benemeritas,* while the supporters of the Liga Federal promoted the more heterogeneous cabildos abiertos as the legitimate system of government.[35]

According to the supporters of the representative system, the cabildo abiertos promoted the rise of demagogues who "inflamed the people with speeches" and could manipulate the vote to serve their own interests.[36] Moreover, they insisted that in cabildos abiertos the system of representation was flawed, because people in the countryside often could not afford to leave their daily affairs to participate in political deliberations. Therefore, according to its detractors, cabildo abiertos suffered from lack of a quorum, which jeopardized the validity of resolutions approved by a small minority that participated in the assemblies. Furthermore, the editor of the *Gazeta* suggested that the common "paysano" (plebeian) was susceptible to bribery and would vote according to his own interest, not taking into consideration the general or common good. The editor concluded, "There is no other advantage in suffrage by representation than more tranquility, without too much agitation," and the "dangerous aspects of freedom," which were characteristics of cabildos abiertos.[37]

The system of representatives, in opposition to the cabildos abiertos, was a clear return to prerevolutionary practices in which involvement in the sovereign body was restricted to local elites, the so-called benemeritos. Moreover, there was the clear objective of demobilizing urban and rural plebeian populations. The representative system was seen as an effective antidote to anarchy and disorder.

In the following years, the Luso-Brazilian government consolidated control of the Banda Oriental. Led by the politically savvy Frederico Lecor, baron of Laguna, the Luso-Brazilian government combined military victories and a successful strategy of co-opting Artiguista leaders. Each capitulation was formalized by the adhesion of the respective cabildo to the Luso-Brazilian empire. In 1819 the terms of the incorporation of Canelones revealed a commitment to the principle of soberanía particular de los pueblos, with "equal but different" rights characteristic of the Iberian Old Regime societies, with "all the *fueros* and privileges to the pueblos of the district, and corporations."[38] After the final victory against Artigas's troops in 1820, the Luso-Brazilian administration incorporated some of the defeated leaders; those who refused to cooperate with the Cisplatine project were imprisoned in Rio de Janeiro.[39] By the end of the year, the Luso-Brazilian authorities called for an Extraordinary General Congress that would decide the future of the Banda Oriental as a polity.

For the Extraordinary General Congress in 1821, all cabildos of the province were supposed to send representatives to decide on its annexation to the Luso-Brazilian empire under the name Cisplatine (aka Oriental) Province. At the congress, despite intense pressure from authorities to incorporate the province in the Portuguese monarchy, the speeches of the representatives showed that the "Sovereign Assembly" had several different options for statehood to choose from. According to representative Bianqui, the Oriental Province had to either become an independent nation or join an already existing one: "These are the alternatives that the circumstances permit; we should ponder if Montevideo and its countryside can become a Nation and maintain its Independence, or if it cannot, to what Nation would be most profitable to join, and which one would offer less dangers."[40]

The representatives of the pueblos of the Banda Oriental voted for the annexation of the province to the Luso-Brazilian empire on the same day. The conditions of incorporation drafted by the congress were similar to the annexation proposal of 1817. The twenty-one articles drafted by representative Larrañaga reinforced the maintenance of "privileges, exemptions, *fueros*, customs, titles, and prerogatives" to all pueblos and guaranteed free trade.[41] The Cisplatine Province would send representatives to the court at Rio de Janeiro and a *síndico procurador*, a delegate who would be named to represent the interest of corporations and cabildos of the Banda Oriental before the provincial government. Moreover, civil and military officers were to be appointed by local authorities, and no additional or extraordinary taxation could be imposed. Language, territory, and the laws of the land were supposed to be maintained as they were under Spanish dominion. The return to monarchy via incorporation in the Brazilian empire meant the maintenance of the colonial status quo, the neutralization of a social revolution from below, and the maintenance of trade networks with Brazil, Britain, and the United States.

The reestablishment of transimperial trade was of primary concern to the elites involved with the Luso-Brazilian occupation. Between 1818 and 1822 the number of ships that entered the port of Montevideo grew, and the pattern of maritime trade routes and the type of goods being transported changed substantially compared to previous years. During this period, Luso-Brazilian ships predominated, while British, Anglo-American, and European ships used Montevideo as a port of call while en route to or from Buenos Aires. More important, there was a marked increase in the activity of smaller ships and in the introduction of food supplies.

THE PORT OF MONTEVIDEO UNDER
LUSO-BRAZILIAN RULE, 1817–1822

In January 1817 the cabildo of Montevideo sent two representatives to the Portuguese court at Rio de Janeiro, which at that time was the capital of the Portuguese empire, to propose the annexation of the Banda Oriental to the United Kingdom of Portugal, Brazil, and Algarves. The representatives carried detailed instructions with the conditions for incorporation of the territory into the Luso-Brazilian monarchy. The instructions tackled matters of sovereignty, administration, and commerce.

Articles 6 and 8 of the instructions issued by the Montevideo junta to these envoys established free trade, gave foreign nationals the liberty to reside and negotiate in the province, and prescribed investments for infrastructural improvements to promote "happiness and aggrandize the maritime commerce," including enhancing the docks, cleaning the port, and building lighthouses.[42] Many of these were old demands that Montevideo merchants had been unsuccessful in obtaining from the Consulado of Buenos Aires since the 1790s. By seeking Montevideo's incorporation in the Brazilian monarchical state, the city's elites were actually securing free trade and preserving their interests in transimperial commerce.

The preoccupation of Montevidean elites with the reestablishment of commerce produced quick results. Between 1818 and 1822, according to the data of the Customs House of Montevideo, a total of 1,124 ships entered the harbor: 109 ships in 1818; 263 in 1820; 404 in the peak year of 1821; and 398 in 1822 (see table 4). The types of ships that engaged in this trade indicated the growth of both coastal and regional trade. While the large Atlantic-crossing brigantines were the most common vessels that entered the port of Montevideo during the period (50.1 percent of all the ships), the increment in the number of sumacas, small ships widely used for regional navigation, is especially noteworthy: from 38 in 1818 to 87 in 1822, or 24.5 percent of the total vessels. There was also an increase in the number of frigates, most likely due to the military operations in the area, and the appearance of smaller boats such as *polacras, sumaquinhas, goletas, chalupas, lanchas,* and *iates.*

Commerce with Brazil flourished during the Luso-Brazilian administration of Montevideo. Table 4 shows the evolution of port movement

Table 4   Ships Entering the Port of Montevideo, 1818–1822

Flag	1818	1819	1820	1821	1822	Total
				Year		
Portuguese	52	4	123	121	0	300
Spanish	2	0	0	0	1	3
British	17	4	49	90	73	233
U.S.	12	2	32	57	68	171
Danish	0	0	1	3	3	7
French	5	0	20	26	18	69
Hamburg	1	0	0	0	0	1
Buenos Aires	18	0	16	18	25	77
Chile	1	0	0	3	0	4
Sardinia	1	1	10	15	7	34
Russia	0	0	1	1	1	3
Sweden	0	0	3	4	2	9
Holland	0	0	1	2	1	4
National	0	0	0	22	187	209
Total	109	11	256	362	386	1,124

SOURCE: AGNU, ExAGA Libro 95, Aduana, Libro de Entrada de Embarcaciones.

during the Luso-Brazilian occupation of Montevideo by the flags of the vessels entering the harbor. The growth and prevalence of Luso-Brazilian trade networks is clear in the data, representing 26.7 percent of total ship movement. If we add the ships under the "National" flag for the year 1822, Luso-Brazilian ships were responsible for 45.2 percent of the maritime activity of Montevideo's port during the period. British ships represented 20.8 percent (233) of total movement during the period, while U.S. vessels represented 15.2 percent. Ships flying the flag of Buenos Aires represented 6.8 percent, and French vessels contributed 6.1 percent of the port's traffic. The remaining vessels were of various origins, including Chile, Sardinia, Sweden, Holland, and Russia. Only three ships with Spanish flags were recorded during the period.

Long-established patterns of transimperial trade remained significant during the Luso-Brazilian occupation. Luso-Brazilian and, after 1822, national ships represented almost half of Montevideo's port activity, while British and Anglo-American ships represented 36 percent (405) of the vessels entering Montevideo's harbor. As the shipping activity in Montevideo demonstrates, a consolidation of Luso-Brazilian commercial hegemony occurred between 1814 and 1822, while exchanges with the region's two main traditional transimperial trade partners, Britain and the United States, also increased at the same time.

A clearer picture of the significance of the increase in Luso-Brazilian shipment becomes available, however, when examined in the context of the Río de la Plata estuary and the changing patterns of Atlantic trade. Between 1818 and 1822, ships from Luso-Brazilian and Río de la Plata (Buenos Aires, Colônia) ports accounted for most of Montevideo's maritime commercial interactions, while ships from other Atlantic ports that had previously enjoyed strong connections with Montevideo lost ground. Even the British, American, or European ships did not necessarily enter Montevideo as their main port of call in the region. Often, British ships would call in Montevideo on leaving Buenos Aires, while U.S. ships tended to call first in Montevideo and then proceed to Buenos Aires. The two main ports of origin of ships entering Montevideo were Buenos Aires, with 18.5 percent (208), and Rio de Janeiro, with 17.9 percent (201). Of the 208 ships arriving from Buenos Aires, 55 flew the flag of Buenos Aires/United Provinces; 46, of Britain; 37, of Portugal; and 41, "National." The combined Portuguese and National vessels amounted to 78 ships navigating under the Luso-Brazilian flag. There were only 13 U.S. ships that entered Montevideo from Buenos Aires, and just 15 vessels arrived from European ports. The heavy traffic connecting Buenos Aires and Montevideo shows that despite the political disarticulation of the port complex of Río de la Plata, both cities still played complementary roles in the logistics and organization of transatlantic trade. Nevertheless, Buenos Aires merchants were much less dependent on their Montevideo agents and were no longer subjected to Montevideo authorities. In practice, Montevideo ceased being the main port of Buenos Aires.

The cargo of the ships entering Montevideo revealed the regional dimension of trade. Most of the ships flying the Luso-Brazilian, National, or Buenos Aires flag were partially loaded with foodstuffs, cattle products including hides, wax, and tallow, and sugar, tobacco, cachaça, and other products from Brazil. Other North Atlantic ships entered Montevideo from Buenos Aires already carrying cattle products, agricultural goods, and other fructos del pais. These data suggest that between 1818 and 1822 Montevideo stopped being the first port of call for transatlantic ships in Río de la Plata and that the city had lost its preeminence as the main entrepôt for transimperial trade in the region.

The growth of contacts between Montevideo and Buenos Aires is best understood within the framework of the treaties celebrated between the Luso-Brazilian empire and the Directorio government at the occasion of the occupation of Montevideo. Both governments saw Artigas as their enemy in 1816, and Buenos Aires's Directorio had agreed on a secret treaty with the court of Rio de Janeiro, which accepted the Luso-Brazilian invasion of Montevideo and the Banda Oriental in exchange for recognizing the independence of Buenos Aires, Santa Fe, and Córdoba.[43] The agreement also established that maritime commercial exchanges between Buenos Aires and Luso-Brazilian ports would be subjected only to a "transit fee," while merchandise from any other port was subjected to all tariffs.[44] Such a privilege provoked complaints from British merchants. On the one hand, the agreement facilitated the Luso-Brazilian invasion of Montevideo and the Banda Oriental; on the other, it opened additional opportunities for direct transimperial trade in Buenos Aires and undermined the interests of merchants established in Montevideo. This situation marked a significant change from the period between 1810 and 1814, when Montevidean ships and merchants blockaded and tried to exclude Buenos Aires from direct transimperial commerce. Between 1818 and 1822, ships from Brazil, England, and the United States often used Montevideo as a port of call but actually bypassed the merchants and warehouses of Montevideo partially or completely.

The number of ships that entered Montevideo from other small ports in the Río de la Plata estuary with cargos of foodstuffs, supplies, and other agricultural goods also grew. A total of 81 vessels docked in Montevideo coming from other ports in the Banda Oriental, such as Maldonado (26), Soriano (24), Colônia (8), and Daiman, Sauce, Rosário, Rio Negro, and Santa Lucia (between 1 and 3 vessels each). Montevideo also received ships from Patagonia (4), Santa Fe (2), and Ensenada, the secondary port of Buenos Aires (6). These were usually small vessels not suitable for transatlantic navigation, and their cargo was mostly destined to supply Montevideo.

From 1818 to 1822 there was a pronounced increase in the number of ships trading from Rio de Janeiro, the second most important port of origin, after Buenos Aires, for ships entering Montevideo. Of the 206 documented vessels that docked in Montevideo from Rio, over half sailed under the flag of the Luso-Brazilian empire: 75 flew the Portuguese flag and 31 the National flag (these all in 1822). British vessels arriving from Rio totaled 41, and 31 ships flew the U.S. flag. Fifteen ships were from European countries, and six ships under the flag of Buenos Aires docked in Montevideo from Rio. The data not only suggest the growth in the commercial links between Rio de Janeiro and Montevideo but also show that U.S. ships used Montevideo as their primary port of call in the region more often than did the British. In addition, the large number of British and U.S. ships that arrived from Rio de Janeiro suggests the strength of a South Atlantic maritime route, in which the coast of Brazil and Río de la Plata were interconnected.[45]

The Luso-Brazilian dominance of Río de la Plata maritime trade was not restricted to the direct connections with Rio de Janeiro. At least 201 ships sailed from other Brazilian ports during the period, and most of the naval movement was concentrated from Rio Grande (80), Bahia (37), and Paranagua (38). The vast majority of the ships sailing from the southern Brazilian ports of Rio Grande and Paranagua were under Luso-Brazilian or National flags (96 percent). Their cargo comprised mostly foodstuffs, wood, and other agricultural products. The emergence of these regional ports suggests a dramatic change in the role of Montevideo as an Atlantic port, and the city's growing demand for and reliance on provisions from other regions, because of ongoing warfare in the countryside. These data suggest a weakening of Montevideo as a hub of transatlantic trade but also the fragility of the Luso-Brazilian administration in the area, since the city needed to import basic necessities and supplies. Luso-Brazilian or National vessels supplying foodstuffs and other basic products for daily life became common at other regional Brazilian ports as well. Southern Brazilian ports such as Santa Catarina (31 ships), Santos (15), Jaguari (3), and Porto Alegre (2) emerged as significant ports of origin for ships entering Montevideo after 1810.

Between 1818 and 1822, there was an increase in ships arriving from the two traditional Luso-Brazilian ports previously connected to Montevideo, Rio de Janeiro and Bahia. But not all the ships entering Montevideo from Luso-Brazilian ports were flying the Luso-Brazilian flag. Roughly 30 percent of the 37 ships from Bahia navigated under British, U.S., or European flags. The ships, in addition to slaves, brought diverse cargo: manufactures, sugar, tobacco, and other Atlantic products that were characteristic of transatlantic trade since the late colonial period. As a result, connections with Portuguese America were not only important for supplying the city but also for the maintenance of broader networks of trade in the Atlantic.

Ships entering Montevideo directly from British and U.S. ports carried cargo that was connected to transatlantic circuits. During the period of Luso-Brazilian control over Montevideo, a total of 77 ships declared as their port of origin locations in the United States, while 72 ships declared sailing from British ports. The ports of New York (29), Baltimore (16), Boston (14), and Philadelphia (13) dominated United States trade with Río de la Plata. Among the British ports of origin, Gibraltar appears 58 times, Liverpool 13 times, and London once. One-third of the ships originating from England and entering the port of Montevideo declared their final destination as Buenos Aires, while less than 20 percent of the U.S. ships declared the same place as their point of navigation. The cargo transported into Río de la Plata included manufactured and iron goods, wheat, and liquor.

The data on origin/itinerary and flag of the ships entering the port of Montevideo allow us to conclude that there was a clear increase in the number of maritime contacts between Montevideo and Luso-Brazilian, British, U.S., and French ports in 1818 and 1822. Specifically, ships from Luso-Brazilian ports such as Rio de Janeiro and Bahia increased their significance in supplying the city with sugar, tobacco, slaves, and furniture and the transshipment of manufactured goods. A number of other southern Brazilian ports also emerged as important routes for supplying Montevideo. The increase in transimperial trade, however, did not mean an increase in the volume of Montevideo's trade. Despite the upsurge in commerce with Luso-Brazilian ports, small vessels for coastal navigation became more common than the large vessels capable of transatlantic voyages.

During this period, a large number of British (52 percent), U.S. (20 percent), and French ships stopped in Montevideo on their way to or return from Buenos Aires. With the end of the Spanish imperial political connections and the colonial regulations on transatlantic trade, Montevideo became less attractive or necessary to agents interested in trading directly with Buenos Aires. After Montevideo lost its status as the mandatory port of call in Río de la Plata, which it had enjoyed during Spanish rule, many foreign merchants conducted only part of their business in Montevideo and used the port city in conjunction with Buenos Aires. Furthermore, prolonged warfare in the countryside of the Banda Oriental had an adverse effect on Montevideo's commerce. Although there was a clear increase in commercial interactions between Montevideo and British and Anglo-American ports, Montevideo lost the centrality in the Río de la Plata port complex that it had enjoyed during the colonial period.

During this period, powerful merchants involved in transatlantic trade, such as Matteo Magariños and Francisco Joanico, remained key players in the commerce and politics of monarchism and the maintenance of Old Regime political institutions in Montevideo.[46] Between 1817 and 1822, the roster of merchants involved in trade with Brazil included a number of agents directly involved with the Luso-Brazilian administration, such as Juan José Duran (governor of Montevideo), Nicolas de Herrera (secretary of the province) and Lucas Obes (senator of the province in Rio de Janeiro), and the brothers Rafael and Carlos Camuso.[47] These prominent characters were members of the inner circle of informal advisers called "Club del Baron," in reference to Carlos Lecor, baron of Laguna. Other merchants heavily involved in transimperial shipping to Montevideo were Juan Villegas, Juan Antonio Bellastegui, and Francisco Martinez. Moreover, the period was marked by an increased number of Luso-Brazilian merchants operating in Montevideo, such as João Luis Ribeiro, Jorge Ribeiro, Manoel João Ribeiro, Manoel José da Costa, and Antonio Pereira. At the height of the Cisplatine Province, the traditional commercial elites of Montevideo had solidified their participation in transimperial trade with Brazil, and Luso-Brazilian traders found opportunities to increase their presence in Río de la Plata. Such a moment marked the emergence of Rio de Janeiro as the main Atlantic port connected to Montevideo.

After 1817 Montevideo lost importance as a transatlantic center for transimperial trade and assumed the character of a regional port, or a subsidiary of Brazil and Buenos Aires. With the end of the Spanish mercantile system, Montevideo lost its role as the prime port of call, transshipment, and bureaucratic authorizations. During the period, however, Rio de Janeiro increased its role as the main Atlantic port in contact with Montevideo. Rio de Janeiro not only increased its commercial exchanges with Montevideo but also became the chief port of call for U.S. and British vessels en route to Montevideo. The involvement of Montevideo merchants in the Cisplatine administration contributed to the increase in Luso-Brazilian vessels in the port of Montevideo.

THE DEMISE OF THE CISPLATINE PROVINCE

The incorporation of the Cisplatine Province in the Luso-Brazilian empire faced insurmountable challenges unfolding in other regions of the Atlantic basin. In 1821 the Constitutionalist Movement of Oporto, in Portugal, promulgated a new constitution that aimed to curb the power of the Portuguese king and demanded his return to Lisbon from Rio. As a consequence, King Joao VI returned to Portugal, but the prince regent, Pedro, stayed in Brazil. The tensions between Portuguese and Brazilian factions culminated in 1822, with the refusal of the prince regent to return to Portugal and the subsequent independence of Brazil. This crisis provoked a deep division among the Luso-Brazilian troops occupying the Banda Oriental. In 1822 three thousand troops faithful to Portugal rebelled against the rule of Carlos Frederico Lecor, invaded Montevideo, and expelled the provincial authorities from the capital city. The Luso-Brazilian civil war in the Banda Oriental between troops loyal to Lisbon and those loyal to Rio had calamitous consequences for the monarchist political project.

Due to the military conflict over Montevideo, the implementation of the Cisplatine government according to the stipulations of the Extraordinary Congress were delayed. In August 1822, Nicolas de Herrera, the province's secretary, expressed his worries to Lucas Obes, representative of the province in Rio de Janeiro. According to Herrera, it was urgent to end military rule in the province and establish a civil branch of government. Herrera was also emphatic about the need to have representatives of pueblos in the provincial government. Even if the creation of a regular bureaucratic body was not possible at the moment, "if the Pueblos and Cabildos elected representatives for a Junta" the representative body would create viable political conditions because "the Pueblos would receive with less dissatisfaction the difficulties of a new war."[48] Herrera was realistic about the "illnesses and vices" that affected the Cisplatine project, and he was adamant about the necessity of "convincing the Pueblos that they are not being ruled by a military government." The aggravation of the political situation was directly connected to the deterioration of maritime trade.

The Portuguese Royalist (Voluntarios Reais) control of the port of Montevideo disrupted trade for Montevidean merchant elites. The military conflict caused the cessation of revenue of long-distance commerce for the administration, a situation that led the Cisplatine authorities to open the ports of Colônia and Maldonado to transatlantic vessels in an attempt to circumvent Montevideo's harbor. Maritime trade in Montevideo was restricted to short-distance trade in food supplies. Although there was an increase in the number of U.S. and British vessels entering Montevideo, after the split between troops loyal to Portugal and Brazil, foreign vessels used Montevideo mostly as a port of call. The disarticulation of established local networks led merchants to conduct most of their business via Buenos Aires. By the end of 1822, Herrera admitted that the situation presented serious risks for the maintenance of the Banda Oriental as part of the Brazilian empire. According to him, "there is no trade, nor stability," and the "revenue of the customs house is weak due to the low volume of trade which generates uncertainty and uneasiness among the people."[49] The pillars of the Cisplatine project—the conservative interpretation of particular sovereignty of the pueblos and transimperial trade—were jeopardized.

In the following years, the Luso-Brazilian civil war continued with intensity. The Brazilian forces were only able to reenter Montevideo in 1824, but by then the Cisplatine project had lost support among the city's principal merchants and political leaders as well as plebeians. A few months later, in 1825, a group of caudillos invaded the Banda Oriental with support from Buenos Aires to end Brazilian rule. From 1825 to 1828, the United Provinces and the Brazilian empire fought over the territory. The armistice, mediated by Britain, stipulated the creation of the independent Republic of Uruguay.

The crisis of legitimacy in Spain provoked different reactions in different regions of Spanish America. In several politically peripheral regions from New Granada to Río de la Plata, political projects emerged in support of autonomy and free trade. However, a closer look at trade patterns of royalist bastions shows that trade with foreigners and the redefinition of legal and illegal commerce was not necessarily connected with revolutionary projects. In the case of Montevideo, the decision to remain faithful to the Spanish monarchy provided the opportunity to not only maintain but also strengthen transimperial networks with Portuguese, British, and U.S. traders. Furthermore, it allowed Montevideo's mercantile community to pursue a separate political path from that of Buenos Aires. In the 1810s, monarchism meant the continuation of transimperial trade in the South Atlantic.

At the same time different political projects emerged in Río de la Plata. The port city of Montevideo became a monarchist bastion. Initially the city remained loyal to the Spanish monarch; later it became the capital of a province of the Luso-Brazilian empire. The support of the monarchist projects by Montevidean elites was directly connected to the maintenance of transimperial trade and Old Regime political principles. The monarchical projects espoused by Montevidean elites protected economic interest of groups connected to transatlantic networks and maintained the principle of soberanía particular de los pueblos, which centered on the cabildos and their representatives. Montevidean monarchism aimed to counterbalance revolutionary political projects based on broad popular participation centered in Buenos Aires and to maintain the status quo of the colonial landed elite. In Montevideo and the Banda Oriental, monarchism represented the strength of transimperial networks of trade and politics. Loyalism to Spain and annexation to the Luso-Brazilian empire were attempts to maintain the control of trade and institutional stability—attempts to postpone the impact of the revolutionary tidal waves that were transforming the Atlantic World.

Conclusion

On September 21, 1808, a multitude gathered in front of Montevideo's cabildo in support of the newly created Junta de Gobierno, loyal to Ferdinand VII. The news that the French-born interim viceroy Santiago de Liniers, in Buenos Aires, had appointed Angel Michelena, a ship captain, to replace Montevideo's governor Francisco Javier de Elío prompted widespread popular mobilization in the city. Elío, a seasoned Spanish field marshal, had strong support from the city's merchants, bureaucrats, and plebeians. Not surprisingly, Michelena was received with hostility by authorities and plebeians alike, he was not allowed to take office and had to flee the city during the night fearing for his safety. As a result, the rise of Montevideo's junta not only maintained Governor Elío in power (by electing him the junta's president), but rejected the authority of Buenos Aires' interim viceroy Santiago de Liniers. The creation of Montevideo's junta effectively severed the political links between Buenos Aires and Montevideo. From this moment on, Buenos Aires was never able to reestablish control over Montevideo. In the following years, Montevideo became the bastion of Spanish loyalism and Luso-Brazilian monarchism. Eventually the city emerged as the capital of independent Uruguay. The events of September 1808, although triggered by the crisis of legitimacy in

Spain, were the culmination of deep rivalries between the two communities in Río de la Plata that had been developing over the previous three decades, since the expulsion of the Portuguese from Colônia do Sacramento and the creation of the viceroyalty of Río de la Plata.

The creation of the viceroyalty and the Spanish conquest of Portuguese Colônia triggered deep regional changes. While Buenos Aires became the seat of the new viceroy and the Audiencia, Montevideo became the primary port for transatlantic trade in the estuary, the base of the Spanish South Atlantic fleet, and the seat of a the newly created agency to repress contraband trade. Moreover, Montevideo profited from the relocation of Luso-Brazilian merchants, ship captains, and other émigrés from Colônia. This engendered significant demographic changes, namely, the relocation of approximately two thousand Portuguese subjects in the region. In the three decades between the creation of the viceroyalty and the political crisis of 1808, Montevideo emerged as the hub for transimperial trade in the Río de la Plata interaction zone. Although Montevideo and Buenos Aires were commercially and politically intertwined, the development of Montevideo's merchant community was marked by progressive conflicts with Buenos Aires over commercial and territorial jurisdictions. The emergence of Montevideo as a commercial hub allowed local elites to advance the city's position within the empire and the Atlantic World.

The changes unfolding in the Atlantic World underlined the growing importance of transimperial networks of trade and politics in the last decades of the eighteenth century. Intermittent warfare had provoked a rearrangement of commercial routes in the Atlantic World. During the last decades of colonial rule, intercolonial trade and trade with foreign nations became crucial for the economy of Spanish American colonies. In Río de la Plata, hundreds of Portuguese and British merchant ships supplied cheap textiles, manufactures, sugar, tobacco, liquor, and a large slave trade to Spanish American possessions. The impressive growth of the slave trade and the increased demand for Atlantic goods ensured the strategic position of Montevideo as the main Atlantic port in the region. As the last decades of the eighteenth century unfolded, disputes over trade fees, regulations, and jurisdiction revealed the competing interests of Buenos Aires's merchants and the emergent Montevideo mercantile community.

This study has examined the emergence of a region (Banda Oriental) within a viceroyalty (Río de la Plata) in the Spanish borderlands of South America, an area contested by the Portuguese and by indigenous groups. As a result, internal and external imperial dynamics appear interlocked. In highlighting the importance of transimperial interaction, this book has showed that networks of trade, family, religion, information, and friendship had a profound impact on local communities situated in Atlantic borderlands. Despite the unequal balance of power between the parties involved, colonial subjects were able to leverage their regional and imperial positions by manipulating imperial and transimperial networks. In contested territories, local groups developed specific notions of community and regional identity that were derived from their interactions within and beyond imperial borders. It was the porous nature of the Río de la Plata interaction zone that permitted the rise of Montevideo's community, by combining political and economic opportunities within the Spanish empire with opportunities offered by networks with foreign powers.

Río de la Plata had been an area of intense transimperial interaction since the early days of the European presence in the sixteenth century. The Spanish and Portuguese empires formally competed for territory, but the Dutch, the British, and the French also had commercial and political interests in the area. During the eighteenth century, the Spanish consolidated their supremacy over the region. Nevertheless, until 1777 the Portuguese town of Colônia do Sacramento was a busy contraband center that furnished cheap goods to the merchants of Buenos Aires. The contraband trade flourished. Through Colônia, Buenos Aires merchants acquired furniture, paper, iron, sugar, tobacco, cachaça, textiles, medicine, and other Atlantic products and even slaves. The Portuguese and their associates, often British merchants, obtained hides, tallow, cacao, wool, and silver from the region in copious quantities. The networks that crossed imperial boundaries in the region were strong and enduring, involving large as well as petty merchants and peasants and authorities alike. Moreover, Colônia's role as the main hub for the introduction of slaves in the region reveals the key significance of transimperial interactions in the shaping of colonial society.

The creation of the viceroyalty of Río de la Plata in 1776 was soon followed by the expulsion of the Portuguese from Colônia (1777) and by the establishment of free trade with other Spanish colonies (1778). The obliteration of Colônia meant the end of an official Portuguese colonial project in the region. Nevertheless, many Luso-Brazilians stayed in the area and swore loyalty to the king of Spain. The Luso-Platine merchants who relocated to Montevideo brought with them capital, know-how, connections, and transimperial networks.

Montevideo replaced Colônia do Sacramento as the transimperial port in Río de la Plata. During the period 1780–1800, more than two hundred ships sailed between Montevideo and Portuguese America. The elites of Montevideo and their Luso-Brazilian associates rapidly reestablished the commercial routes that once went through Colônia. Adopting a specific interpretation of imperial laws originally intended to foster the trade in slaves and guarantee trade with foreigners during periods of war, merchants and authorities of Montevideo justified the transimperial trade. Trade with foreigners involved Luso-Brazilian merchants of Montevideo and Rio de Janeiro who had been previously active in trade during the Colônia era.

Montevideo profited from the reforms of the late 1770s in Río de la Plata in other ways. The decree that established free trade within the Spanish empire opened the ports of Montevideo and Buenos Aires for Atlantic trade. Montevideo, however, because of its excellent natural harbor, was declared the mandatory port of call for all vessels entering or leaving the estuary. Moreover, Montevideo's port was the only one authorized to disembark slaves and the base for the South Atlantic Spanish fleet. As a consequence, new offices charged with suppressing contraband were established in the city. The elites of Montevideo interpreted these new regulations to gain control over terrestrial as well as maritime transimperial routes. Between 1780 and 1805, the jurisdiction of Montevideo, which originally comprised only the surrounding areas of the city, expanded to the borderlands of Portuguese America, toward the Siete Pueblos missions, and to the surrounding areas of Colônia. Most important, the authorities of Montevideo gained the power to police crime and contraband in the countryside and borderlands. Progressively, they consolidated their influence over the population and the countryside by creating patrols, guards, and forts along the border to suppress criminal activities and exert control over contraband in the region.

The ascension of Montevideo as an administrative, social, and economic center was apparent in the commercial flows and in the expansion of the city's jurisdiction. Because the region was a contested territory, subjects of different Atlantic empires produced a plethora of material about it. European and locally born imperial agents, travelers, and merchants produced maps and descriptions of the area in which the centrality of Montevideo was apparent. The toponymy used to describe Montevideo's adjacent countryside changed, from Otra Banda to Banda Norte to Banda Oriental, reflecting the region's new jurisdictional arrangements in the eighteenth century. In addition to jurisdictional change, travelers and inhabitants of the region alike participated in a process of spatial transformation, giving rise to a new space, the Banda Oriental, with its capital in Montevideo.

The conflicts and enterprises in which colonial subjects were engaged, their loyalties and their perceptions of community, are at the core of this study. In examining the microhistory of one individual and his connections illuminates the relationship between transimperial networks, local community, and economic and social processes. The story of don Manuel Cipriano de Melo is illustrative of how individual agents lived their lives in a zone of imperial interaction, switching loyalties between the Portuguese and the Spanish empires, engaging in transatlantic enterprises, and at the same time becoming active members of the local community. Although Cipriano de Melo changed his political loyalty several times, his familial, religious, commercial, and friendship networks remained substantially the same throughout the years. He was able to channel resources through his transimperial networks, giving him and his associates a qualitative advantage in improving their status within the empire. As the head of the imperial agency in charge of suppressing contraband, Cipriano de Melo actively participated in many of the disputes and legal maneuvers that allowed Montevideo to expand its influence in the countryside and to improve the community's status within the viceroyalty and the empire.

Transimperial networks were also crucial in shaping the path to independence in the Atlantic World. With the crisis of legitimacy triggered by Napoleon's invasion of the Iberian Peninsula in 1808, different reactions and political projects emerged in the colonies. Montevideo was the first Spanish American city to break away from the regional center of power, namely, the viceregal capital, Buenos Aires, by creating the autonomous Junta de Gobierno in 1808. If Buenos Aires was not able to control Montevideo under the Spanish monarchy, with the creation of the revolutionary Buenos Aires Junta of 1810, Montevideo became the bastion of Spanish loyalism in the South Atlantic and the main opposition to Buenos Aires. The elites of Montevideo initially remained loyal to Spain but later espoused Portuguese monarchism; loyalism and monarchism were means to maintain existing transimperial networks of trade and politics with Brazil and Britain. From 1816 to 1822 Montevideo and the Banda Oriental were integrated into the Luso-Brazilian empire. During this period, trade with foreigners constituted more than 50 percent of the city's naval movement. After the independence of Brazil (1822), rearrangements of power culminated in the War of the Cisplatine, opposing Brazil and the United Provinces of Río de la Plata. Monarchism was intimately associated with the maintenance of transimperial trade networks and with keeping the political and economic order of the colonial period. Monarchism represented the continuity of the Old Regime's legal principles, provided safety and stability for transimperial trade, and, above all, prevented the economic, political, and social changes proposed by revolutionary projects.

In the late eighteenth-century Atlantic World, internal and external dynamics were intertwined: metropoles and colonial possessions constituted an interdependent, interlocked imperial unit that was shaped by the relationship with other polities and territories. Furthermore, the processes unfolding in Río de la Plata and the South Atlantic demonstrates how local communities, structured around networks that went beyond imperial limits, were able to resist and influence centers of imperial power, thereby creating social and political coherence on an imperial scale. *Edge of Empires* emphasizes the significance of transimperial dynamics and regional processes in shaping these polycentric monarchies. The case of Montevideo and the Banda Oriental adds a new layer to our understanding of the creation and maintenance of regional and Atlantic dynamics. By tracing the emergence of a late colonial provincial center that became the capital of a sovereign state, this book argues that disputes between regional elites and the new interpretations of law and sovereignty, coupled with transimperial networks, shaped institutions, the political culture, and the social dynamics in the age of Atlantic revolutions.

Notes

INTRODUCTION

1. Arquivo Histórico do Itamaraty, Invasão e Anexação da Banda Oriental, Lata 194 Maços 1 and 2, 1816–21.

2. In recent years, a new wave of scholarship has begun to reinterpret the processes of independence in Latin America within the framework of the Atlantic World. New historical works on the late colonial and revolutionary decades in Latin America have successfully argued for the significance of plural and competing political projects and ideas of sovereignty. Most important are Lauren Benton, *A Search for Sovereignty* (Cambridge: Cambridge University Press, 2010); and Ana Frega, *Soberanía y revolución* (Montevideo: EBO, 2006).

3. John Lynch, *Latin American Revolutions, 1808–1826: Old and New World Origins* (Norman: University of Oklahoma Press, 1994); Jaime Rodriguez, *The Independence of Spanish America* (New York: Cambridge University Press, 1998): Carlos Chiaramonte, *Mercaderes del Litoral: Economía y sociedad en la provincia de Corrientes, primera mitad del siglo XIX* (Buenos Aires: Fondo de Cultura Económica, 1991); Jay Kinsbruner, *Independence in Spanish America* (Albuquerque: University of New Mexico Press, 1994).

4. For the economic development of late colonial Buenos Aires: Lyman Johnson, *Workshop of Revolution* (Durham, NC: Duke University Press, 2011), Introduction.

5. Treaty of Utrecht (1715), Treaty of Paris (1737), Treaty of Madrid (1750), Treaty of El Pardo (1762), Treaty of San Ildefonso (1777).

6. Alejandra Irigoin and Regina Grafe, "Bargaining for Absolutism: A Spanish Path to Nation-State and Empire Building," *Hispanic American Historical Review* 88, no. 2 (2008): 173–209.

7. Jeremy Adelman, *Sovereignty and Revolution in the Iberian Atlantic* (Princeton: Princeton University Press, 2006), 5.

8. Pedro Cardim, Tamar Herzog, José Javier Ruiz Ibáñez, and Gaetano Sabatini, eds., *Polycentric Monarchies* (Sussex: Sussex Academic Press, 2012), 4. For the development of a similar concept for the Portuguese empire (pluricontinental monarchy), see João Fragoso, org., *Na trama das redes: Políticas e negocios no Império Português séculos XVI ao XIX* (Rio de Janeiro: Civilização Brasileira, 2010).

9. Jack P. Greene, *Negotiated Authorities* (Charlottesville: University of Virginia Press, 1994); John Elliot, *Empires of the Atlantic World* (New Haven: Yale University Press, 2006); David Eltis, *Coerced and Free Migrations: Global Perspectives* (Stanford, CA: Stanford University Press, 2002); Alfred Crosby, *The Ecological Imperialism* (Cambridge: Cambridge University Press, 2004); Bernard Bailyn, *Atlantic History* (Cambridge, MA: Harvard University Press, 2005). More recently: Jorge Canizares-Esguerra and Ben Breen, "Hybrid Atlantics: Future Directions for the History of the Atlantic World," *History Compass* 11, no. 8 (2013): 597–609, 10.1111/hic3.12051.

10. Carlos Sempat Assadourian, *El sistema de la economía colonial—mercado interno, regiones y espacio económico* (Lima: Instituto de Estudios Peruanos, 1982); Susan Socolow, *Los mercaderes de Buenos Aires virreinal* (Buenos Aires: Ed. De la Flor, 1992); João Fragoso and Manolo Florentino, *Arcaísmo como projeto: Mercado atlântico, sociedade agrária em uma economia colonial tardia—Rio de Janeiro c. 1790–c. 1840* (Rio de Janeiro: Civilização Brasileira, 2001): Manolo Florentino, *Em costas negras* (São Paulo: Companhia das Letras, 1997).

11. Elizabeth Mancke and Carole Shammas, eds., *The Creation of the British Atlantic* (Baltimore: Johns Hopkins University Press, 2005), 2. Recently, Cañizares-Esguerra and Breen have pointed to the notion of "hybrid Atlantics" in order to understand the multiple historical processes that crossed political, religious, and cultural borders in the Atlantic. Canizares-Esguerra and Breen, "Hybrid Atlantics."

12. Susan Socolow, *The Bureaucrats of Buenos Aires* (Durham, NC: Duke University Press, 1987); João Fragoso, "Nas rotas do império: Eixos mercantis, tráfico de escravos e relações sociais no mundo português" (Seminário Internacional, Universidade Federal do Rio de Janeiro, Programa de Pós-Graduação em História Social, 2006); Alida Metcalf, *Family and Frontier in Colonial Brazil* (Berkeley: University of California Press, 1992).

13. Bartolomé Salvador Clavero, *Antidora, antropología católica de la economía moderna* (Milan: Giuffrè Editore, 1991); Jose Maria Imizcoz, ed., *Casa, familia y sociedad: País Vasco, España y América, siglos XV–XIX* (Bilbao: Servicio Editorial, Universidad del País Vasco = Euskal Herriko Unibertsitatea, Argitalpen Zerbitzua, 2004).

14. Socolow, *Los mercaderes de Buenos Aires virreinal;* Imizcoz, *Casa, familia y sociedad.*

15. Socolow, *Bureaucrats of Buenos Aires;* Zacarías Moutoukias, "Redes personales y autoridad colonial," *Annales: Histoire, Sciences Sociales* (May–June 1992): 889–915.

16. Michel Bertrand, "De la familia a la red de sociabilidad," *Revista Mexicana de Sociología* 61, no. 2 (1999): 107–35.

17. Tiago Gil, "Infieis transgresores" (Master's thesis, PPG UFRJ, Rio de Janeiro, 2002).

18. Mary Louise Pratt, *Imperial Eyes* (London: Routledge, 1992), 6–9.

19. Ibid.

CHAPTER 1. A PORTUGUESE TOWN
IN RÍO DE LA PLATA

1. For the urban, agrarian, and commercial evolution of Colônia in the first half of the eighteenth century, see Fabrício Prado, *A Colônia do Sacramento—o extremo sul da América portuguesa* (Porto Alegre: Fumproarte, 2002).

2. Alex Borucki, "From Shipmates to Soldiers: Emerging Black Identities in Montevideo, 1770–1850" (PhD diss., Emory University, 2011), 47.

3. Fernando Jumar, "La región Río de la Plata y su complejo portuario durante el Antiguo Régimen," in *Historia de la provincia de Buenos Aires*, vol. 2, *De la Conquista a la crisis de 1820*, ed. Raúl O. Fradkin (Buenos Aires: UNIPE/ EDHASA, 2012), 123–58.

4. Zacarías Moutoukias, *Contrabando y control colonial en el siglo XVII: Buenos Aires, el Atlántico y el espacio peruano*, Biblioteca Universitarias (Buenos Aires: Centro Editor de América Latina,1988); Jorge Gelman, *De mercanchifle a gran comerciante* (La Rabida: Universidad Internacional de Andalucia, 1996); Socolow, *Los mercaderes de Buenos Aires virreinal;;* Fernando Jumar, "Le commerce atlantique au Rio de la Plata" (PhD diss., École des Hautes Études en Sciences Sociales, 2000); Dennis Owen Flynn, *World Silver and Monetary History in the 16th and 17th Centuries*, Collected Studies (Aldershot: Variorum, 1996); Enrique Tandeter and Nathan Wachtel, *Precios y producción agraria: Potosí y Charcas en el siglo XVIII*, Estudios Cedes (Buenos Aires: Centro de Estudios de Estado y Sociedad, 1983).

5. Alice P. Canabrava, *O comércio português no Rio da Prata, 1580-1640* (São Paulo: USP, [1942] 1984).

6. Mario Rodriguez, "Don Pedro de Braganza and Colônia do Sacramento, 1680-1705," *Hispanic American Historical Review* 8, no. 2 (May 1958): 179-208.

7. Moutoukias, *Contrabando y control colonial*, 25-26. In this work, I use the term *direct trade* as synonymous with contraband trade.

8. See also Moutoukias, *Contrabando y control colonial*, Conclusion.

9. Jumar, "Le commerce atlantique au Río de la Plata," chap. 4.

10. Aníbal Riveros Tula, *Historia de la Colonia del Sacramento* (Montevideo: IHGU, 1951), 191-200.

11. Sebastião da Veiga Cabral, *Historia corographica da Colônia do Sacramento* (1711); Jônathas da Costa Rego Monteiro, *A Colônia do Sacramento, 1680-1777* (Porto Alegre: Globo, 1937).

12. Simão Pereira de Sá, *História topográfica e bélica da nova Colônia do Sacramento do Rio da Prata, escrita por ordem do Governador e Capitão Geral do Rio de Janeiro em 1737 e 1777* (1747; repr. Porto Alegre: Arcano 17, 1993); Prado, *A Colônia do Sacramento*.

13. For a detailed analysis of the commercial development of Sacramento and the presence of British merchants among the local mercantile elite, see Prado, *A Colônia do Sacramento*, chap. 4.

14. Population maps were less detailed types of censuses, often crafted for military purposes.

15. Arquivo Histórico da Cúria Metropolitana do Rio de Janeiro (AHCRJ)—Colônia do Sacramento, Livro 5, Batismos.

16. For more on creolization and maritime borderlands, see Linda Rupert, *Creolization and Contraband: Curaçao in the Early Modern Atlantic World* (Athens: University of Georgia Press, 2012).

17. AHCRJ, Sacramento Livro 5, 20 Oct. 1775.

18. AHU, Colônia do Sacramento, Doc. 86, Dec. 1722. Costa Rego Monteiro, *A Colônia do Sacramento*, vol. 2. For the significance of Rosário's brotherhoods among people of African descent in the Americas, see Mariza Soares, *People of Faith: Slavery and African Catholics in Eighteenth-Century Rio de Janeiro* (Durham, NC: Duke University Press, 2011).

19. For the significance of slave networks created in Colônia del Sacramento, see Borucki, "From Shipmates to Soldiers," 89-135.

20. The auction for both taxes was managed in Colonia. In comparison, in 1726 the wheat tithe was 172$155 and the corn tithe 25$000.

21. For the use of slaves in the urban environment, as social status, and as source of income, see Fragoso and Florentino, *O arcaísmo como projeto*.

22. In other Brazilian ports, such as Recife and Rio de Janeiro, slaves accounted for nearly 40 percent of the population.

23. AHU, Colônia do Sacramento, Doc. 409, 18 Apr. 1746.

24. Fábio Kuhn, "Clandestino e ilegal: O contrabando de escravos na Colônia do Sacramento, 1740–1777," in *Escravidão e liberdade*, ed. Regina Xavier Lima (Porto Alegre: Alameda, 2010), 184. Also: Paulo C. Possamai, "O tráfico de escravos na Colônia do Sacramento" (5o. Encontro de Escravidão e Liberdade no Brasil Meridional, Porto Alegre, 2010), 1–15, www.escravidaoeliberdade.com.br/site/images/Textos5/possamai%20paulo%20cesar.pdf. Accessed 29 Jan. 2014.

25. AHU, Colônia do Sacramento, Doc. 49, 18 Apr. 1746.

26. AHU, Colônia do Sacramento, Doc. 408, 1746.

27. *Voyages: Online Slave Trade Database*, www.slavevoyages.org.

28. Alexandre Vieira Ribeiro, "O tráfico atlântico de escravos e a praça mercantil de Salvador, c. 1678–1830" (Master's thesis, UFRJ/PPGHIS, 2005), 108.

29. AHU, RJ Doc. 9294, 20 Mar. 1780.

30. Biblioteca Nacional Lisboa—*Manuscritos Pombalinos*, Códice 10855, 8 Feb. 1776.

31. Real Biblioteca—Madrid (RBM), II/2825, 13, *Discursos sobre el Comercio Legitimo de Buenos Aires con la España, el Clandestino de la Colonia del Sacramento: Medios de Embarazo en la mayor parte y poner cubierto de enemigos aquella provincia* (1766).

32. Ibid., 43.

33. Ibid., 48–50.

34. Several recent studies have examined the existence of multiple enterprises dedicated to contraband trade and networks involving merchants and authorities in both cities. See Prado, *A Colônia do Sacramento;* Jumar, "Le commerce atlantique au Rio de la Plata"; Kuhn, *Clandestino e ilegal.*

35. Jumar "La región," 143.

36. Prado, *A Colônia do Sacramento*, 143–44.

37. Fabio Kuhn, "Os comerciantes da Colônia do Sacramento e o tráfico de escravos para o Rio da Prata (1732–1777)" (Paper presented at the Fifth Río de la Plata Seminar, Williamsburg, 2014), 5. The number of self-declared traders between 1737 and 1762.

38. Paulo Possamai, "Aspectos do cotidiano dos mercadores na Colônia do Sacramento durante o governo de Antonio Pedro de Vasconcelos (1722–1749)," *Revista de Estudos Ibero-Americanos* 28, no. 2 (Dec. 2002): 57–61.

39. AHU, Rio de Janeiro, Doc. 16844, 25 Feb. 1737.

40. Ibid.

41. Ibid.

42. Prado, *A Colônia do Sacramento*, 142.

43. Mestre de campo is equivalent to the office of colonel and granted high status to the officeholder.

44. Manuel Botelho had written many letters of recommendation for his subordinates trying to obtain higher positions in the Portuguese bureaucracy. His

letters usually were cited together with those of other governors. AHU, Colônia do Sacramento, Doc. 514, [Ant.] 19/IV/1760.

45. AHU, Colônia do Sacramento, Doc. 460, 1752.

46. I thank João Fragoso for this information. Records in personal database: fichas 6628, 6795, 1469, and 2003.

47. Arquivo da Curia Metropolitana do Rio de Janeiro, Colônia do Sacramento, Série A.R. Notação 335, Petição, 28 May 1773.

48. Archivo General de la Nación, Buenos Aires (AGN), Colônia do Sacramento, Sala IX, 3.8.2, 12 Mar. 1774.

49. Links of solidarity could also represent peer pressure to honor business transactions. Considering the extralegal characteristics of transimperial trade, an interconnected community provided access to information on the merchants involved. Moutoukias, "Redes personales y autoridad colonial."

50. AHU, Rio de Janeiro, Doc. 16844, 25 Feb. 1737.

51. Joao Fragoso, ed., *Conquistadores e negociantes: História de elites no Antigo Regime nos trópicos* (Rio de Janeiro: Civilização Brasileira, 2007).

52. Caio Boschi, *Irmandades religiosas nas Minas setecentistas* (São Paulo: Atica, Coleção Brasiliana, 1986), 162–63. According to Caio Boschi, belonging to a lay brotherhood was one of the most important ways of displaying social status. Thus, because of living in a reduced space, religious activity was an important for of showing the social hierarchy. Arquivo da Curia Metropolitana do Rio de Janeiro, Colônia do Sacramento, Série A.R. Notação 417, 21 June 1760, Notação 335, 28 May 1773.

53. A.J.R Russel-Wood, *Fidalgos and Philanthropists* (Berkeley: University of California Press, 1968), 346–47.

54. AHU, Colônia do Sacramento, Doc. 86; AHU, RJ, Doc. 04081, 1722. The brotherhoods were Santíssimo Sacramento, Nossa Senhora do Pilar, Nossa Senhora Sant'Anna, Nossa Senhora do Rosário, Santo Antônio, and Irmandade das Almas.

55. Luis Enrique Azarola Gil, *A Colônia do Sacramento, 1680-1828* (Montevideo: Casa Barrero y Ramos, 1940), 224. For instance, Governor Vasconcelos was the "protector" of the Chapel of São Pedro de Alcântara, and the Chapel of Santa Rita was "protected" by mestre de campo Manoel Botelho de Lacerda.

56. AHCRJ, Serie A.R., Not. 335, 1773.

57. Antonio Pedro de Vasconcelos, *Relação que da um tronco* (1732), Archivo Regional de Colonia. There is also a copy in the Bibliotheca Rio-Grandense, Rio Grande, Brazil. This piece is a literary description of the parties celebrated in Sacramento. Although it was printed in Portugal, it is written in Spanish. The language choice reveals the audience of Sacramento's poetic governor.

58. Luis Garcia de Bivar, *Relação das festas* (1753), Archivo Regional Colônia.

59. AHCRJ, Death Records Third Book, Colônia do Sacramento. This book contains only records of free people.

60. AHCRJ, Serie A. R. Not. 417. 1760.

61. The sample that I am using includes 47 record from 1776, 1 record from 1777, and 53 records from 1760. The dates were defined randomly and tried to capture two different moments in the second half of the eighteenth century.

62. I did not estimate the participation of people in the brotherhoods because of the lack of information about slaves, which would undercount the participation of Rosário's brotherhood in the religious life of the town.

63. For a comparison with Minas Gerais, see Boschi, *Irmandades,* 187. The top three brotherhoods in the Minas Gerais region were Rosário, Santíssimo Sacramento, and Almas.

64. Socolow, *Los mercaderes,* 216. Among the Portuguese population living in Buenos Aires in the same period, 47 percent had chosen to be buried in the São Francisco habit.

65. Archivo General de Indias (AGI), Audiencia de Buenos Aires, Leg. 162, 1763.

66. Ibid.

67. AGI, Audiencia de Buenos Aires, Leg. 162, Nov. 1761. Cevallos cited the case of the Franciscan Azurara, Portuguese resident in the convent in Buenos Aires since 1757.

68. AGI, Audiencia de Buenos Aires, Leg. 162, 1763.

69. Luis E. Azarola Gil, *La epopeya de Manuel Lobo* (Buenos Aires: Compañía Ibero Americana de Publicaciones, 1931), 229.

CHAPTER 2. DEPARTING WITHOUT LEAVING

1. I am using the words *Portuguese* and *Luso-Brazilian* synonymously in reference to subjects of the Portuguese Crown living in the Americas.

2. Arquivo Histórico do Itamaraty, Lata 188, Maço 1. It is unclear whether this group of people remained in Colônia or in the adjacent locations.

3. The contingent of foreigners residing in Buenos Aires amounts to 1.1 percent of the population (481 individuals), while in Montevideo the foreign population represented 1.45 percent of the total population (165 individuals). *Documentos para la historia argentina,* vol. 12; AGN, Montevideo, AGA Caja 20, Padron de Estranjeros, 1807.

4. Prado, *A Colônia do Sacramento;* Jumar, "Le commerce atlantique."

5. Rodrigo Ceballos, "Uma Buenos Aires lusitana: A presença portuguesa no rio da Prata (séc. XVII)," *Mneme Revista de Humanidades* 9, no. 24 (2008): 7, www.cerescaico.ufrn.br/mneme/anais/st_suma_pg/st11.html (accessed Mar. 2009); Emir Reitano, "Los portugueses del Buenos Aires tardo colonial" (PhD diss., Universidad Nacional de La Plata, 2004), 78. For 1641, Ceballos found 270 (54 percent) Portuguese in the city out of 500 foreigners. For 1744, Reitano has

identified 47 Portuguese (69.1%) among the foreign population. In 1804, 262 (53 percent) Portuguese were living in Buenos Aires out of 455 foreigners.

6. Canabrava, *O comércio português no Rio da Prata.*

7. Jorge Gelman, "Economía natural y economía monetaria: Los grupos dirigentes del Buenos Aires a principios del siglo XVII," *Anuario de Estudios Americanos* 44 (1987): 1–19; Eduardo Saguier, "The Uneven Incorporation of Buenos Aires into the World Trade in the 17th Century" (PhD diss., Washington University, 1982); Ceballos, "Uma Buenos Aires lusitana," 7.

8. Ceballos, "Uma Buenos Aires lusitana," 6–7.

9. Ceballos summarizes the debate on the topic in his "Uma Buenos Aires lusitana," 7–12. For the full debate on the social dynamics among elite groups in Buenos Aires, see Gelman "Economía natural y economía monetaria," 1–19; Saguier," The Uneven Incorporation of Buenos Aires."

10. Ceballos, "Uma Buenos Aires lusitana," 6–11. For the eighteenth century see the following bandos: AGN, Sala IX, 39.7.3. 1749; AGN, Sala IX, 8.10.16–26. I.1763; AGN, Sala IX, 8.10.2–04.X.1762. See also *Documentos para la historia argentina,* vol. 12 (Buenos Aires: Facultad de Filosfia y Letras de la UBA, 1919.

11. Maria José Goulão, "La puerta falsa de América—Influência artística portuguesa no Rio da Prata colonial" (PhD diss., Universidade de Coimbra, 2005).

12. Ibid. See the example of Antonio Pinho.

13. Ceballos, "Uma Buenos Aires lusitana," 7.

14. Prado, *A Colônia do Sacramento,* chap. 2.

15. For the case of Juan de Mosqueria, who owned a shop allegedly supplied by contraband trade, see AGN, Sala IX, 3.8.2, 1734.

16. The arrival of Portuguese traders provoked "scandals" at the Riachuelo docks, as they would openly throw bags with merchandise from ships and sometimes even jump off to meet their partners and avoid docking in the port. See AGN, Sala IX 3.8.2 [1745].

17. AGN, Sala IX, 3.8.2, 9 Jul. 1749. I could not find information on whether this measure was implemented.

18. AGN, Sala IX, 8.10.2, 4 Dec. 1762; AGN, Sala IX, 8.10.2, 3 Jan. 1763; AGN, Sala IX, 8.10.2, 26 Jan. 1763.

19. AGN, Sala IX, 8.10.13, 22 Feb. 1765.

20. I was not able to find information regarding the social and civil status of the subjects who were expelled. However, considering the doctrines of Natural Law and Derecho de Gentes, the individuals expelled were likely neither vecinos nor married into local families.

21. The motivation for such an action is not clear. Juan Alejandro Apoland, *Genesis de la familia uruguaya,* vol. 1 (Montevideo: Linardi, 1975), 246; AGN, Sala IX, 2.1.4, 27 Sept. 1730; AGN, Sala IX, 2.1.4, 22 July 1729.

22. AGN, Sala IX, 4.3.1. 5 Feb. 1747; AGN, Sala IX, 4.3.1. 3 Nov. 1746; AGN, Sala IX, 4.3.1 24 Oct. 1746.

23. AGNM, AGA, Caja 2, Exp. 15.

24. Apoland, *Genesis de la familia uruguaya*. I was able to identify twenty-one Portuguese subjects married to Spanish women.

25. Ibid., 1:97, "Plan de los Solares Originales."

26. For example, Antonio Cuello, in 1729, married to Maria del Rosario. For other cases, see Apoland, *Genesis de la familia uruguaya*, vol. 1, pts. 3, 5, 12, 15, 24, 32, 41.

27. Apoland, *Genesis de la familia uruguaya*, 2:852, pt. 55.

28. AGN, Sala IX, 2.2.3, 25 Feb. 1763.

29. AGN, Sala IX, 2.2.3, 25 Feb. 1763. Also Apoland, *Genesis de la familia uruguaya*, 1:535–40.

30. Apoland was able to identify only one Luso-Brazilian who had relocated, even though this individual reappeared in the city later in the 1760s. See Apoland, *Genesis de la familia uruguaya*, 1:535–40.

31. Archivo General de la Nación—Montevideo (AGNM), Colección Falcao Espalter, 82, 20 Feb. 1766.

32. AGNM, Colección Falcao Espalter, 81–82, 20 Feb. 1766.

33. AGN, Sala IX, 24.7.8. Reales Ordenes. The king had declared "perpetual silence" on such matters.

34. Apoland, *Genesis de la familia uruguaya*, 2:935, 967.

35. Moacyr Domingues, *Portugueses no Uruguai: São Carlos de Maldonado, 1764* (Porto Alegre: Edições EST, 1994).

36. Prado, *A Colônia do Sacramento*, 96–102. Because of the nature of the data used to build such a genealogy, we cannot calculate either the total number of Portuguese settlers who relocated or the average size of the household. Studies on Azorean casais for Colônia do Sacramento and Rio Grande for previous years suggest an average family size ranging from 3.2 to 3.8 inhabitants per household, respectively.

37. Gelman, *Estancieros y campesinos* (Buenos Aires: Libros del Riel, 1998), 285–87.

38. Ibid., 42–43. Gelman considers the fall of Colônia a turning point for wheat production in the region. According to the Argentine historian, the expulsion of the Portuguese from Colônia led to an agrarian expansion in the region. Social mobility was intimately connected with building a family and starting agrarian production. Gelman shows that after 1777, ascendant social mobility was a viable option in the region, and the Portuguese inhabitants also climbed the social ladder.

39. Ana Frega, *Pueblos y soberanía en la revolución artiguista* (Montevideo: Ediciones de la Banda Oriental, 2007), 359. Frega, in analyzing the same region in the 1810s, suggests that origin was not a determinant factor for social integration and political participation. In analyzing the local political dynamics of Soriano and Mercedes during the Artigas revolution, Frega identified 20 heads of house-

hold of Luso-Brazilian origin between the years 1793 and 1810. According to the author, they were all married into local families. Furthermore, these individuals had political and social connections with local factions that did not support the Luso-Brazilian interventions in the region in 1811 and 1816. According to Frega, Portuguese authorities complained about the large number of Luso-Brazilians that sided with the "enemies" instead of supporting the Luso-imperial cause.

40. Pedro Pereira Mesquita, *Relación de la conquista de la colonia por don Pedro de Cevallos* (Buenos Aires: Municipalidade de la Ciudad de Buenos Aires, 1980), 30.

41. AGI (Buenos Aires), Gobierno, 333–13 [Jan.] 1798; 333 s-f 1785.

42. AGNM, AGA, Caja 92—24 Mar, 1779.

43. AGN, Sala IX, 8.10.8. 11, Dec. 1801.

44. AGNM, AGA, Libro 44, "Fidelidad de los Portugueses, 1801."

45. Padrón 1778, in *Documentos para la historia argentina*, XII.

46. These data were extensively analyzed in Marcela Tejerina, *Luso-Brasileños and la Plaza Mercantil de Buenos Ayres virreynal* (Bahia Blanca: Ed Univ. Bahia Blanca, 2004); and Reitano, "Los portugueses del Buenos Aires tardo colonial." The numbers presented here are similar to the ones found by Tejerina, and they are slightly higher than the ones presented by Reitano, including twenty more foreigners.

47. I am using the figure of 45,000 inhabitants for Buenos Aires, estimated for 1810 by Susan Socolow and L. Johnson, "Población y espacio en el Buenos Aires del siglo XVIII," *Desarollo Económico* 20, no. 19 (1980): 329–49. Although there must have been variations in the population, these are still the best data available. As a result this analysis is affected by a possible bias for using a bigger value for the total population. Nevertheless, all conclusions and estimates presented downplay the weight of the foreigners in Buenos Aires. As a result, my conclusions are based on minimum figures.

48. Padrón 1778, in *Documentos para la historia argentina*, XII.

49. For the sale of British products in Montevideo after the invasion and the profit of Montevidean merchants, see Anónimo, *Razões dos lavradores do Vice-reinado de Buenos Ayres para a franqueza com comércio com os ingleses contra a representação de alguns comerciantes e resolução do governo com o apêndice de observações e exame dos efeitos do novo regulamento nos interesses comerciais do Brazil*, trans. José da Silva Lisboa (Rio de Janeiro: Impressão Régia,1810), John Carter Brown Library, C810, R278d.

50. AGNM, AGA, Caja 20, "Padron de Estranjeros, 1807."

51. I am using the data available for 1810 of 10,500 inhabitants for Montevideo collected by Andres Lamas. These data present the same type of bias as that for Buenos Aires. These figures represent the minimum estimation for the weight of foreigners in Montevideo.

52. Padrón 1778, in *Documentos para la historia argentina*, XII.

CHAPTER 3. TRANSIMPERIAL COOPERATION

1. This explanation was originally advanced by John Fisher, "Commerce and Imperial Decline: Spanish Trade with Spanish America 1797–1820," *Journal of Latin American Studies* 30 (1998): 459–79; and Lynch, *Latin American Revolutions*. This interpretation still permeates recent historical works, especially the significance of war in disrupting trade and interrupting commerce between Spain and its colonies: Stein and Stein, *The Edge of Crisis*, 207; Richard Graham, *Independence in Latin America: A Comparative Approach* (Austin: University of Texas Press, 2013); and Elliot, *Empires of the Atlantic World*. A notable exception is Adelman, *Sovereignty and Revolution in the Iberian Atlantic*.

2. During wartime British privateers confiscated Spanish vessels and took them to Jamaica or other Caribbean islands. Spanish American merchants were able to regain their vessels and cargo by paying a ransom. Merchants abused this practice, often using the ransoming of a ship to introduce more goods than the original confiscated shipment. Adrian Pearce, *British Trade with Spanish America, 1763–1808* (Liverpool: Liverpool University Press, 2007), 80–119.

3. Stein and Stein, *Edge of Crisis*, chap. 8. See also Jerry Cooney, "Oceanic Commerce and Platine Merchants, 1796–1806: The Challenge of War," *The Americas* 45, no. 4 (Apr. 1989): 509–24.

4. Pearce emphasizes the role of Colonia del Sacramento for British trade with the Spanish empires before 1777. The author suggests that up to 40 percent of the British trade conducted with Brazil was destined for Río de la Plata. See Pearce, *British Trade with Spanish America*, 10.

5. Juan Carlos Garavaglia, "Economic Growth and Regional Differentiations: The River Plate Region at the End of the Eighteenth Century," *Hispanic American Historical Review* 65, no. 1 (Feb. 1985): 57.

6. Ibid., 53.

7. Ibid., 54.

8. Bentancur, *El puerto colonial*, 1:204.

9. Archivo General de la Nación—Montevideo, Protocolos de Marina—Registro de Protocolizaciones, 1803–9.

10. Bentancur, *El puerto colonial*, 1:148. AGN, Montevideo, Protocolos de Marina—Registro de Protocolizaciones, 1803–9.

11. Merchants obtaining loans from Buenos Aires merchants included Matteo Magariños, Francisco Xavier Ferrer, Eusebio Vidal, Jaime Posadas, Juan Francisco Zuñiga, and Jorge de la Carreras. The 25,000 pesos were provided by Buenos Aires's Maria Bernarda Lezica, Jose Inchaguerri, Benito de Olazabal, and Esteban de Villanueva. Bentancour, *El puerto colonial*, 1:42–43.

12. *Semanario de Agricultura*, 1803–4.

13. Such phenomena have been recorded for the Caribbean region as well. Pearce has examined in detail the use of pretexts such as *rescates* (ransom of

ships) as a means to sail to British colonies in order to conduct trade. See Pearce, *British Trade with Spanish America,* chap. 4.

14. I was unable to find any records of rescate expeditions conducted from Río de la Plata to any foreign port. Pearce has identified twelve rescate operations between 1798 and 1803 but estimates that this number was just a fraction of the total carried out. See Pearce, *British Trade with Spanish America,* 138–39.

15. Moutoukias, *Contrabando e control colonial,* chap. 4.

16. AHU—Rio de Janeiro D. 9294, 30 Mar. 1780.

17. Moutoukias, *Contrabando y control colonial.* For the standard formulaic text of *autos de embarcação,* see AN Cx 492 Pc 02.

18. I use administrative reports, autos de embarcações, and letters exchanged by Portuguese and Spanish authorities between 1778 and 1806 in order to examine the scale, route, and significance of the trade between Spanish colonial subjects from Río de la Plata and Portuguese merchants from Brazil. These sources were deposited in the Archivo General de la Nación, Montevideo (AGNM), in the Arquivo Nacional, Rio de Janeiro (AN), in the Arquivo Histórico Ultramarino of Lisbon (AHU), and in the Archivo General de Indias, Seville (AGI). The cross-referencing of such information allowed me to detect a high degree of association between colonial subjects of different empires, especially during periods of war.

19. AGNM, EHG Caja 2, Auto de Embarcación, 2 Nov. 1784.

20. IANTT—MNE Livro 199. For 1789, the arrival of 160 Portuguese ships was recorded in Cádiz. Only one of these vessels carried silver, and the most common products were oranges, fish, olive oil, rocks, salt, and Brazil wood. Montevideo became the primary port city of Río de la Plata because of its privileged natural harbor, which was more protected and larger than the port of Buenos Aires. Thus, in the last decades of the eighteenth century, Montevideo was the gateway for most Río de la Plata commerce, and to a certain extent it became the port of Buenos Aires. See Bentancur, *El puerto colonial.*

21. One ship, originally of Portuguese origin but nationalized by Spanish authorities and merchants, is counted as Portuguese and Spanish. In other words, it was registered twice because it falls into both categories.

22. Not enough information for twenty-seven ships.

23. The numbers presented in this work are part of a database collected from the following sources: AN Cx 492 Pct 02; AGNM, EHG Cj. 34, 18, 40, 2, 24, 15, 23, 27, 28, 31, 32, 34, 41, 56, 55, 54, 48, 45, 28; AGNM Ex-Museo Histórico Cj. 4; AHU RJ D. 10056, 10215, 10532, 10607, 11714, 13396, 13397, 13398, 13399, 13406, 13405, 13407, 13408, 13412, 13413, 13415, 13418, 13419, 13421, 13422, 13436, 13437, 13438, 13441, 13446, 13452,13458, 13462, 13470, 14058, 14121, 14099, 14500, 14506, 14500, 14511, 15946, 15953, 15958, 15959, 16130, 16233, 16268, 16341, A16541, 16824, 18013, 9567, 9028, 9326, 9772, 9859, 9772, 9932, 10052; AGI Buenos Aires, Gobierno Leg. 141; *Declaración de Entrada de Puerto.*

Additional information is provided by Alex Borucki's database, including slave vessels; information about its sources can be found in Borucki, "The Slave Trade to Río de la Plata, 1777–1812: Trans-Imperial Networks and Atlantic Warfare," *Colonial Latin American Review* 20, no. 1 (2011): 81–107.

24. Borucki, "Slave Trade to Río de la Plata."

25. Ernst Pijning, "Controlling Contraband: Mentality, Economy and Society in Eighteenth-Century Rio de Janeiro" (PhD diss., Johns Hopkins University, 1997), 163.

26. Bentancur, *El puerto colonial*, 1:265.

27. AGN, Montevideo, Libro de Fianzas y protocolizaciones.

28. Bentancur, *El puerto colonial*, 1:36.

29. *Semanario de Agricultura Industria y Comercio*, Junta de Historia Numismatica Americana, Buenos Aires, 1928–37; AGN, Montevideo; AGA, Libros de Aduana 95, 96, 99.

30. "RELAÇÃO dos GENEROS e Fazendas proprios do consumo da Colonia do Rio da Prata, Reyno do Perú e Prezidencia do Chili: os preços que permitem na prz. guerra, e os que demosntrão mayor utilidade," AHU, RJ doc. 12655, 4 Apr. 1799.

31. Pijning, "Controlling Contraband," chap. 4.

32. Dauril Alden, "The Undeclared War of 1773–1777: Climax of Luso-Spanish Platine Rivalry," *Hispanic American Historical Review* 41, no. 1 (Feb. 1961): 55–74.

33. In addition to the Portuguese settlers, demographic growth was due to a new wave of immigrants from Spain and the interior provinces of Río de la Plata and to the growing slave trade.

34. Tejerina, *Luso-Brasileños en el Buenos Aires virreinal*; Reitano, "Los portugueses del Buenos Aires tardo colonial"; *Documentos para la historia argentina* (Buenos Aires: Senado de la Nación, 1960), vol. 12, Padron de 1778. The following decrees targeted specifically the Portuguese population in Buenos Aires, imposing restrictions on mobility, residence, and property. AGN, IX 8.10.8, 11 Dec. 1801; AGN, IX 8.10.13, 22 Feb. 1765; AGN, IX 8.10.2, 26 Jan. 1763; AGN, IX 8.10.4, 11 Oct. 1777.

35. For more on Cipriano de Melo and his role in Montevideo's community, see Fabricio Prado, "A carreira trans-imperial de don Manuel Cipriano de Melo," *Topoi, Revista de História* (Rio de Janeiro) 13, no. 25 (July–Dec. 2012): 168–84.

36. AGI, Buenos Aires, Códice 333, 24 May 1785. Regarding exchange rates: for this period 1 peso = $760 réis.

37. Moutoukias, *Contrabando y control colonial*; Pijning, "Controlling Contraband"; Bentancur, *El cuerto colonial*.

38. Bentancur, *El puerto colonial*, 1:289–98.

39. On 30 September. AHU, RJ D. 9028. Although the ships are Spanish, the sources record the names using Portuguese spellings.

40. AHU, RJ D. 9294, 30 Mar. 1780. Pijning also identified this ship and this letter as being the key moment in the La Plata contraband trade for the period.

41. Ibid.

42. See Borucki, "From Shipmates to Soldiers," 51.

43. The 1751 ordinance must be understood in the context of the negotiations of the Treaty of Madrid. For Spanish authorities, the main goal of the accord in Río de la Plata was to put an end to contraband trade.

44. AHU, RJ D. 9561, 12 June 1781.

45. Ibid.

46. "avultadissima quantidade de coiros, e prata . . . para Corte e dela para Espanha." AHU, RJ D. 9561, 12 June 1781.

47. The price for a shipment from Rio to Lisbon was 20 cruzados, while from the River Plate the price was 60 cruzados on average. AHU, RJ D. 9561.

48. Biblioteca Nacional (BN) Lisboa, Manuscritos Pombalinos, Códice 10855, Colônia do Sacramento, 8 June 1776; AGI, Buenos Aires 333, 14 June 1785. In 1783 transactions involving Cipriano de Melo, Francisco Maciel, and Brás Carneiro Leão involved more than 13,000 pesos.

49. AHU, RJ D. 9561, 12 June 1781.

50. IANTT—MNE Cx 915—Papéis Varios de Hespanha, Pasta No. 3, "Primeiro e Segundo Compêndio que o Marques de Pombal entregou a Raynha Nossa Senhora para Ser Apresentado ao Rey D. José," 1776–77.

51. AGN, IX 25.5.6—Reales Comunicaciones, 7 Jan. 1781.

52. AHU, RJ D. 9772, 19 Mar. 1783.

53. AHU, RJ D. 9622, 20 Apr. 1782.

54. AHU, RJ D. 12729, 11 June 1799.

55. AHU, RJ D. 13319, 8 Jan. 1800.

56. AHU, RJ D. 9326, 10052, 9567, 10215, 10607, 10056.

57. AHU, RJ D. 10052, 29 Apr. 1785.

58. From 1791 on, a series of royal orders allowed Spanish merchants to acquire slaves in Brazil and foreign ships to introduce slaves. Real Academía de Historia de Madrid, Colección Mata Linares, Tomo LXVIII, 9, 1723; fols. 998–1001.

59. Borucki, "Slave Trade to Río de la Plata."

60. Laws liberalizing the slave trade were enacted in 1789–91 in the Spanish empire. See Adelman, *Sovereignty and Revolution*, chap. 2; and Borucki, "Slave Trade to Río de la Plata."

61. AGNM, EHG Cj. 40, 7 Nov. 1799, 25 Dec. 1799, 18 Nov. 1799; IANTT–MNE Cx 915, 17 May 1802.

62. AGNM, EHG Cj. 55.1802, Cj. 55.1802 exp. 194; Cj. 56 exp. 216, Cj. 40, 21 Jan. 1799; Cj. 40, 16 Sept. 1798; Cj. 40, 5 Sept. 1799.

63. AGNM, AHG Cj. 40, 5 Sept. 1799.

64. AGNM, EHG Cj. 55, 1802.

65. AHU, RJ 10215, 10532, 10607, 13396, 13397, 13398, 13399, 13407, 13412, 13408.

66. "Com prerrogativas que lhe guardam as leis do Estado."AN, RJ Cx 492, Pct. 02, 10 Oct. 1796.

67. I have information for twenty-six vessels in the 1800s. Captains on eighteen of those vessels alleged that storms were the reason they sought entry at Rio de Janeiro.

68. AGNM, EHG Cx 79. 1788, 12 Jun. 1788; and AGI, Buenos Aires, Códice 346, 30 Apr. 1798.

69. For a detailed analysis, see Borucki, "Slave Trade to Río de la Plata."

70. AHU, RJ D. 12265, 28 Apr. 1798.

71. AHU, RJ D. 11714, 17 July 1795.

72. AGNM, EHG Cj. 34 and 40. Among the products imported were wax, sugar, cachaça, iron, rice, and indigo. For an extensive analysis of the acquisition of foreign vessels by Río de la Plata merchants, see Jerry W. Cooney, "Neutral Vessels and Platine Slavers: Building a Viceregal Merchant Marine," *Journal of Latin American Studies* 18, no. 1 (May 1986): 25–39.

73. AGNM, EHG Cj 34, 20 Feb. 1797; Cj. 34, 12 Dec. 1797; Cj. 34, 15 Dec. 1797; Cj 40, 5 Apr. 1799; AGNM, AGA, *Libro de Fianzas del Puerto de Montevideo.*

74. AGNM EHG Cj. 34, 15 Dec. 1797.

CHAPTER 4. THE MAKING OF MONTEVIDEO

1. Jacques Barbier, *Reform and Politics in Bourbon Chile, 1775–1796* (Ottawa: University of Ottawa Press, 1980); Adelman, *Sovereignty and Revolution in the Iberian Atlantic.*

2. For overlapping jurisdictions and local disputes, see Frank Jay Moreno, "The Spanish Colonial System: An Institutional Approach," *Western Political Quarterly* 20 (1967): 59–101; Cardim et al., *Polycentric Monarchies;* John Elliot, "An Europe of Composite Monarchies,"*Past & Present,* no. 137 (Nov. 1992): 48–71. For a more comprehensive discussion of colonial jurisdiction and sovereignty, see Benton, *A Search for Sovereignty.*

3. The northwestern Banda Oriental was formally under three distinct and overlapping jurisdictions during the last part of the colonial period: the intendancy of Buenos Aires, the governorship of Montevideo, and the governorship of Misiones. Frega, *Pueblos y Soberanía,* 2.

4. German Tjarks, *El Consulado de Montevideo y su proyección en la História del Río de la Plata* (Buenos Aires: Instituto Emilio Ravignani, 1962), 1:632–35.

5. Ibid., 637.

6. The governorship of Montevideo was responsible for the founding of Maldonado (1757) and Minas (1786).

7. Real Academia Española, *Nuevo tesoro lexicográfico de la lengua española* (1780), Academia Usual, 568, http://ntlle.rae.es/ntlle/SrvltGUIMenuNtlle?cmd= Lema&sec=1.0.0.0.0. Accessed 23 May 2015.

8. The alcalde of Santa Hermandad was the delegate of this philanthropic institution, which was supported by a religious brotherhood and owned property in Montevideo and the countryside. This position, although honorific, carried prestige and influence over political matters in Montevideo.William Pierson Jr., "Some Reflections on the Cabildo as an Institution," *Hispanic American Historical Review* 5, no. 4 (Nov. 1922): 573–96.

9. This assessment is strengthened by the prominent role of the cabildos during the revolutionary period., See Pierson, "Some Reflections on the Cabildo as an Institution"; Frega, *Pueblos y soberanía;* Lynch, *Latin American Revolutions;* Fredrick Pike, "The Municipality and the System of Checks and Balances in Spanish American Colonial Administration," *The Americas* 15, no. 2 (1958): 139–58. The central role of the cabildo of Montevideo is discussed in further detail in chapter 7 of this book.

10. For a comprehensive discussion of jurisdictions and cabildo politics in colonial Mexico, see Frances Ramos, *Identity, Ritual, and Power in Colonial Puebla* (Tucson: University of Arizona Press, 2012). For violence and cabildo politics, see Oscar Cornblit, *Power and Violence in the Colonial City* (Cambridge: Cambridge University Press, 1995).

11. For the role of the cabildos in regional disputes in rural settings and the ways this institution shaped the political and social tissue in the colonial period, see Frega, *Pueblos y soberanía,* 56–64. For a broader analysis of the role of the juridical culture centered on cabildos and natural law, see Jose Carlos Chiaramonte, "La cuestión iusnaturalista en los movimientos de independencia," *Boletín del Instituto de Historia Argentina y Americana Dr. Emilio Ravignani,* 3rd ser., no. 22 (2000): 33–71.

12. John Lynch, "Intendants and Cabildos in the Viceroyalty of La Plata, 1782– 1810," *Hispanic American Historical Review,* 35 no. 3 (Aug. 1955): 337–62. According to Lynch, it was the creation of the intendant system (later superintendancy) in the late 1770s that most seriously affected the power of the cabildos both in Buenos Aires and in Montevideo, because the intendant had competing jurisdiction over city regulations and taxation.

13. Frega, *Pueblos y soberanía,* 56–57.

14. Alzaybar had the right to patrol the River Plate with corsair vessels. AGN, Sala IX 2.8.1; Bentancur, *El puerto colonial,* 178.

15. Bentancur, *El puerto colonial,* 178.

16. Arturo Ariel Bentancur, *Cipriano de Melo, Señor de fronteras* (Montevideo: ARCA, 1985), 14. The Resguardo consisted of "un comandante de barco, un visitador, un teniente de este, un guardamayor, seis dependientes de numero,

diez soldados, un cabo, asi como un contramestre y 12 marineros que tripulaban la embarcación."

17. For the importance of the initial proceedings and the generation of the sumaria in shaping the outcome of the legal procedures, see Barreneche, *Crime and Administration of Justice in Buenos Aires;* Bentancur, *El puerto colonial,* 180–84.

18. The Comandancia del Resguardo was the office in charge of repressing contraband trade, of the ports, and of patrolling the coastal areas as well as the borderlands.

19. AGN, Sala IX, Serie Montevideo, 3.2.4–3.7.10; AGN, Sala XI Montevideo, 3.2.1; Sala IX, 2.4.1; Sala IX, 2.7.5.

20. Julio Djenderedjian, "Roots of Revolution: Frontier Settlement Policy and the Emergence of New Spaces of Power in the Río de la Plata Borderlands, 1777–1810," *Hispanic American Historical Review* 88, no. 4 (Nov. 2008): 639–68.

21. AGN, Sala IX, 3.1.2, the following letters specifically: 25 Jan. 1772, 14 Jan. 1773, 25 Jan. 1773, 20 Apr. 1773, 29 Jan. 1773.

22. AGN, Sala IX, Montevideo 3.2.1, 26 Feb. 1773, 25 Jan. 1773, 24 Apr. 1773, 13 Apr. 1773, 10 Jan. 1773; Sala 2.1.4, Montevideo, 1731–51.

23. Moutoukias, *Contraband y control colonial;* Prado, *A Colônia do Sacramento.*

24. AGN, Sala IX, 2.7.5.

25. Ibid., reports of 31 May 1792, 29 May 1792, 22 June 1792.

26. AGN, Sala IX, 2.7.5, 29 May 1792.

27. AGN, Sala IX, 2.7.5, 16 June 1792.

28. AGN, Sala IX, 2.7.5, 21 May 1792.

29. AGN, Sala IX, 2.7.5, 29 May 1792, for Laguna Mirin Jurisdiction, 28 July 1792 for formal jurisdiction over matters in the borderland forts.

30. AGN, Sala IX, 2.7.5, 30 Aug. 1792: "sobre envio de cueros decomisados a Montevideo."

31. AGN, Sala IX, 2.7.5, 23 May 1792, 29 Nov. 1792, 4 July 1792, 16 Apr. 1792.

32. AGN, Sala IX, 2.7.5, 30 July 1792, 31 May 1792, 27 June 1792, 29 June 1792.

33. AGN, Sala IX, 8.10.4, 11 Oct. 1777.

34. AGN, Sala IX, 2.4.1, 9 July 1781; AGI, Buenos Aires Gobierno 333, 22 Feb. 1783, 5 Dec. 1781, 23 Dec. 1782, 5 Aug. 1783, 7 Nov. 1783.

35. AGI, Buenos Aires 333, Arreglo de los Campos de Montevideo, 1785, Punto 1—Carta 295. Edicts of Viceroy Vertiz and Intendant Sanz favored Montevideo's groups.

36. AGI, Buenos Aires 333, Arreglo de los Campos de Montevideo, 1785. "Despues de haver llevado la tolerancia y el disimula hasta el estremo, haver agotado quantos medios le ha sugerido su genial deseo de la buena armonia y su

poco apego a la obstentacion de autoridad cree que talvez habra sido su exceso de sufrimento en esta parte cauxa de haver llegado el Virrey a tal punto; pues valiendose de la expresion qual usa el articulo 2º de la ordenanza de Intendentes acerca de las omnimodas facultades del Virrey, y sin embargo de la excepcion que hace en todos negocios de Real Hacienda cree que su autoridad no tiente limites."

37. AGI, Buenos Aires 333, Arreglo de los Campos de Montevideo, 1785, Comandante Pereira, defensa de Vertiz.

38. AGI, Buenos Aires 333, Arreglo de los Campos de Montevideo, 1785.

39. AGN, Sala IX, 25.1.8, Reales Ordenes, 5 June 1786. "La Jurisdicion de la campaña enquanto se dirije a contravando extraccion de cueros, ganados y fraude pertenece al Superintendente. Asi como los efectos producidos en dominios de Portugal, como de la introduccion de Tabacos del Brasil y otros generos de ilicito comercio."

40. AGN, Sala IX, 25.1.8, Reales Ordenes, 6 Mar. 1786: "precaver rovos y violencias q en ella se cometan, y la seguridad de los campos para que se prevenga la internacion de PORTUGUESES y estrangeros y cutodiar las fronteras." The Real Orden was specific in stating that the viceroyal authorities were not supposed to intervene in the Arreglo of the countryside and its police, as well as the rules applied to the land and cattle herds on the Neutral Fields. "Deve V.Exa. inivirse absolutamente de conocimiento del arreglo de la campaña y su peculiar policia enquanto se dirije a precaver y cortar el contravando . . . tambien la reduccion de estancias de los hacendados dela parte de Montevideo con declaracion de las reglas con declaracion de las reglas que han de observar para errar los ganados y sobre la pertenencia de los terrenos realengos."

41. Socolow, *Bureaucrats of Buenos Aires,* Appendix D.

42. These areas ended up as part of modern Brazil.

43. Socolow, *Bureaucrats of Buenos Aires,* Appendix D. For the significance of the summary, see Oswaldo Barreneche, *Crime and Administration of Justice in Buenos Aires* (Lincoln: University of Nebraska Press, 2006).

44. Bentancur, *El puerto colonial,* 178: "continuacion del Trafico Ultramarino exclusivamente por Montevideo."

45. AGI, Buenos Aires Gobierno, Leg. 346, 3 Mar. 1798: "El querer distinguir una ciudad subalterna [Montevideo] mas que a la Capital [Buenos Aires] es el motivo de unas providencias irritantes . . . cuyos resultados perjudiciales los hemos tenido a la vista."

46. Enrique Martin de Alzaga, *Cartas (1806–1807)* (Buenos Aires: Emece, 1972), 1–32.

47. Ibid., 31–64.

48. AGNM, Archivos Particulares, Correspondencia Comercial Alzaga, 1803–4, Cj. 332, Carpetas 1–10. Specifically, letters of 30 Mar., 13 Apr., 20 Apr. 1803.

49. AGNM, Protocolos de Marina, Fianzas y Protocolizaciones, 1805–9.

50. Ibid.

51. Bentancur, *El puerto colonial*, 42–45.

52. AGNM, *Actas y Acuerdo del Consulado de Comercio de Montevideo*, 1794.

53. The Buenos Aires merchants' donation was to finance the war against the French Consulate. Tjarks, *El Consulado*, 627–29.

54. The creation of the Consulado was a long-standing demand of Buenos Aires merchants. The 100,000-peso donativo to the Crown is perceived as crucial to the creation of the guild. This impressive sum advanced to the Crown was financed by important Buenos Aires merchants who belonged to the Consulado. The *averia* was used to pay interest on the merchants' loan to the Consulado. For detailed analysis of the role of donativos in imperial politics and regional economy, see Viviana Grieco, *The Politics of Giving* (Albuquerque: University of New Mexico Press, 2013), 82–85.

55. During the 1790s, the Crown allowed the creation of consulates in Caracas, Guatemala, Havana, Buenos Aires, Cartagena, Vera Cruz, Guadalajara, and Santiago de Chile while weakening the power of the traditional corporations of Lima and Mexico. Part of the justification for creating consulados was the commitment of local merchants to improve and maintain commercial infrastructure and local commercial justice. See Gabriel Paquette, "State and Civil Society Cooperation: The Intellectual and Political Activities of the Ultramarine *Consulados* and Economic Societies," *Journal of Latin American Studies* 39, no. 2 (May 2007): 263–98. For the *averia*, Tjarks, *El Consulado*, 624–40; and Grieco, *The Politics of Giving*, 83.

56. Grieco *The Politics of Giving*, 2–13.

57. AGNM, *Actas y Acuerdos del Consulado de Montevideo*, 14 Jan. 1794, p. 6v.

58. Ibid., p. 7.

59. AGI, Buenos Aires Gobierno, Leg. 346, 3 Mar. 1798.

60. Ibid., 30 Apr. 1798.

61. Ibid., [between 13 and 27] Feb. 1797: "nadie podra negar que el puerto de Buenos Aires lleva conocidas ventajas sobre el de Montevideo."

62. The almojarifazgo was a fee for operating warehouses in the port area.

63. AGI, Buenos Aires Gobierno, Leg. 346, 27 Feb. 1797.

64. Ibid.

65. Ibid., 23 [Jan.] 17[97–98].

66. Ibid., 13 [Jan.] 1798.

67. AGNM, *Actas y Acuerdos del Consulado de Montevideo*, pp. 1–13; and Luis Aguirre, "Los Consulados de Comerciantes en la independencia de Hispanoamérica: El caso del Consulado de Montevideo, 1794–1838" (Master's thesis, UNAM, 2014), 98–109.

68. The Crown stipulated that consulados should repair and improve infrastructure such as roads, ports, and docks. See Paquette, "State and Civil Society Cooperation and Conflict," 263–98; and Grieco, *The Politics of Giving*, 83.

69. Javier Kraselski, "De las Juntas de Comercio al Consulado: Los comerciantes rioplatenses y sus estrategias corporativas, 1779–1794," *Anuario de Estudios Americanos* 64, no. 2 (July–Sept. 2007): 145–70; Tjarks, *El Consulado,* 634–36.

70. Tjarks, *El Consulado,* 805.

71. *Semanario de Agricultura,* June 1803–June 1804.

72. Alzaga, *Cartas,* 62–64.

73. Ibid., 53; Com Luis de Gardezabal, 1 May, 1709.

74. AGI, Buenos Aires Gobierno, Leg. 346, 30 Dec. 1797, 15 [Jan.] 1798.

CHAPTER 5. CHANGING TOPONYMY AND THE EMERGENCE OF THE BANDA ORIENTAL

1. Nonassimilated indigenous populations were not included in these descriptions. Indigenous groups were referred to by their "nation" (e.g., Guaranís, Minuanes, and Charruas).

2. I am using the concept of representations as discursive and symbolic constructions that were embedded in power relations and ethical and political values. The competing representations reflected power struggles between diverse social groups, diverse interests, and perspectives about the future. See Carlo Ginzburg, *Wooden Eyes: Nine Reflections on Distance* (New York: Columbia University Press, 2001), especially the chapter, "Representation: The Word, the Thing, the Idea."

3. Although this area was claimed by European empires, sovereign equestrian nomadic indigenous groups were present in the region and did not recognize European sovereignty over the territory.

4. Chiefly, Montevideo was the only port that was allowed to disembark slaves in the Rio de la Plata—a trade that brought approximately 90,000 enslaved Africans to the region according to the newest numbers presented by Alex Borucki. Before the late 1770s, slaves were disembarked at Buenos Aires or Colônia do Sacramento. The trade via Colônia was illegal in the eyes of Spanish authorities. See Borucki, "Slave Trade to Río de la Plata," 81–107.

5. J. A. B. Beaumont, *Viajes por Buenos Aires, Entre Rios y la Banda Oriental, 1826–27* (Buenos Aires: Hachette, 1957), 88–89.

6. Don Francisco Joanico, a merchant from Montevideo, hosted Thomas Kinder in 1809 and J. A. Beaumont in 1827/28. Both men spoke highly of their host and mentioned that he introduced them to local society and other foreigners residing in Montevideo, shared information about the region and its customs, and provided letters of reference.

7. Sá, *História topográfica e bélica da nova Colônia do Sacramento do Rio da Prata;* Emeric Essex Vidal, *Picturesque Illustrations of Buenos Ayres and Mon-*

tevideo consisting of 24 views accompanied with description of the scenery (London: Ackerman, 1820); Beaumont, *Viajes por Buenos Aires*, 53–61.

8. Beaumont, *Viajes por Buenos Aires*, 108.

9. Hispanic Society of America, "Journal and Logbook of an Anonymous Scotch Sailor," New York, HC 363–1299, 1726–28; I thank Prof. David Eltis for this material. And see Anónimo, *Noticias sobre el Rio de la Plata* (Madrid: Historia 16, 1988); Vidal, *Picturesque Illustrations of Buenos Ayres and Montevideo;* Auguste de Saint-Hilaire, *Viagem ao Rio Grande do Sul* (Brasília: Senado Federal, 2002); John Luccock, *Notes on Rio de Janeiro and the Southern Parts of Brazil: Taken during a residence of ten years in that country from 1808 to 1818* (London: Samuel Leigh, 1820); and Beaumont, *Viajes por Buenos Aires*.

10. Beaumont, *Viajes por Buenos Aires*, 109–12.

11. Ibid., 108–13.

12. For the centrality of the urban space, see Angel Rama, *La ciudad letrada* (Hanover, NH: Ediciones del Norte, 1984).

13. Sá, *História topográfica e bélica da nova Colônia do Sacramento do Rio da Prata;* Silvestre Ferreira da Silva, *Relação do sítio da nova Colônia do Sacramento* (1748; repr. Porto Alegre: Arcano 21, 1977). Anonymous, "Journal and Logbook." Also, Portuguese and Spanish authorities produced a plethora of classified documents, specifically correspondence between governors and the Overseas Council and the Council of the Indies, respectively.

14. Anónimo, *Noticias sobre el Río de la Plata;* Bartolomé Cosme Bueno, *El Aragones Cosme Bueno y la descripción geográfica del Río de la Plata, 1768–1776* (Huesca: Instituto de Estudios Altoaragoneses, 1996); Felix de Azara, *Memoria sobre el estado rural del Río de la Plata* (Buenos Aires: Editorial Bajel, 1943); Damaso Larrañaga, *Diario del viaje de Montevideo a Paysandu* (Montevideo: Instituto Nacional del Libro, 1994); Luccock, *Notes on Rio de Janeiro and the Southern Parts of Brazil;* Beaumont, *Viajes por Buenos Aires;* Vidal, *Picturesque Illustrations of Buenos Ayres and Montevideo.*

15. For more thoughts on the Atlantic audience and information networks, see also Gustavo Paz, "Reporting Atlantic News" (Paper presented at Emory University, 6 Jan. 2006); Elizabeth Elbourne, "The Sin of the Settler," *Journal of Colonialism and Colonial History* 4, no. 3 (2003): 2–3. Here I am appropriating Bennedict Anderson's concept of imagined communities, suggesting that the eighteenth-century Atlantic World also connected people through imaginary ties to the European colonial system. However, I am not suggesting the existence of modern nation-states or national identities in Latin America for the period in question. Rather, I am arguing for the existence of a transimperial community conscious of themselves as a group.

16. Corographies were descriptions of a region or a colony that included information on geography, fauna, flora, weather, peoples, and economy. This was a popular genre in the eighteenth century.

17. For the importance of written accounts for colonial identity in British America and in the Caribbean, see Jack Greene, "Reformulando a identidade inglesa na América britânica colonial: Adaptação cultural e experiência provincial na construção das identidades corporativas," *Almanack Braziliense*, no. 4 (Nov. 2006): 5–36.

18. Elizabeth Elbourne, "Indigenous Peoples and Imperial Networks in the Early Nineteenth Century: The Politics of Knowledge," in *Rediscovering the British World*, ed. Phillip Buckner and Douglas Francis (Calgary: University of Calgary Press, 2003). See also Karl Offen, "Creating Mosquitia: Mapping Amerindian Spatial Practices in Eastern Central America, 1629–1779," *Journal of Historical Geography* 33 (2007): 254–82.

19. Pratt, *Imperial Eyes*, 6–9.

20. Pratt's concept of the contact zone has been challenged for other part of the Americas as well. Mathew Brown probes the use of contact zones for Venezuela and Colombia through the writing of the British mercenary Richard Vowell: "Richard Vowell's Not So Imperial Eyes: Travel Writing and Adventure in Nineteenth-Century Hispanic Latin America," *Journal of Latin American Studies* 38 (2006): 95–122. For the discussion on contact zones and a review of recent historiography on travel writing, see 98–101.

21. Pratt, *Imperial Eyes*, 6–9.

22. For contact with the other and the process of cultural interaction during the European Expansion, see Stuart Schwartz, ed., *Implicit Understandings: Observing, Reporting, and Reflecting on the Encounters between Europeans and Other Peoples in the Early Modern Era* (New York: Cambridge University Press, 1994), especially Schwartz's introduction, 3–4.

23. Anonymous, "Journal and Logbook." The parts referred to here are mainly from 1727–28. *Voyages—Online Slave Trade Database* records this ship under ID no. 76203.

24. Anonymous, "Journal and Logbook." The parts referred to here are mainly from 1727–28, 2–8.

25. Sá, *História topográfica e bélica*, 25, 51, 53, 90; Silva, *Relação do sítio da nova Colônia do Sacramento*, 74, 75, 77, 95. For the reference to "Castellanos" de Montevideo, see Silva, 22.

26. Sá, *História topográfica e bélica;* Silva, *Relação do sítio da nova Colônia do Sacramento*, 95.

27. "Ingleses q. tomarão nosso partido, mas tb. negociavão com os castelhanos." Sá, *História topográfica e bélica*, 97, 101.

28. Cosme Bueno, *El Aragones Cosme Bueno*, 135.

29. Ibid., 136: "Mas al oriente [de Montevideo] esta el puerto de Maldonado con una Bahia espaciosa."

30. Francisco Millau, *Descripción de la província del Rio de la Plata* (Buenos Aires and Mexico: Espasa Calpe, 1947), 95–124.

31. Ibid., 103.

32. Ibid., 94.

33. Ibid., 99.

34. Ibid., 100.

35. Ibid., 101.

36. Ibid., 103.

37. Ibid., 105.

38. Ibid., 108.

39. Ibid., 110.

40. Cosme Bueno, *El Aragones Cosme Bueno*, 132–36.

41. Creoles were natives of European descent. Jose Manuel Perez Castellano, "Descripción de Montevideo y la campaña de la Banda Oriental," in *Seleccion de Escritos, 1787–1814* (Montevideo: Biblioteca Artigas, 1968), 5–15.

42. Ibid., 5.

43. Ibid., 35–37.

44. Ibid., 13–14.

45. Ibid., 6–7.

46. This trend becomes clearer especially in Perez Castellano's letters about the British invasion and the role of Montevideo in liberating Buenos Aires. He also mentions the "honor" of Montevideo as defined by the actions of its inhabitants. See Perez Castellano, "Descripción de Montevideo y la campaña de la Banda Oriental," 46, 52–56, 125.

47. Paula Sanz a Marques de Loreto, AGI-GOB-BA-333-014.

48. Ibid.

49. Anónimo, *Noticias sobre el Río de la Plata,* especially the introduction. Because the manuscript was not dated, there is some debate about when it was written, and the years 1792, 1794, and 1797 have all been suggested. However, it is possible that the account was produced at various times.

50. Anónimo, *Noticias sobre el Río de la Plata,* Motivos a Escribir, y Capitulo 1.

51. The narrative is titled, *Noticia para el arreglo de los campos de Buenos Aires y Montevideo* (Information for the Improvement of the Buenos Aires and Montevideo Countrysides)." Anónimo, *Noticias sobre el Río de la Plata,* 43.

52. Anónimo, *Noticias sobre el Río de la Plata,* 51 and 90 passim.

53. Ibid., 91.

54. Ibid., 70–71.

55. Viana (1760–1820) was the son of Francisco Viana, who governed Montevideo in the 1750s and 1760s. His family remained very influential in Montevideo in subsequent decades.

56. Francisco Javier de Viana, *Diarios de viaje* (Montevideo: Biblioteca Artigas, 1958), 36–39.

57. Ibid., 13.

58. Ibid., 25.

59. Ibid., 26–34.

60. Ibid.,, 23.

61. Real Academia de la Historia, Colección de La Mata Linares CVLLL.

62. Azara, *Memoria,* 11, 13, 15, 30 passim.

63. Large portions of the text are dedicated to descriptions of the Paraguay province, north of Buenos Aires.

64. Azara, *Memoria,* 12.

65. Ibid., 5–6.

66. Ibid., 6.

67. William Gregory, *A Visible Display of Divine Providence* (London, 1802); John Carter Brown Library, Thomas Kinder, *The Kinder Manuscript* (1808–10).

68. Gregory, *A Visible Display,* 175.

69. Ibid., 175, 176.

70. John Carter Brown Library, Kinder, 83, 84.

71. Ibid., 98.

72. Johnson, *Workshop of Revolution,* 169–271. Elío gave the order to rescue Martin de Alzaga and other conspirators from Patagones.

73. John Carter Brown Library, "Proclama. Del excelentisimo señor don Xavier Elio Mariscal de Campo de los Reales Exercitos, Virrey, Gobernador, y Capitan General de las Provincias del Rio de la Plata, etc. etc," 1811.

74. John Carter Brown Library, B81 A692c V.2, Gaspar Vigodet, 1810; Jose Artigas, 1811.

75. These opposing proclamations show a lack of unity and the plurality of ideas and projects linked to the notion of *orientalidad.* Although not homogeneous, the existence of a regional identity connected to the territory was indisputable. For the political implications of the term *orientales,* see Frega, *Soberanía y revolución.* Frega argues that after 1816 the term *orientales* was associated with Artiguismo.

76. Larrañaga, *Diario del viaje de Montevideo a Paysandu,* 21.

77. Ibid., 19, 39, 43.

78. Ibid., 63, 79–85.

79. This situation lasted until 1825, when a group of caudillos entered the region from Buenos Aires to liberate it from Brazilian rule.

80. For the alliance between the Portuguese and the British, see Alan Manchester, *The British Preeminence in Brazil* (New York: Octagon Publishers, 1972); and Peter Winn, *Inglaterra y la tierra purpurea* (Montevideo: EBO, 2000).

81. R. A. Humpheys, ed., *British Consular Reports on the Trade and Politics of Latin America, 1824–1826* (London: Offices of the Royal Historical Society, 1940); Luccock, *Notes on Rio de Janeiro and the Southern Parts of Brazil.*

CHAPTER 6. TRAVERSING EMPIRES

1. For a review of this trend, see the introduction to Mancke and Shammas, *The Creation of the British Atlantic World*, 2–5. Regarding efforts to connect the history of different empires, see Peggy K. Liss, *Atlantic Empires: The Network of Trade and Revolution, 1713–1826* (Baltimore: Johns Hopkins University Press, 1983);

2. For the significance of networks and processes that unfolded beyond imperial borders, see the pioneering work of Charles Boxer, *Salvador de Sá e a luta pelo Brasil e Angola* (São Paulo: Editora Nacional, EDUSP, 1973). Recently, expanding the analysis into the Iberian Atlantic: Adelman, *Revolution and Sovereignty;* and, examining networks in the Portuguese Atlantic, James Sweet, *Domingos Alvares, African Healking, and the Intellectual History of the Atlantic World* (Chapel Hill: University of North Carolina Press, 2011).

3. For a discussion of regional colonial identity formation in this context, see Anthony Pagden and Nicholas P. Canny, eds., *Colonial Identity in the Atlantic World, 1500–1800* (Princeton: Princeton University Press, 1987); and João Fragoso, "A nobreza da República: notas sobre a formação da primeira elite senhorial do Rio de Janeiro (séculos XVI e XVII)," in *Topói, Revista de História* 1 (2000):45–122.

4. For a discussion of the importance of networks in peripheral areas, see Giovanni Levi, *A herança imaterial: Trajetória de um exorcista no Piemonte do século XVII* (Rio de Janeiro: Civilização Brasileira, 2000); Zacarías Moutoukias, "Las formas complejas de la acción politica: justicia corporativa, faccionalismo y redes sociales (Buenos Aires 1750–1760)," *Jarbuch für Geschichte Lateinamerikas* 39 (2002): 69–102; Imízcoz, ed., *Casa, familia y sociedad;*; and Bertrand, "De la familia a la red de sociabilidad."

5. For the increasing dependence of Portugal and Spain in relation to Britain and France, see Stein and Stein, *Trade and War,* 120–41; and H. E. S. Fisher, *The Portugal Trade: A Study of Anglo Portuguese Commerce* Repr. New York: Routledge, 2006.30–42.

6. Dauril Alden, "The Undeclared War of 1773–1777: Climax of Luso-Spanish Platine Rivalry," *Hispanic American Historical Review* 41, no. 1 (Feb. 1961): 55–74.

7. Prado, *A Colônia do Sacramento,*191–93.

8. For more information on the impact of Bourbon reforms on the Spanish administrative system in Río de la Plata, see Socolow, *The Bureaucrats of Buenos Aires;* and John Lynch, *Spanish Colonial Administration, 1782–1810: The Intendant System in the Viceroyalty of the Río de la Plata* (New York: Greenwood Press, 1969).

9. Vicente Osvaldo Cutolo, *Nuevo diccionario biográfico argentino.* (Buenos Aires: Editorial Elche, 1975), 520.

10. Bentancur, *Don Cipriano de Melo,* 9–12; Cutolo, *Nuevo diccionario,* 520–21.

11. Termo de Asentada, Colônia do Sacramento, 19 Feb. 1776, Biblioteca Nacional Lisboa (hereafter cited as BNL), Manuscritos Pombalinos, Cod. 10855.

12. Cutolo, *Nuevo diccionario,* 520–21.

13. Ibid.

14. Termo de Asentada, Colônia do Sacramento, 19 Feb. 1776. BNL, Manuscritos Pombalinos, Cod. 10855.

15. Lista das Letras que se passaram sobre a thezouraria Geral do Erario da Cap. do Rio de Janeiro (hereafter Lista das Letras), Colônia do Sacramento, 8 June 1776. BNL, Manuscritos Pombalinos, Cod. 10855,

16. Cartas do Governador Francisco José da Rocha, Colônia do Sacramento, 8 Feb. 1776. BNL, Manuscritos Pombalinos, Cod. 10855.

17. Francisco Antonio Maciel a Francisco Jose de Luzena. Montevideo, 12 Nov. 1783, AGI, Buenos Aires Gobierno, Leg. 333. See also João Fragoso, *Homens de Grossa Ventura: Acumulação e hierarquia na praça mercantil do Rio de Janeiro, 1790-1830* (Rio de Janeiro: Civilização Brasileira, 1992), 319–32.

18. Representacion de Don Manuel Cipriano de Melo para que se declare se debe ser considerado extranjero o sudito de SMC y goce de los fueros apropriados (hereafter Representacion de Don Manuel Cipriano de Melo). AGI, Buenos Aires Gobierno, Leg. 311, 1783.

19. Representacion de Don Manuel Cipriano de Melo. AGI, Buenos Aires Gobierno, Leg. 311, 1783. Expediente del Virrey Marques de Loreto con el Intendente de Buenos Aires Francisco Paula Sanz sobre el Arreglo de los Campos de Montevideo. AGI, Buenos Aires Gobierno, Leg. 333, 1786.

20. Francisco Antonio Maciel a Luis de Vasconcelos, Rio de Janeiro, 30 March, 1780, AHU, Rio de Janeiro, D. 9294. For a comprehensive analysis of contraband trade in Rio de Janeiro, see Pijning, "Controlling Contraband," 148–82.

21. Luís de Vasconcelos e Sousa ao Martinho de Melo e Castro, Rio de Janeiro, 12 July, 1781, AHU, Rio de Janerio, doc. 9561; and Representacion de Don Manuel Cipriano de Melo, AGI, Buenos Aires Gobierno, Leg 311, 1783. Brás Carneiro Leão had been involved in trade with Colônia do Sacramento in the past and had declared to the Spanish Crown that he owed money to Cipriano de Melo.

22. Autos Seguidos entre Dn. Manuel Perez y Dn. Miguel Josef de Fleitas sobre anular la venta de unos esclavos que el segundo hizo al primero, 1794, AGN, Montevideo, Escribanía de Gobierno y Hacienda (hereinafter EGH), caja 22, exp. 38. The pilots were Miguel de Fleitas, Antonio João da Cunha, and Leonardo Perdigão. Miguel de Fleitas and Cipriano de Melo severed their partnership during this case.

23. Autos Formados por la Prision del Portugues Juan de Acuña, AGI, Buenos Aires Gobierno, Leg. 333, 1785; Francisco de Paula Sanz, Buenos Aires, 6 Oct. 1784, AGI, Buenos Aires Gobierno, Leg. 333.

24. Apoland, *Génesis de la familia uruguaya: Los habitantes de Montevideo en sus primeros 40 años, filiaciones, ascendencias, entronques, descendencias* (Montevideo: n.p., 1975), 931–40.

25. For more details about the Alzaybar family and their influence in early Montevideo, see Fabricio Prado, "In the Shadows of Empires: Trans-Imperial Networks and Colonial Identity in Bourbon Río de la Plata" (PhD diss., Emory University, 2009), chap. 3.

26. Apoland, *Génesis de la familia uruguaya*, 931–33.

27. A saladero was an estate for the production of dried meat through the process of dehydration with salt. Turning meat into *tasajo* or *charque* extended the shelf life of the meat and offered a cheap protein diet to slaves in plantation areas. Bentancur, *Cipriano de Melo*, 20–25. As reported in Medina's probate records, Cipriano de Melo had credits of more than 2,000 pesos.

28. Apoland, *Génesis de la familia uruguaya*, 935–37, 967.

29. Autos Formados por la Prision del portugues Juan de Acuña, AGI, Buenos Aires Gobierno, Leg. 333, 1785.

30. Ibid.

31. The group identified as "monopolist" merchants is the group that has traditionally operated within the monopolistic system centered on the Cádiz–Río de la Plata axis. For a fuller analysis of the merchants of Buenos Aires, see Socolow, *Los mercaderes de Buenos Aires virreinal;* and Viviana L. Grieco, "Politics and Public Credit: The Limits of Absolutism in Late Colonial Buenos Aires" (PhD diss., Emory University, 2005).

32. Autos Formados por la Prision del Portugues Juan de Acuña, AGI, Buenos Aires Gobierno, Leg. 333, 1785.

33. For the bureaucracy in Río de la Plata, see Socolow, *The Bureaucrats of Buenos Aires.*

34. Autos Formados por la Prision del Portugues Juan de Acuña, AGI, Buenos Aires Gobierno, Leg. 333, 1785. Juan de Acuña, or João da Cunha in Portuguese, was know as "capitán Barriga" (Captain Belly) among Montevideo's mercantile circles.

35. Ibid.

36. Ibid. The operations involved the purchasing of slaves, sugar, tobacco, furniture, textiles and clothing. The values mentioned in individual receipts were 30,000 pesos, 1,400 pesos, 13,000 pesos, and 7,000 pesos.

37. Autos Formados por la Prision del Portugues Juan de Acuña, AGI, Buenos Aires Gobierno, Leg. 333, 1785.

38. Ibid.

39. Ibid.

40. AGI, Buenos Aires Gobierno, Leg. 311, Representación de Manuel Cipriano de Melo.

41. Ibid.

42. Parecer sobre pedido de Francisco Mendes Ribeyro para pasar al Rio de Geneiro, Buenos Aires, 24 May 1785. AGI, Buenos Aires Gobierno, Leg. 333. In addition to the case of Cipriano de Melo, Sanz cited the case of Francisco Mendez Ribeyro, a Portuguese man living in Buenos Aires, who had his request denied to import from Rio de Janeiro an inheritance from a deceased brother.

43. AGN, Sala IX, 33.4.5, Hacienda, exp. 41; AGN, Sala IX, 31.16.6, Justicia, 1791.

44. AGN, Sala IX, 31.16.6, Justicia, 1791. Rl. Orden que Remitan los Documentos relativos a la defensa de Dn. Man. Cipriano de Melo 2º. Comandte. de los Resguardos y de Dn. Manuel Diago.

45. Archivo Judicial, Uruguay, Cj. 203, Civil 1, 1821, Probate records of Ana Joaquina da Silva. I thank Alex Borucki for providing the reference for this record.

46. AGI, Indiferente General, Leg. 2466, 1799, Statement signed by Marques de Aviles.

47. AGNM, EGH, Cj. 34, Auto de Embarcación, Montevideo, 20 Feb. 1797, 18 Feb. 1797, 14 Dec. 1799; EGH, Cj. 40, Auto de Embarcación, Montevideo, 19 Dec. 1799, 23 Nov. 1799; EGH, Cj. 18, Auto de Embarcación, Montevideo, 13 Mar. 1793.

48. AGN, Montevideo, *Actas y Acuerdos del Consulado de Montevideo.*

49. Bentancur, *El puerto colonial*, 1:176; AGN, Montevideo, *Libro de Fianzas y Protocolizaciones.*

50. AGNM, Escribanía de Gobierno y Hacienda, Auto de Embarcación, Cj. 18, 9 May 1792.

51. Gil, "Infiéis transgressores."

52. Juez de Arribadas, AGNM, EGH, Cj. 25, exp. 89, 1794.

53. Dna. Maria del Carmen vs. Dn. Miguel de Fleytas, Montevideo, 19 Sept. 1794, AGNM, Escribanía de Gobierno y Hacienda, Cj. 22. In this case, Cipriano de Melo testified against Miguel de Fleytas, who worked for Tomás Antonio Romero. Decomiso de Pedro Duval, Casimiro Necochea, Miguel Josef Fleytas, et al., Montevideo, 22 Feb. 22, 1800, AGNM, Escribanía de Gobierno y Hacienda, caja 46.

54. Grieco, "Politics and Public Credit."

55. Statement signed by Jose de Maria, Buenos Aires, 1798. AGI, Buenos Aires Gobierno, Leg. 346. The merchant defends trade with neutrals but argues against the primacy of Montevideo.

56. "Representación del Real Consulado contra el Comercio de Frutos de esta Provincia con las Colonia Estranjeras," AGI, Buenos Aires Gobierno, Leg. 346, 1797.

57. Ibid.

58. Ibid.

59. *"malos y infieles servidores."* Statement signed by Pedro Duval, Buenos Aires, 30 Apr. 1798, AGI, Buenos Aires Gobierno, Leg. 346.

60. Representación del Real Consulado contra el Comercio de Frutos de esta Provincia con las Colonia Estranjeras, AGI, Buenos Aires Gobierno, Leg. 346. Statement signed by Pedro Duval, Buenos Aires, 30 Apr. 1798, AGI, Buenos Aires Gobierno, Leg. 346.

61. Representación del Real Consulado contra el Comercio de Frutos de esta Provincia con las Colonia Estranjeras, AGI, Buenos Aires Gobierno, Leg. 346.

62. Ibid.

63. Ibid.

64. Hugo Raúl Galmarini also reports that the conflict between monopolist and nonmonopolist merchants in the Consulado de Comercio also affected the people on the streets of Buenos Aires. These examples show that in late colonial Río de la Plata, social factions were composed of individuals of different classes and social status. Hugo Raúl Galmarini, *Los negocios del poder: Reforma y crisis del estado, 1776–1826* (Buenos Aires: Corregidor, 2000), 53.

65. Representación del Real Consulado contra el Comercio de Frutos de esta Provincia con las Colonia Estranjeras, AGI, Buenos Aires Gobierno, Leg. 346.

66. Diogo de Souza a Manuel Cipriano de Melo, Porto Alegre, 1810, Arquivo Histórico do Rio Grande do Sul, A1.06; Diogo de Souza a Manuel Cipriano de Melo, Porto Alegre, 1810, Arquivo Histórico do Rio Grande do Sul, A1.02.

67. Bentancur, *Don Cipriano de Melo*, 126–27. Cipriano de Melo's house actually is located in the Ciudad Vieja of Montevideo and currently serves as the Museo Casa de Lavalleja.

CHAPTER 7. POSTPONING THE REVOLUTION

1. John Fisher, "Commerce and Imperial Decline"; Lynch, *Latin American Revolutions;* and, to a lesser extent, Elliot, *Empires of the Atlantic World.*

2. For other interpretations of the meanings of royalism, see Marcela Echeverri, "Popular Royalists, Empire and Politics in Southwestern New Granada," *Hispanic American Historical Review* 91, no. 2 (2011): 237–69. For broader theoretical considerations on Iberian monarchies and the role of colonial subjects in distant geographies of empire, see Cardim et al., *Polycentric Monarchies.*

3. Bentancur. *El puerto colonial,* 2:15–16.

4. Aurora Capilla de Castellanos, *Historia del consulado de Montevideo* (Montevideo: Museo Historico Nacional, 1962), 1:67–69.

5. JCB, Documentos 1807-9, B81 A692c V.1 1-Size, Observaciones de los Recientes Acontecimentos en Montevideo, Anonymous, ca. 1810. The anonymous writer from Buenos Aires refers to Montevidean merchants as "!Reptiles de la sociedad!" On a less dramatic note: John Mawe, *Voyage in the Interior of Brazil, particularly in the Gold and Diamond Districts of that Country, by Authority of*

the Prince Regent of Portugal, Including a Voyage to the Río de la Plata, and a Historical Sketch of the Revolucion of Buenos Ayres (London: Longman, Hurst, Rees, Orme and Brown, Paternoster-Row, 1812), 40–53. Mawe also mentions a large number of former British soldiers who took up residence in Montevideo after swearing loyalty to the king of Spain. These former British subjects were easy to recognize as they were still wearing British military uniforms.

6. John Street, *Artigas and the Emancipation of Uruguay* (Cambridge: Cambridge University Press, 1959), 53–62.

7. Bentancur, *El puerto colonial,* 2:17. Among the merchants who supplied funds for the defense of Río de la Plata were Francisco Antonio Maciel, Matteo Magariños, Juan Francisco de Zuñiga, Jose Battle y Carrio, and Miguel Antonio Vilardebo.

8. Bentancur, *El puerto colonial,* 2:17–18.

9. The representatives to the cabildo abierto were Juan Francisco Garcia de Zuñiga, José Manuel Perez Castellano (Guardian del Convento de San Francisco), Francisco Xavier Carvallo, Matteo Magariños, Joaquin de Chopitea, Manuel Diago, Ildefonso Garcia, Jaime Ylla, Crival Salvañach, José Antonio Zubillaga, Matteo Gallego, José Cardoso, Antonio Pereyra, Antonio de San Vicente, Rafael Fernandez, Juan Ignacio Martinez, Miguel Vilardebó, Juan Manuel de la Serna, and Manuel Tejidor.

10. Baltasar Hidalgo de Cisneros took office as viceroy of Río de la Plata in 1809.

11. John Carter Brown Library, B81 A692c V.1 1-Size—REGLAMENTO Formado por la Junta de Comercio de Montevideo Sobre El Metodo y Formalidades que Deben Observarse en las Expediciones Procedentes de Extrangeros aprobado por el Superior Gobierno. 1811.

12. Ibid.

13. Data regarding port of origin are not available for all records.

14. "Apresentación," *Gazeta de Montevideo* (1810; repr. Montevideo: Biblioteca de Impresos Raros Americanos, 1954), vol. 1.

15. Arthur P. Whitaker, *The United States and the Independence of Latin America, 1800–1830* (New York: Norton, 1964), 1–20, 50–57, 119–20. For a detailed account of U.S.-Peninsular trade in flour, see Edward Pompeian, "Spirited Enterprises: Venezuela, the United States, and the Independence of Spanish America, 1789–1823" (PhD diss., College of William and Mary, 2012).

16. AGNM, EHG Cj. 107, exp. 73 and 93, 1812. JCB, BUENOS AYRES 1810–19, B81 A962c V.2. 1-Size, Proclama, Virrey Vigodet, Montevideo, 1811.

17. AGNM, Libro de Entradas 95.

18. John Carter Brown Library, Kinder, *Kinder Manuscript.*

19. The Liga Federal, the political project led by José Artigas, comprised a federation of provinces including the Banda Oriental, Corrientes, Córdoba, Santa Fe, and Entre Rios.

20. The Directorio of the United Provinces accepted the Portuguese intervention against Artigas conditioned on the recognition of the United Provinces, Paraguay, and Santa Fe. For the juridical aspects of the invasion, see Ana Frega, "Cidadania e representação em tempos revolucionários: A banda/província oriental, 1810–1820," in *Perspectivas da cidadania no Brasil Império*, ed. José Murilo de Carvalho and Adriana Campos (Rio de Janeiro: Civilização Brasiliera, 2011), 66.

21. For a detailed analysis of the Spanish monarchical plans and conspiracies to reconquer Río de la Plata and Montevideo, see Frega, "Alianzas y proyectos independentistas en los inicios del 'Estado Cisplatino,'" 20–21.

22. Frega, *Revolución e soberanía*, Introduction.

23. For more information on the radical program of land redistribution and concession of property titles, see Frega, *Revolución e soberanía*, 272–78.

24. Ibid., 272.

25. Frega, *Revolución y soberanía*, 273.

26. "Instrucciones," in Pivel Devoto, *El Congreso Cisplatino (1821)* (Montevideo, Imprenta "El Siglo ilustrado," 1937), 343, 344. The other articles included religion, bureaucratic administration, security in the countryside, and promotion of general happiness.

27. AGNM, Herrera, Comentario Acerca de los Limites de la Provincia de Montevideo e la Capitania de Rio Grande, 1820.

28. Devoto, *El Congreso Cisplatino (1821)*. Autorización a Bianqui y Larrañaga, Montevideo, 31 Jan. 1817, pp. 341, 342.

29. Ana Frega, "Cidadania e representação em tempos revolucionários," 59–86.

30. Ibid., 76. Also, the province was to keep its legal and political autonomy while part of the United Kingdom of Brazil, Portugal, and Algarve.

31. Alvaro Caso Bello, "The Language of Patriotism" (Paper presented at the Fifth Rio de la Plata Seminar, Williamsburg, 2014), 8.

32. Johnson, *Workshop of Revolution*, 1–15.

33. Gabriel Di Meglio, *Viva el bajo pueblo* (Buenos Aires: Prometeo Libros), 3–22.

34. In the last decades of the colonial period in the Banda Oriental, elections for regidores, alcaldes, and síndico procuradores tended to endorse the social status already acquired by individuals within the community. Frega, *Revolución y sobranía*, 58.

35. *Gazeta de Buenos Aires*, 5 June 1816. Although the polemic appeared in the *Gazeta de Buenos Aires*, the issues discussed included political agents and pueblos of all Río de la Plata provinces, including Buenos Aires, the Banda Oriental, Santa Fe, and Corrientes. Therefore, this debate represented the political challenges and instabilities unfolding in the region as a whole.

36. *Gazeta de Buenos Aires*, 16 June 1816.

37. Ibid., 5 July 1816.

38. Ibid., 12 Jan. 1820. "Se les guardaran a los pueblos del distrito todos sus fueros y privilegios."

39. The most prominent caudillo to join the Luso-Brazilian project was Fructuoso Rivera. Former Artigas leaders Fernando Otorgues and Juan Lavalleja were imprisoned in Rio de Janeiro. Although the Luso-Brazilian occupation had prevailed, opposition to the project within the Banda Oriental remained.

40. Arquivo Histórico do Itamaraty, Invasão e Anexação da Banda Oriental, Lata 194, Maços 1 and 2, 1816–21.

41. Ibid.

42. Devoto, *El Congreso Cisplatino*, 341–57.

43. John Carter Brown Library, *Gazeta de Buenos Aires*, 10 Mar. 1820.

44. José Pedro Barrán, Ana Frega, and Monica Nicoliello, *El cónsul británico en Montevideo y la independencia del Uruguay: Selección de los informes de Thomas Samuel Hood (1824–1829)* (Montevideo: Facultad de Humanidades, 1999), 76.

45. Rhode Island Historical Society, Traders Book, 151–71, Rio de Janeiro, 1810.

46. Frega, *Historia regional e independencia del Uruguay*, 19–23.

47. AGNM, Aduana, Libro de Entradas, 99.

48. AGNM, Lucas Obes, Cj. 16, Carp. 2, Nicolas de Herrera a Lucas Obes, 10 Aug. 1822.

49. Ibid., 28 Oct. 1822.

Archive Abbreviations

AGI	Archivo General de Indias, Seville
AGN	Archivo General de la Nación, Buenos Aires, Argentina
AGNM	Archivo General de la Nación, Montevideo, Uruguay
AH Itamaraty	Arquivo Histórico do Itamaraty, Rio de Janeiro
AHCMPA	Arquivo Histórico da Curia Metropolitana de Porto Alegre
AHCMRJ	Arquivo Histórico da Curia Metropolitana do Rio de Janeiro
AHRGS	Arquivo Histórico do Rio Grande do Sul
AHU	Arquivo Histórico Ultramarino, Projeto Resgate Barão do Rio Branco
AJ	Archivo Historico Judicial, Montevideo, Uruguay
AN	Arquivo Nacional, Rio de Janeiro, Brazil
ARCS	Archivo Regional de Colonia del Sacramento
BN	Biblioteca Nacional de Lisboa, Lisbon, Portugal
JCB	John Carter Brown Library, Providence, RI
IANTT	Arquivo Nacional da Torre do Tombo, Lisbon
LL	Lilly Library, Bloomington, IN
RAH	Real Academia de la Historia, Madrid, Spain
RBM	Real Biblioteca, Madrid
RIHS	Rhode Island Historical Society, Providence, RI

Bibliography

MANUSCRIPT PRIMARY SOURCES

Archivo General de Indias

Buenos Aires Gobierno—Legajos 31, 141, 311, 333, 346

Archivo General de la Nación—Buenos Aires

Sala IX, Legajos 1.2.5, 2.1.4, 2.2.3, 2.4.1, 2.7.5, 2.8.1, 3.1.2, 3.2.1, 3.8.2, 4.3.1,
    8.10.2, 8.10.3, 8.10.4, 8.10.8, 8.10.16,15.1.8, 24.7.8, 25.1.8, 25.5.6, 33.4.5,
    39.7.3,31.16.6
Sala IX—Serie Montevideo—Legajos 3.2.4 to 3.7.10

Archivo General de la Nación—Montevideo

AGA—Actas y Acuerdo del Consulado de Comercio de Montevideo, 1794
AGA Libro 44—Fidelidad de los Portugueses, 1801
AGA Libros Aduana 95, 96, 99
AGA Cajas 2, 92
AGA Caja 20, 1807, Padron de Estranjeros
AGA Libro de Fianzas del Puerto de Montevideo
AGA Protocolos de Marina—Fianzas y Protocolizaciones, 1805–1809

Colección Falcao Espalter
EGH Cajas 2, 15, 18 ,22, 23, 24, 27, 28, 31, 32, 34, 40, 41, 45, 46, 48, 54, 55, 56,
    79, 207
Ex-Museo Histórico Caja 4
Particulares Lucas Obes Cajas 15, 16.16
Particulares Martín de Alzaga Caja 332

Arquivo Histórico do Itamaraty

Lata 188 Maço 1
Lata 194 Maços 1, 2 (1816–21)

Arquivo Histórico da Curia Metropolitana de Porto Alegre

Rol dos Confessados de Viamão, 1756

Arquivo Histórico da Curia Metropolitana do Rio de Janeiro

Colônia do Sacramento—Livro 3º. Batismos
Colônia do Sacramento—Livro 5º. Batismos
Colônia do Sacramento—Livro 3º. Óbitos

Arquivo Histórico Ultramarino, Lisboa

Colônia do Sacramento, Documentos: 27, 47, 49, 56, 86, 106, 107, 196, 408, 409,
    513
Rio de Janeiro, Documentos: 7286, 9028, 9294 ,9294 ,9326, 9561, 9567, 9622,
    9772, 9859, 9932, 10052, 10056, 10215, 10532, 10607, 11714, 12265, 12655,
    12729, 12895, 13319, 13396, 13397, 13399, 13405, 13406, 13408, 13413,
    13415, 13418, 13419, 13421, 13422, 13436, 13437, 13438, 13441, 13446, 13452,
    13458, 13462, 13470, 14058, 14099, 14121, 14500, 14506, 14511, 15946, 15953,
    15958, 15959, 16130, 16233, 16268, 16541, 16824, 18013

Archivo Nacional de la Nación, Judiciales—Uruguay

Caja 203

Arquivo Nacional—Brazil

Cx 492 Pc 02

Archivo Histórico de la Catedral de Montevideo

Livro de Bautizmos años 1777–98

Arquivo Histórico do Rio Grande do Sul

A1.02. 1810
A1.06. 1810

John Carter Brown Library

B81 A962c V.1 1-Size
B81 A962c V.2. 1-Size
Gazeta de Buenos Aires

Biblioteca Nacional, Lisboa

Manuscritos Época Pompalina, Códice 10855

Hispanic Society of America

Journal and Logbook of an Anonymous Scotch Sailor. New York. HC 363–1299.
    1726–28

Instituto Arquivos Nacionais—Torre do Tombo

MNE Caixas 427–46, 455–58, 915
MNE Livros 132,134,133, 199, 622, 642
MNEJ Maços 48, 60, 63, 67, 73
Papéis do Brasil—Codices 1, 14

Real Academia de la Historia, Madrid

Colección de La Mata Linares CVLLL

Real Biblioteca de Madrid

II/2825, 13. *Discursos sobre el Comercio Legitimo de Buenos Aires con la
    España, el Clandestino de la Colônia del Sacramento: Medios de Embarazo
    en la mayor parte y poner cubierto de enemigos aquella provincia*, 1766.

PRINTED PRIMARY SOURCES

Abreu, Cristovão Pereira de. "3ª. Pratica—Notícia dada pelo Coronel Cristovão
    Pereira de Abreu, sobre o mesmo Caminho ao R. P. Me. Diogo Soares" (1731).
    Revista do Instituto Histórico e Geográfico Brasileiro 69, no. 1 (1908). Rio de
    Janeiro.

Alzaga, Enrique Martin de. *Cartas (1806–1807)*. Buenos Aires: Emece, 1972.

Anónimo. *Notícias sobre el Río de la Plata*. Madrid: Historia 16, 1988.

Anónimo. *Razões dos lavradores do vice-reinado de Buenos Ayres para a franqueza do comércio com os inglezes contra a representação de alguns comerciantes e resolução do governo com appendice de observações dos efeitos do novo regulamento nos interesses comerciais do Brazil*. Trans. José da Silva Lisboa. Rio de Janeiro: Impressão Régia, 1810. John Carter Brown Library C810, R278d.

Azara, Felix de. *Memoria sobre el estado rural del Río de la Plata*. Buenos Aires: Editorial Bajel, 1943.

Barrán, José Pedro, Ana Frega, and Monica Nicoliello. *El cónsul británico en Montevideo y la independencia del Uruguay: Selección de los informes de Thomas Samuel Hood (1824–1829)*. Montevideo: Facultad de Humanidades, 1999.

Beaumont, J.A.B. *Viajes por Buenos Aires, Entre Ríos y la Banda Oriental, 1826–27*. Buenos Aires: Hachette, 1957.

Cabral, Sebastião da Veiga. *Historia corographica da Colônia do Sacramento* [1711].

Cosme Bueno, Bartolomé. *El Aragones Cosme Bueno y la Descripción Geográfica del Río de la Plata, 1768–1776*. Huesca: Instituto de Estudios Altoaragoneses, 1996.

Documentos para la Historia argentina. Vol. 12. Buenos Aires: Facultad de Filosofía y Letras de la UBA, 1919.

Gazeta de Montevideo. "Apresentación." Vol. 1. Repr. Montevideo: Biblioteca de Impresos Raros Americanos, 1954.

Gregory, William. *A Visible Display of Divine Providence*. London, 1802.

Larrañaga, Damaso. *Diario del viaje de Montevideo a Paysandu*. Montevideo: Instituto Nacional del Libro, 1994.

Lisanti Filho, Luis. *Negócios coloniais*. Rio de Janeiro: Casa da Moeda, 1973.

London Times. Col B, 4 Aug. 1800.

Mawe, John. *Voyage in the Interior of Brazil, particularly in the Gold and Diamond Districts of that Country, by Authority of the Prince Regent of Portugal, Including a Voyage to the Río de la Plata, and a Historical Sketch of the Revolución of Buenos Ayres*. London: Longman, Hurst, Rees, Orme and Brown, Paternoster-Row, 1812

Mesquita, Pedro Pereira. *Relación de la conquista de la colonia por don Pedro de Cevallos*. Buenos Aires: Municipalidade de la Ciudad de Buenos Aires, 1980.

Millau, Francisco. *Descripción de la provincia del Río de la Plata*. Buenos Aires and Mexico: Espasa Calpe, 1947.

Perez Castellanos, Jose Manuel. *Selección de escritos, 1787–1814*. Montevideo: Biblioteca Artigas, 1968.

Sá, Simão Pereira de. *História topográfica e bélica da nova Colônia do Sacramento do Rio da Prata, escrita por ordem do Governador e Capitão Geral do Rio de Janeiro em 1737 e 1777.* 1747; repr. Porto Alegre: Arcano 17, 1993.

Saint-Hilaire, Auguste de. *Viagem ao Rio Grande do Sul.* Brasília: Senado Federal, 2002.

Semanario de Agricultura Industria y Comercio. Buenos Aires: Junta de Historia Numismatica Americana, 1928–37.

Silva, Silvestre Ferreira da. *Relação do sítio da nova Colônia do Sacramento.* Porto Alegre: Arcano 17, [1748] 1977.

Viana, Francisco Javier de. *Diarios de Viaje.* Montevideo: Biblioteca Artigas, 1958.

Vidal, Emeric Essex. *Picturesque Illustrations of Buenos Ayres and Montevideo consisting of 24 views accompanied with description of the scenery.* London: Ackerman, 1820.

Voyages—Online Slave Trade Database. www.slavevoyages.org.

SECONDARY SOURCES

Abreu, Capistrano de. *Capítulos de história colonial, 1500–1800 & Os caminhos antigos e o povoamento do Brasil.* Brasília: Ed. Universidade de Brasília, 1982.

Adelman, Jeremy. *Sovereignty and Revolution in the Iberian Atlantic.* Princeton: Princeton University Press, 2006.

Aguirre, Luis. "Los Consulados de Comerciantes en la independencia de Hispanoamérica: El caso del Consulado de Montevideo, 1794–1838." Master's thesis, UNAM, 2014.

Alden, Dauril. "The Undeclared War of 1773–1777: Climax of Luso-Spanish Platine Rivalry." *Hispanic American Historical Review* 41, no. 1 (Feb. 1961): 55–74.

Almeida, Luis Ferrand de. *A Colônia do Sacramento a época de sucessão de Espanha: Anais do Simpósio Comemorativo do Bicentenário da Restauração do Rio Grande.* Rio de Janeiro: Instituto Histórico Geográfico Brasileiro, 1979.

Alzaga, Enrique Martín de. *Cartas.* Buenos Aires: Emece, 1972.

Anderson, Benedict. *Imagined Communities: Reflections on the Origin and Spread of Nationalism.* New York: Routledge, 1983.

Apoland, Juan Alejandro. *Génesis de la familia uruguaya: Los habitantes de Montevideo en sus primeros 40 años, filiaciones, ascendencias, entronques, descendencias.* Montevideo: n.p, 1975.

Arruda, José Jobson, "Decadence or Crisis in the Luso-Brazilian Empire: A New Model of Colonization in the Eighteenth Century." *Hispanic American Historical Review* 81, no. 3–4 (2000): 839–64.

Assadourian, Carlos Sempat. *El sistema de la economía colonial—mercado interno, regiones y espacio económico.* Lima: Instituto de Estudios Peruanos, 1982.

Azarola Gil, Luis E. *A Colônia do Sacramento, 1680–1828.* Montevideo: Casa Barrero y Ramos, 1940.

———. *La epopeya de Manuel Lobo.* Buenos Aires: Compañía Ibero Americana de Publicaciones, 1931.

Bailyn, Bernard. *Atlantic History.* Cambridge, MA: Harvard University Press, 2005.

Barbier, Jaques. *Reform and Politics in Bourbon Chile, 1775–1796.* Ottawa: University of Ottawa Press, 1980.

Barreneche, Oswaldo. *Crime and Administration of Justice in Buenos Aires.* Lincoln: University of Nebraska Press, 2006.

Barth, Fredrik. *Nomads of South Persia: The Basseri Tribe of the Khamseh Confederacy.* Boston: Little, Brown, 1961.

Bartlett, Robert. *The Making of Europe: Conquest, Colonization, and Cultural Change, 950–1350.* Princeton: Princeton University Press, 1993.

Bauza, Francisco. "A independência nacional." In *A questão da independência nacional,* ed. Pivel Devoto. Montevideo: Col. Clásicos Uruguaios, 1960.

Bentancur, Arturo Ariel. *Cipriano de Melo: Señor de fronteras.* Montevideo: ARCA, 1985.

———. *El puerto colonial de Montevideo.* Montevideo: Universidade de la República—FHCE, 1997.

Benton, Lauren. *A Search for Sovereignty.* Cambridge: Cambridge University Press, 2010.

Bertrand, Michel. "De la familia a la red de sociabilidad." *Revista Mexicana de Sociología* 61, no. 2 (Apr.–June 1999): 107–35.

Bhabha, Homi. "Of Mimicry and Man: The Ambivalence of Colonial Discourse." In *Colonialism in Question,* ed. Fredrick Cooper and Ann L. Stoler. Berkeley: University of California Press, 1997.

Blanco Acevedo, Pablo. *La dominación española en el Uruguay.* Montevideo: Barreiro y Ramos, 1944.

Boccara, Guillaume. "Etnogenesis Mapuche: Resistencia y restructuración entre los indígenas del Centro-Sur de Chile (siglos XVI–XVIII)." *Hispanic American Historical Review* 79, no. 3 (1999): 425–61.

Borucki, Alex. "From Shipmates to Soldiers: Emerging Black Identities in Montevideo, 1770–1850." PhD diss., Emory University, 2011.

———. "The Slave Trade in the Making of the Late-Colonial Rio de la Plata, 1786–1806." Paper presented at the annual meeting of the Social Science History Association, Chicago, 15–18 Nov. 2007.

———. "The Slave Trade to Río de la Plata, 1777–1812: Trans-Imperial Networks and Atlantic Warfare." *Colonial Latin American Review* 20, no. 1 (2011): 81–107.

Boschi, Caio. *Irmandades religiosas nas Minas setecentistas.* São Paulo: Atica. Coleção Brasiliana, 1986.

Boxer, Charles. *The Golden Age of Brazil.* Berkeley: University of California Press, in cooperation with the Sociedade de Estudos Históricos Dom Pedro Segundo, Rio de Janeiro, 1962.

———. *Salvador de Sá e a luta pelo Brasil e Angola.* São Paulo: Editora Nacional, EDUSP, 1973.

Brown, Peter. "Richard Vowell's Not So Imperial Eyes: Travel Writing and Adventure in 19th Century Hispanic Latin America." *Journal of Latin American Studies* 38 (2006): 95–122.

Buarque de Hollanda, Sergio. *Raizes do Brasil.* São Paulo: Cia das Letras, 1992.

Canabrava, Alice P. *O comércio português no Rio da Prata (1580–1640).* São Paulo: USP, [1942] 1984.

Canizares-Esguerra, Jorge. *Puritan Conquistadors.* Stanford, CA: Stanford University Press, 2006.

Canizares-Esguerra, Jorge, and Ben Breen. "Hybrid Atlantics: Future Directions for the History of the Atlantic World." *History Compass* 11, no. 8 (2013): 597–609, 10.1111/hic3.12051.

Capilla de Castellanos, Aurora. *Historia del consulado de Montevideo.* Vol. 1. Montevideo: Museo Historico Nacional, 1962.

Cardim, Pedro, Tamar Herzog, José Javier Ruiz Ibáñez, and Gaetano Sabatini, eds. *Polycentric Monarchies.* Sussex: Sussex Academic Press, 2012.

Cardim, Pedro, and Nuno Monteiro, eds. *Optima pars elites do antigo regime.* Lisbon: ICS, 2005.

Caso Bello, Alvaro. "The Language of Patriotism." Paper presented at the Fifth Rio de la Plata Seminar, Williamsburg, 2014.

Ceballos, Rodrigo. "Uma Buenos Aires lusitana: A presença portuguesa no Rio da Prata (séc. XVII)." *Mneme Revista de Humanidades* 9, no. 24 (2008): 1–16. www.cerescaico.ufrn.br/mneme/anais/st_suma_pg/st11.html.

Chasteen, John. *Heroes on Horseback.* Albuquerque: University of New Mexico Press, 1995.

Chiaramonte, Jose Carlos. "La cuestión iusnaturalista en los movimientos de independencia." *Boletín del Instituto de Historia Argentina y Americana Dr. Emilio Ravignani,* 3rd ser., no. 22 (2000): 33–71.

———. "Legalidad constitucional o caudillismo." *Desarollo Económico* 26, no. 102 (1986): 175–96.

———. *Mercaderes del Litoral: Economía y sociedad en la provincia de Corrientes, primera mitad del siglo XIX.* Buenos Aires: Fondo de Cultura Económica, 1991.

Clavero, Bartolomé Salvador. *Antidora, antropología católica de la economía moderna*. Milan: Giuffrè Editore, 1991.

Coates, Timothy J. *Convicts and Orphans: Forced and State-Sponsored Colonizers in the Portuguese Empire, 1550–1755*. Stanford, CA: Stanford University Press, 2001.

Cohen, Anthony. "Culture as Identity: An Anthropologist's View." *New Literary History* 24, no. 1 (Winter 1993): 195–209.

Cooney, Jerry W. "Neutral Vessels and Platine Slavers: Building a Viceregal Merchant Marine." *Journal of Latin American Studies* 18, no. 1 (May 1986): 25–39.

———. "Oceanic Commerce and Platine Merchants, 1796–1806: The Challenge of War." *The Americas* 45, no. 4 (April 1989): 509–24.

Cornblit, Oscar. *Power and Violence in the Colonial City*. Cambridge: Cambridge University Press, 1995.

Cortesão, Jaime. *Do tratado de Madri a conquista dos Sete Povos*. Rio de Janeiro: Biblioteca Nacional, Divisão de Publicações e Divulgação, 1969.

Craib, Raymond. *Cartographic Mexico: A History of State Fixations and Fugitive Landscapes*. Durham, NC: Duke University Press, 2004.

Crais, Clifton. "Custom and the Politics of Sovereignty in South Africa." *Journal of Social History* 39, no. 3 (2006): 721–40.

Crosby, Alfred. *The Ecological Imperialism*. Cambridge: Cambridge University Press, 2004.

Cutolo, Vicente Osvaldo. *Nuevo diccionario biográfico argentino*. Buenos Aires: Editorial Elche, 1975.

Degler, Carl. *Neither Black nor White: Slavery and Race Relations in Brazil and the United States*. New York: Cambridge University Press, 1995.

Devoto, Pivel. *El Congreso Cisplatino (1821)*. Montevideo: Imprenta "El Siglo ilustrado," 1937.

Di Meglio, Gabriel. *Viva el bajo pueblo*. Buenos Aires: Prometeo Libros, 2006.

Djenderedjian, Julio. "Roots of Revolution: Frontier Settlement Policy and the Emergence of New Spaces of Power in the Río de la Plata Borderlands, 1777—1810." *Hispanic American Historical Review* 88, no. 4 (Nov. 2008): 639–68.

Domingues, Moacyr. *Portugueses no Uruguai: São Carlos de Maldonado, 1764*. Porto Alegre: Edições EST, 1994.

Duara, Prasenjit. *Sovereignty and Authenticity: Manchukuo and the East Asian Modern*. New York: Rowman & Littlefield, 2003.

Echeverri, Marcela. "Popular Royalists, Empire and Politics in Southwestern New Granada." *Hispanic American Historical Review* 91, no. 2 (2011): 237–69.

Elbourne, Elizabeth. *Blood Ground: Colonialism, Missions, and the Contest for Christianity in the Cape Colony and Britain, 1799–1853*. McGill-Queen's

Studies in the History of Religion. Montreal: McGill-Queen's University Press, 2002.

———. "Indigenous Peoples and Imperial Networks in the Early Nineteenth Century: The Politics of Knowledge." In *Rediscovering the British World,* ed. Alfred Buckner and Douglas Francis. Calgary: University of Calgary Press, 2003.

———. "The Sin of the Settler." *Journal of Colonialism and Colonial History* 4, no. 3 (2003).

Elliott, John. "An Europe of Composite Monarchies." *Past & Present,* no. 137 (Nov. 1992): 48–71.

———. *Empires of the Atlantic World.* New Haven: Yale University Press, 2006.

Eltis, David. *Coerced and Free Migrations: Global Perspectives.* Stanford, CA: Stanford University Press, 2002.

Esherick, Joseph, Hasan Kayali, and Eric Van Young. *Empire to Nation: Historical Perspective on the Making of the Modern World.* New York: Rowman & Littlefield, 2006.

Fisher, H. E. S. *The Portugal Trade: A Study of Anglo Portuguese Commerce.* Repr. New York: Routledge, 2006.

Fisher, John. "Commerce and Imperial Decline: Spanish Trade with Spanish America 1797–1820." *Journal of Latin American Studies* 30 (1998): 459–79.

———. "The Imperial Response to 'Free Trade': Spanish Imports from Spanish America, 1778–1796." *Journal of Latin American Studies* 17, no. 1 (May 1985): 35–78.

Florentino, Manolo. *Em costas negras.* São Paulo: Companhia das Letras, 1997.

Flynn, Dennis Owen. *World Silver and Monetary History in the 16th and 17th Centuries.* Collected Studies. Aldershot: Variorum, 1996.

Fradkin, Raúl, and Jorge Gelman, eds. *Desafíos al orden: Política y sociedades rurales durante la Revolución de Independencia.* Rosario: Prohistoria Ediciones, 2008.

Fragoso, João Luís R. "Bandos e redes imperiais nas primeiras décadas do século XVIII." Conferência "À espera das frotas: Micro-história tapuia e a nobreza principal da terra (Rio de Janeiro, c. 1600—c. 1750)," apresentada no Concurso Público para Professor Titular de Teoria da História do Departamento de História da Universidade Federal do Rio de Janeiro, 2005. Unpublished.

———. *Homens de Grossa Ventura: Acumulação e hierarquia na praça mercantil do Rio de Janeiro, 1790-1830.* Rio de Janeiro: Civilização Brasileira, 1992.

———. "Nas rotas do império: Eixos mercantis, tráfico de escravos e relações sociais no mundo português." Seminário Internacional, Universidade Federal do Rio de Janeiro, Programa de Pós-Graduação em História Social, 2006.

———. "A nobreza da República: Notas sobre a formação da primeira elite senhorial do Rio de Janeiro (séculos XVI e XVII)." *Topói, Revista de História*, no. 1 (2000): 45–122.

———, ed. *Conquistadores e negociantes: História de elites no Antigo Regime nos trópicos*. Rio de Janeiro: Civilização Brasileira, 2007.

———. *Na trama das redes: politicas e negócios no Império Português séculos XVI ao XIX*. Rio de Janeiro: Civilização Brasileira, 2010.

Fragoso, João, and Manolo Florentino. *Arcaísmo como projeto: Mercado atlântico, sociedade agrária em uma economia colonial tardia—Rio de Janeiro c. 1790—c. 1840*. Rio de Janeiro: Civilização Brasileira, 2001.

Fragoso, João, Maria de Fátima Gouvea, and Maria Fernanda Bicalho, eds. *O antigo regime nos trópicos*. Rio de Janeiro: Civilização Brasileira, 2001.

Frega, Ana. "Alianzas y proyectos independentistas en los inicios del 'Estado Cisplatino." In *Historia regional e independencia del Uruguay*, ed. Ana Frega. Montevideo: EBO, 2009.

———. "Cidadania e representação em tempos revolucionários: A banda/ província oriental, 1810–1820." In *Perspectivas da cidadania no Brasil Império*, ed. José Murilo de Carvalho and Adriana Campos, 59–86. Rio de Janeiro: Civilização Brasiliera, 2011.

———. *Pueblos y soberanía en la revolución artiguista*. Montevideo: Ediciones de la Banda Oriental, 2007.

———. *Soberanía y revolución*. Montevideo: EBO, 2006.

Freyre, Gilberto. *Casa grande e senzala*. Rio de Janeiro: Editora Record, 2002.

Fuente, Ariel de la. *Children of Facundo*. Durham, NC: Duke University Press, 2000.

Gallagher John, and Ronald Robinson. "The Imperialism of the Free Trade" (1953). In *The Decline, Revival and Fall of the British Empire*, ed. John Gallagher and Anil Seal. Cambridge: Oxford University Press, 1982.

Galmarini, Hugo Raul. *Los negocios del poder: Reforma y crisis del estado, 1776–1826*. Buenos Aires: Corregidor, 2000.

Garavaglia, Juan Carlos. "Economic Growth and Regional Differentiations: The River Plate Region at the End of the Eighteenth Century." *Hispanic American Historical Review* 65, no. 1 (Feb. 1985): 51–89.

Gellner, Ernest. *Nações e nacionalismo*. Lisbon: Gradiva, 1993.

Gelman, Jorge. "Economía natural y economía monetaria: Los grupos dirigentes del Buenos Aires a principios del siglo XVII." *Anuario de Estudios Americanos* 44 (1987): 1–19.

———. *Estancieros y campesinos*. Buenos Aires: Libros del Riel, 1998.

———. *De Mercanchifle a gran comerciante*. La Rabida: Universidad Internacional de Andalucia, 1996.

Gil, Tiago. "Infieis transgresores." Master's thesis, PPG UFRJ, Rio de Janeiro, 2002.

————. "Sobre o comércio ilícito: A visão dos demarcadores de limites sobre o contrabando terrestre na fronteira entre os domínios lusos e espanhóis no Rio da Prata (1774–1801)." Paper presented at the II Jornadas de Historia Regional Comparada Porto Alegre, 12–15 Oct. 2005.

Ginzburg, Carlo. *Wooden Eyes: Nine Reflections on Distance*. New York: Columbia University Press, 2001.

Gonzalez Gimenez, Manuel. "Frontier and Settlement in Castile." In *Medieval Frontier Societies*, ed. Robert Barttlet and Angus Mackay. Oxford: Clarendon Press, 1989.

Goulão, Maria José. "La puerta falsa de América—Influência artística portuguesa no Rio da Prata colonial." PhD diss., Universidade de Coimbra, 2005.

Graham, Richard. *Independence in Latin America: A Comparative Approach*. Austin: University of Texas Press, 2013.

Greene, Jack P. *Negotiated Authorities: Essays in Colonial, Political, and Constitutional History*. Charlottesville: University of Virginia Press, 1994.

————. "Reformulando a identidade inglesa na América britânica colonial: Adaptação cultural e experiência provincial na construção das identidades corporativas." *Almanack Braziliense*, no. 4 (Nov. 2006): 5–36.

Grieco, Viviana. "Politics and Public Credit: The Limits of Absolutism in Late Colonial Buenos Aires." PhD diss., Emory University, 2005.

————. *The Politics of Giving*. Albuquerque: University of New Mexico Press, 2013.

Grinberg, Carla. *Os Judeus no Brasil*. Rio de Janeiro: Civilização Brasileira, 2005.

Grotius, Hugo, Richard Hakluyt, William Welwood, and David Armitage. *The Free Sea*. Natural Law and Enlightenment Classics. Indianapolis, IN: Liberty Fund, 2004.

Grotius, Hugo, and Richard Tuck. *The Rights of War and Peace*. Natural Law and Enlightenment Classics. Indianapolis, IN: Liberty Fund, 2005.

Gruzinsky, Serge. *Mestizo Mind*. New York: Routledge, 2002.

Guardino, Peter. *Peasants, Politics, and the Formation of Mexico's National State*. Stanford, CA: Stanford University Press, 1996.

Gutfreind, Ieda. *A historiografía rio-grandense*. Porto Alegre: Editora da Universidade/UFRGS, 1998.

Guy, Donna, and Thomas Sheridan, eds. *Contested Grounds*. Tucson: University of Arizona Press, 1998.

Hespanha, Antonio Manoel *As vésperas do Leviatã*. Lisbon: Almedina, 1994.

Hoberman, Louisa. *Mexico's Merchant Elite, 1590–1660: Silver, State, and Society*. Durham, NC: Duke University Press, 1991.

Hobsbawn, Eric. *Nações e nacionalismo desde 1780*. São Paulo: Paz e Terra, 1991.

Humpheys, R. A. *British Consular Reports on the Trade and Politics of Latin America, 1824–1826*. London: Offices of the Royal Historical Society, 1940.

Imízcoz, José María, ed. *Casa, familia y sociedad: País Vasco, España y América, siglos XV–XIX*. Bilbao: Servicio Editorial, Universidad del País Vasco = Euskal Herriko Unibertsitatea, Argitalpen Zerbitzua, 2004.

Irigoin, Alejandra, and Regina Grafe. "Bargaining for Absolutism: A Spanish Path to Nation-State and Empire Building." *Hispanic American Historical Review* 88, no. 2 (2008): 173–209.

Johnson, Alvin Saunders. "Commerce and War." *Political Science Quarterly* 29, no. 1 (Mar. 1914): 47–56.

Johnson, Lyman. *Workshop of Revolution*. Durham, NC: Duke University Press, 2011.

Johnson, Lyman, and Susan Socolow. "Población y espacio en el Buenos Aires del siglo XVIII." *Desarollo Económico* 20, no. 19 (1980): 329–49.

Jumar, Fernando. "Le commerce atlantique au Rio de la Plata." PhD diss., École des Hautes Études en Science Sociales, Paris, 2000.

———. "La región Río de la Plata y su complejo portuario durante el Antiguo Régimen." In *Historia de la provincia de Buenos Aires*, vol. 2, *De la Conquista a la crisis de 1820*, ed. Raúl O. Fradkin. Buenos Aires: UNIPE/EDHASA, 2012.

Kinsbruner, Jay. *Independence in Spanish America*. Albuquerque: University of New Mexico Press, 1994.

———. *Petty Capitalism in Spanish America: The Pulperos of Puebla, Mexico City, Caracas, and Buenos Aires*. Boulder, CO: Westview Press, 1987.

Klooster, Wim. *Illicit Riches: Dutch Trade in the Caribbean, 1648–1795*. Leiden: KITLV Press, 1998.

Komroff, Manuel. *Contemporaries of Marco Polo, consisting of the travel records to the eastern parts of the world of William of Rubruck (1253–1255), the journey of John of Pian de Capini (1245–1247), the journal of Friar Odoric (1318–1330) & the oriental travels of Rabb*. New York: Boni & Liveright, 1928.

Kraselski, Javier. "De las Juntas de Comercio al Consulado: Los comerciantes rioplatenses y sus estrategias corporativas, 1779–1794." *Anuario de Estudios Americanos*, 64, no. 2 (July–Sept. 2007): 145–70.

Krasner, Stephen. "Sovereignty." *Foreign Policy* 122 (2001): 20–29.

Kuhn, Fábio. "Clandestino e ilegal: O contrabando de escravos na Colônia do Sacramento 1740–1777." In *Escravidão e liberdade*, ed. Regina Xavier Lima. Porto Alegre: Alameda, 2010.

———. "Os comerciantes da Colônia do Sacramento e o tráfico de escravos para o Rio da Prata (1732–1777)." Paper presented at the Fifth Rio de la Plata Seminar, Williamsburg, 2014.

Langfur, Hal. *Forbidden Lands: Colonial Identity, Frontier Violence, and the Persistence of Brazil's Eastern Indians, 1750–1830*. Stanford, CA: Stanford University Press, 2006.

Larner, John. *Marco Polo and the Discovery of the World*. New Haven: Yale University Press, 1999.

Larranaga, Damaso. *Diario del viaje de Montevideo a Paysandu*. Montevideo: Instituto Nacional del Libro, 1994.

Levene, Ricardo. *Los origenes de la democracia: Argentina*. Buenos Aires: Librería Nacional, 1911.

Levi, Giovanni. *A herança imaterial: Trajetória de um exorcista no Piemonte do século XVII*. Rio de Janeiro: Civilização Brasileira, 2000.

Liss, Peggy K. *Atlantic Empires: The Network of Trade and Revolution, 1713-1826*. Baltimore: Johns Hopkins University Press, 1983.

Luccock, John. *Notes on Rio de Janeiro and the Southern Parts of Brazil: taken during a residence of ten years in that country from 1808 to 1818*. London: Samuel Leigh, 1820.

Lynch, John. "Intendants and Cabildos in the Viceroyalty of La Plata, 1782–1810." *Hispanic American Historical Review* 35, no. 3 (August 1955): 337–62.

———. *Latin American Revolutions, 1808-1826: Old and New World Origins*. Norman: University of Oklahoma Press, 1994.

———. *Spanish Colonial Administration: The Intendant System in the Viceroyalty of the Río de la Plata*. New York: Greenwood Press, 1979.

Mallon, Florencia. *Peasant and Nation*. Berkeley: University of California Press, 1995.

Manchester, Alan. *The British Preeminence in Brazil*. Oxford: Oxford University Press, 1933; repr. New York: Octagon, 1972.

Mancke, Elizabeth, and Carole Shammas, eds. *The Creation of the British Atlantic*. Baltimore: Johns Hopkins University Press, 2005.

Mayo, Carlos. *Puperos y pulperías en Buenos Aires*. Buenos Aires: Editorial Biblos, 2000.

Metcalf, Alida. *Family and Frontier in Colonial Brazil*. Berkeley: University of California Press, 1992.

———. *The Go-Betweens and the Colonization of Brazil*. Austin: University of Texas Press, 2005.

Monteiro, John M. *Negros da terra: Índios e bandeirantes nas origens de São Paulo*. São Paulo: Companhia das Letras, 1994.

Monteiro, Jonathas da Costa Rego. *A Colônia do Sacramento, 1680-1777*. 2 vols. Porto Alegre: Livrarias do Globo, 1937.

Moreno, Frank Jay. "The Spanish Colonial System: An Institutional Approach." *Western Political Quarterly* 20 (1967): 59–101.

Moutoukias, Zacarías. *Contrabando y control colonial en el siglo XVII: Buenos Aires, el Atlántico y el espacio peruano*. Bibliotecas Universitarias. Buenos Aires: Centro Editor de América Latina, 1988.

——. "Las formas complejas de la acción política: Justicia corporativa, faccionalismo y redes sociales (Buenos Aires, 1750–1760)." *Jarbuch für Geschichte Lateinamerikas* 39 (2002): 69–102.

——. "Redes personales y autoridad colonial." *Annales: Histoire, Sciences sociales* (May–June 1992): 889–915.

Neumann, Eduardo. "A fronteira tripartida: Índios, espanhóis e lusitanos na formação do Continente do Rio Grande." XXI Simpósio Nacional de História—ANPUH, Niterói, 2001.

——. *O trabalho guaraní misioneiro no Rio da Prata colonial, 1640–1750.* Porto Alegre: Martins Livreiro, 1996.

Novais, Fernando. *Portugal e Brasil na crise do antigo sistema colonial, 1777–1808.* São Paulo: Hucitec, 1986.

Offen, Karl. "Creating Mosquitia: Mapping Amerindian Spatial Practices in Eastern Central America, 1629-1779." *Journal of Historical Geography* 33 (2007): 254–82.

Ortiz, Fernando. *Cuban Counterpoints.* Lanham, MD: Lexington Books, 2005.

Osorio, Helen. "Estanceiros, lavradores e comerciantes na Constituição da Estremadura portuguesa na América: Rio Grande de São Pedro, 1737–1822." PhD diss., PPGHIS-UFF, Niterói, 1999.

Pagden, Anthony, and Nicholas Canny, eds. *Colonial Identity in the Atlantic World.* Princeton: Princeton University Press, 1987.

Paquette, Gabriel. "State and Civil Society Cooperation: The Intellectual and Political Activities of the Ultramarine *Consulados* and Economic Societies." *Journal of Latin American Studies* 39, no. 2 (May 2007): 263–98.

Paz, Gustavo. "Reporting Atlantic News." Paper presented at Emory University, 6 Jan. 2006.

Pearce, Adrian. *British Trade with Spanish America, 1763–1808.* Liverpool: Liverpool University Press, 2007.

Pedreira, Jorge Miguel Viana. "From Growth to Collapse: Portugal, Brazil, and the Breakdown of the Old Colonial System, 1750–1830." *Hispanic American Historical Review* 81, no. 3–4 (2000): 865–78.

Peregalli, Henrique. *O recrutamento no Brasil colonial.* São Paulo: UNICAMP, 1986.

Pesavento, Fábio. "Um pouco antes da Corte: A economia do Rio de Janeiro na segunda metade do setecentos." PhD diss., PPGE-UFF, Niterói, 2009.

Pierson, William, Jr. "Some Reflections on the Cabildo as an Institution." *Hispanic American Historical Review* 5, no. 4 (Nov. 1922): 573–96.

Pijning, Ernst. "Controlling Contraband: Mentality, Economy, and Society in Eighteenth-Century Rio de Janeiro." PhD diss., Johns Hopkins University, 1997.

——. "A New Interpretation of Contraband Trade." *Hispanic American Historical Review* 81, no. 3-4 (2001): 733–38.

Pike, Fredrick. "The Municipality and the System of Checks and Balances in Spanish American Colonial Administration." *The Americas* 15, no. 2 (1958): 139–58.

Polo, Marco. *The Travels of Marco Polo: With 25 illus. in full color from a 14th century MS. in the Bibliothèque nationale, Paris.* New York: Orion Press, 1958.

Pompeian, Edward. "Spirited Enterprises: Venezuela, the United States, and the Independence of Spanish America, 1789–1823 (PhD diss., College of William and Mary, 2012).

Porto, Aurélio. *História das missões orientais do Uruguai.* Porto Alegre: Livraria Selbach, 1954.

Possamai, Paulo. "Aspectos do cotidiano dos mercadores na Colônia do Sacramento durante o governo de António Pedro de Vasconcelos (1722–1749)." *Revista de Estudos Ibero-Americanos* 28, no. 2 (Dec. 2002): 53–73.

————. "O tráfico de escravos na Colônia do Sacramento." 5o. Encontro de Escravidão e Liberdade no Brasil Meridional. Porto Alegre, 2010. www .escravidaoeliberdade.com.br/site/images/Textos5/possamai%20paulo %20cesar.pdf.

————. *A vida quotidiana na Colónia do Sacramento.* Lisboa: Livros do Brasil, 2006.

Prado, Fabricio. "A carreira trans-imperial de Don Manuel Cipriano de Melo." *Topoi, Revista de História* 13, no. 25 (July–Dec. 2012): 168–84.

————. *A Colônia do Sacramento—O extremo sul da América portuguesa.* Porto Alegre: Fumproarte, 2002.

————. "In the Shadows of Empires: Trans-Imperial Networks and Colonial Identity in Bourbon Río de la Plata." PhD diss., Emory University, 2009.

Pratt, Mary Louise. *Imperial Eyes.* London: Routledge, 1992.

Proctor III, Frank T. "Slavery, Identity, and Culture: An Afro-Mexican Counterpoint, 1640–1763." PhD diss., Emory University, 2003.

Rama, Angel. *La ciudad letrada.* Hanover, NH: Ediciones del Norte, 1984.

Ramos, Frances. *Identity, Ritual, and Power in Colonial Puebla.* Tucson: University of Arizona Press, 2012.

Real Academia Española. *Nuevo tesoro lexicográfico de la lengua española.* U 1780, Academia Usual. http://ntlle.rae.es/ntlle/SrvltGUIMenuNtlle?cmd=Le ma&sec=1.0.0.0.0.

Reitano, Emir. "Los portugueses del Buenos Aires tardo colonial." PhD diss., Universidad Nacional de La Plata, 2004.

Ribeiro, Alexandre Vieira. "O tráfico atlântico de escravos e a praça mercantil de Salvador (c. 1678–1830)." Master's thesis, UFRJ/PPGHIS, Rio de Janeiro, 2005.

Riveros Tula, Aníbal. *La Colonia del Sacramento.* Montevideo: EBO, 1959.

Rodriguez, Jaime. *The Independence of Spanish America.* New York: Cambridge University Press, 1998.

Rodriguez, Mario. "Don Pedro de Braganza and Colônia do Sacramento, 1680–1705." *Hispanic American Historical Review* 8, no. 2 (May 1958): 179–208.

Rupert, Linda. *Creolization and Contraband: Curaçao in the Early Modern Atlantic World.* Athens: University of Georgia Press, 2012.

———. "Introducao." In *O antigo regime nos trópicos,* ed. João Fragoso, Bicalho, Maria Fernanda Bicalho, and Gouvea, Maria de Fatima Bouvea. São Paulo: Civilização Brasileira, 2000.

Saguier, Eduardo. "The Uneven Incorporation of Buenos Aires into the World Trade in the 17th Century." PhD diss., Washington University, 1982.

Said, Edward. *Orientalism.* New York: Pantheon Books, 1978.

Schwartz, Stuart. *Sovereignty and Society: The High Court of Bahia.* Berkeley: University of California Press, 1973.

———, ed. *Implicit Understandings: Observing, Reporting, and Reflecting on the Encounters between Europeans and Other Peoples in the Early Modern Era.* Cambridge: Cambridge University Press, 1994.

Seed, Patricia. *Ceremonies of Possession.* New York: Cambridge University Press, 1995.

Smith, Anthony. *La identidad nacional.* Buenos Aires: Rama, 1991.

Soares, Mariza. *People of Faith: Slavery and African Catholics in Eighteenth-Century Rio de Janeiro.* Durham, NC: Duke University Press, 2011.

Socolow, Susan. *The Bureaucrats of Buenos Aires.* Durham, NC: Duke University Press, 1987.

———. *Los mercaderes de Buenos Aires virreinal: Familia y comercio.* Trans. Alicia Steimberg. Buenos Aires: Ed. de la Flor, 1991.

Socolow, Susan, and L. Johnson. "Población y espacio en el Buenos Aires del siglo XVIII." *Desarollo Económico* 20, no. 19 (1980): 329–49.

Stavig, Ward. *The World of Tupac Amaru.* Lincoln: University of Nebraska Press, 1999.

Stein, Stanley, and Barbara Stein. *The Colonial Heritage in Latin America.* New York: Oxford University Press, 1970.

———. *The Edge of Crisis: War and Trade in the Spanish Atlantic, 1789–1808.* Baltimore: Johns Hopkins University Press, 2009.

Strang, David. "The Inner Incompatibility of Empire and Nation." *Sociological Perspectives* 35, no. 2 (1992): 367–84.

Street, John. *Artigas and the Emancipation of Uruguay.* Cambridge: Cambridge University Press, 1959.

Sweet, James. *Domingos Alvares, African Healing, and the Intellectual History of the Atlantic World.* Chapel Hill: University of North Carolina Press, 2011.

Tandeter, Enrique, and Nathan Wachtel. *Precios y producción agraria: Potosí y Charcas en el siglo XVIIIi.* Estudios Cedes. Buenos Aires: Centro de Estudios de Estado y Sociedad, 1983.

Tejerina, Marcela. *Luso-Brasileños and la Plaza Mercantil de Buenos Ayres virreynal* Bahia Blanca: Ed. Universidade Bahia Blanca, 2004.

Tiago, Gil. "Infieis transgresores." Master's thesis, PPG-UFRJ, Rio de Janeiro, 2002.

Tjarks, German. *El Consulado de Buenos Aires y su proyección en la história del Río de la Plata.* Vol. 1. Buenos Aires: Instituto Emilio Ravignani, 1962.

Todorov, Tzvetan. *The Conquest of America: The Question of the Other.* New York: Harper and Row, 1984.

Tuck, Richard. *The Rights of War and Peace: Political Thought and the International Order from Grotius to Kant.* Oxford: New York: Oxford University Press, 1999.

Udaondo, Enrique. *Diccionario biográfico colonial argentino.* Buenos Aires: Editorial Huarpes, 1945.

Van Young, Eric. *The Other Rebellion.* Stanford, CA: Stanford University Press, 2001.

Vasconcellos, Antonio. *La raza cósmica.* Mexico: Espasa-Calpe Mexicana, 1948.

Vellinho, Moysés. *Fronteira.* Porto Alegre: Globo/UFRGS, [1973] 1975.

Whitaker, Arthur P. *The United States and the Independence of Latin America, 1800–1830.* New York: Norton, 1964.

Winn, Peter. *El imperio informal británico en el Plata.* Montevideo: EBO, 1976.

———. *Inglaterra y la tierra purpurea.* Montevideo: EBO, 2000.

Wolf, Eric. *Europe and the People without History.* Berkeley: University of California Press, 1982.

Xavier-Guerra, Francois. "Forms of Communication, Political Spaces, and Cultural Identities in the Creation of Spanish American Nations." In *Beyond Imagined Communities,* ed. John Chasteen and Sandra Castro-Klaren. Baltimore: Johns Hopkins University Press, 2003.

Zulawski, Ann. *They Eat from Their Labor: Work and Social Change in Colonial Bolivia.* Pittsburgh: University of Pittsburgh Press, 1995.

Index